The Advanced Genius Theory

Are They Out of Their Minds

or Ahead of Their Time?

Jason Hartley

Foreword by Chuck Klosterman

Scribner

New York London Toronto Sydney

Scribner
A Division of Simon & Schuster, Inc.
1230 Avenue of the Americas
New York, NY 10020

First Scribner trade paperback edition May 2010

SCRIBNER and design are registered trademarks of The Gale Group, Inc.,
used under license by Simon & Schuster, Inc., the publisher of this work.

For information about special discounts for bulk purchases,
please contact Simon & Schuster Special Sales at
1-866-506-1949 or business@simonandschuster.com.

The Simon & Schuster Speakers Bureau can bring authors to your live event.
For more information or to book an event contact the Simon & Schuster
Speakers Bureau at 1-866-248-3049 or visit our website at
www.simonspeakers.com.

Designed by Carla Jayne Jones

Manufactured in the United States of America

10 9 8 7 6 5 4 3 2 1

Library of Congress Cataloging-in-Publication Data is available

ISBN 978-1-4391-0236-7
ISBN 978-1-4391-1748-4 (ebook)

To Britt, who invented Lou Reed for me

Contents

Foreword

Chuck Klosterman

This is what happened: It was 2003, and I was working at *Spin* magazine in New York. It was the best time of my life, mostly because (a) I was working with a lot of interesting people and (b) most of the time, there was very little actual work to do. Every day, I would sit in somebody's office and have a seventy-five-minute conversation about nothing, although certain topics consistently and mysteriously emerged (Steve Albini, Mike Davis's *City of Quartz,* George Washington, the presence of Cat Power's pubic hair in *The New Yorker,* Felipe Lopez, the drumming on Bob Seger's "Hollywood Nights," someone named Dave living on the grift in Berlin, and the Chapel Hill Police Department). One afternoon, I entered the room while two coworkers were having a (possibly fake) argument I could not comprehend. The debate—as far as I could deduce—mostly involved repeating the words "Advanced" and "Overt" in every single sentence they uttered. This was my introductory lesson in the Ways of Advancement: You simply cannot repeat the words "Advanced" and "Overt" too much. If you've been talking for sixty seconds and no one has said the word "Advanced" at least once, you are probably not talking about Advancement.

Like everyone else who has ever been introduced to Advancement, I did not understand it for a very long time. Was "being Advanced" just another way of describing something as good because it was bad? "No," they told me. "Absolutely not." Was Advancement somehow tied to irony or emotional detachment? "No," my coworkers decreed. "That's even more wrong." Every hypothesis I posed was promptly debunked. But these two men could never directly explain what Advancement was, either; it was an inside joke they were not totally inside of. I would ask questions like "Is Tori Amos Advanced?" and they would say things like "Well, maybe. Her music appeals to Wiccans and she has an album title that references a Brazilian sports legend, so that's Advanced. But her cover of 'Smells like Teen Spirit' was Overt." Over time, they would forward my questions to the resident *Spin* Advancement expert, Andrew Beaujon (a former *Teenbeat* recording star who was now working as a magazine copyeditor). Beaujon would respond to every query by saying "Not Advanced" in a highly menacing fashion. He was an Advancement hard-liner, so almost nothing qualified. These hopeless conversations went on intermittently for several months. The only thing I learned was that Lou Reed was unassailable and that the rapper C-Murder was Advanced because he had literally murdered someone, but Beaujon eventually told me I was wrong about that, too.

A year later, I had lunch with my editor from *Esquire* (where I was writing a monthly column and selling $2,000 watches). We were at the kind of restaurant where they play Sting songs over the sound system, so something off *Soul Cages* started to occupy the gaps in our conversation. "Hey, they're playing Sting," I said. "He's Advanced." My editor asked what this meant. I tried to explain, which (of course) prompted him to ask all the same questions I had asked my two coworkers twelve months before. I could tell he was intrigued; every time our dialogue stalled, he would immediately return to asking me if Liz Phair was Advanced or if Jethro Tull was Overt. He instructed me to write a column about Advancement, which I assumed was impossible. "I don't even know if this Theory is real," I said. "I think two dudes just made it up in a Pizza Hut." This, paradoxically, made him all the more excited. I agreed to try, mostly because writing about Advancement in *Esquire* seemed Advanced.

It was at this point that I contacted Jason Hartley, the cofounder of Advancement Theory and the author of the book you are now holding (I've still never talked to the guy he ate pizza with). I'd never encountered Hartley before, but my *Spin* cohorts told me he was inscrutable—supposedly he was once a member of a Brooklyn-based rock band called Vintage Veal that was fronted by a top hat sitting on a wooden stool (supposedly the band members would place the hat in front of the microphone and perform instrumentally, except when they needed to sing the choruses). He was a former dancer working at a clothing store for teenage girls, yet he was still attracted to women. People told me he often wore a tie to nonformal events. He was, as far as I could tell, completely unfamous in every possible way. This being the case, I assumed he would be shocked when a person he'd never met called him on the telephone and wanted to interview him about a philosophy he had made up during college. He was not. That was the weirdest part: Hartley seemed to think it was a completely predictable request. He was not flattered, confused, or excited. "I'm glad you asked," he said. Then he began teaching me the ancient art of realizing I might be wrong about everything I ever thought I knew.

Part of what makes Advancement Theory so entertaining (at least to me) is the way it outrages so many uncreative music critics, almost all of whom (a) begin by dismissing it completely before (b) spending the next twenty minutes manically fixating on why no one should ever talk about it, even in jest. In many ways, Advancement is a criticism of criticism; it's almost always proartist and eviscerates the very notion of "good taste." The Advancement scholar is kind of like a devout creationist with a master's degree in paleontology: he starts with what he believes in his heart and uses his mind to work backward.

For example, here's the conventional critical take on the Rolling Stones: "The Rolling Stones are brilliant. They made some of the most important albums of all time in the 1960s, although much of their work came in the immediate wake of what the Beatles had already accomplished. They produced the greatest music of the rock genre when Mick Taylor temporarily joined the band, but then they became druggy derivatives of themselves. They had another fleeting period of creative quality around 1978, but they became bloated and bored for all of the '80s. Though still a viable live act, they don't make good albums anymore and are only concerned with money." This, in a nutshell, is how most rock writers would describe the group. But here is how Hartley would do it: "The Rolling Stones are brilliant." That's the only thing we all know to be true. And if we all agree that this is true—if we agree that the Stones are geniuses and that genius is extremely rare and that geniuses evolve in a way that's unlike the rest of us—then the responsibility falls on us to excavate the murky value of "The Harlem Shuffle." That's the real labor. Advancement is a profoundly optimistic way to experience art, and that's what makes it difficult to accept; it requires a flexible mind, a certain kind of intellectual humility, and a willingness to disregard what initially seems obvious. But once you let your mind slide in the Advanced direction, it can never slide back. Not totally. Things will always sound a little different . . . and a little better.

Now, do I believe everything Hartley says? Not exactly. In fact, I may have agreed with the principles of Advancement more *before*

I read this book (a few of Hartley's arguments strike me as a little Overt). But that's exactly what I anticipated. I assumed that parts of this book would befuddle me. I mean, it kind of had to. Because if reading *The Advanced Genius Theory* completely made sense to someone like me, how good could it really be?

The
Advanced
Genius
Theory

Introduction

From Baby Einstein to the Apple Store, the label "genius" has been used so liberally recently that it has virtually lost its meaning. And with so many "geniuses" toddling around the nation's preschools and fixing our MacBooks, it is difficult to recognize actual geniuses in our midst. Further confusing matters are the geniuses themselves, who often use their brilliance in bewildering or disappointing ways, especially when they are older. This Late period is what the Advanced Genius Theory seeks to explain.

Like most of the extraordinary discoveries in human history, the Advanced Genius Theory had its eureka moment in an ordinary place. As gravity had its apple orchard and relativity its patent office, the Advanced Genius Theory had the Pizza Hut in Columbia, South Carolina. Advancement, as the theory came to be known in the halls of *Spin* magazine and later in Chuck Klosterman's seminal *Esquire* article "Real Genius: An Introduction to the Highly Advanced Theory of Advancement," challenged everything we know about the nature of genius. It was a theory so revolutionary that it is barely understood to this day, even by its creators. The basic contention of Advancement, however, is simple: there is a special class of geniuses who were so great when they were young that it is impossible that they could ever become bad, no matter how questionable their judgment might appear to be. Or, as Klosterman put it, "When a genius does something that appears idiotic, it does not necessarily mean he suddenly sucks. What it might mean is that he's doing something you cannot understand, because he has Advanced beyond you."

Though it is difficult to pin down an exact date, the theory came to life sometime around 1992, when Britt Bergman and I got together for that fateful meeting at the Pizza Hut near the University of South Carolina. Somehow we got onto the subject of the decline of Lou Reed, whose music Britt introduced me to in high school. The Velvet Underground was unquestionably one of the greatest bands ever, but we wondered why Reed had made those Honda scooter commercials and why he had such a terrible haircut and why he always played "Walk on the Wild Side" on *Late Night* and, finally, why his music had gotten so embarrassingly bad. And then it hit us: the Velvet Underground was ahead of its time in the '60s, so maybe Reed was ahead of *our* time in the '80s and '90s. Maybe he was just as much of a genius in the days of "The Original Wrapper" as he was when he wrote "Venus in Furs." Maybe he was expressing his genius in a way we didn't yet understand. And if this was true, could it also be true of other geniuses throughout history? We knew that we were onto something bigger than just explaining Lou Reed's haircut, and consequently, for the last fifteen years, I have devoted my life to understanding Advancement.

What Is Genius?

Harold Bloom starts out his book *Genius: A Mosaic of One Hundred Exemplary Creative Minds* with this very question, and thank goodness he starts out with it because otherwise I would have had to read the entire book to find out the answer. (My research budget affords me just enough to pay for the cup of coffee that allows me to loiter in a bookstore and skim through books.) Bloom says that "fierce originality" is a crucial element of genius but that originality is "always canonical, in that it recognizes and comes to terms with precursors." He adds that the great geniuses are "clearly both of and above the age." Finally, he agrees with Ralph Waldo Emerson that genius is "God within, the self in 'Self-Reliance.'" In other words, a genius is someone who is completely original yet derivative, dated yet timeless, divine yet human, particle yet wave, yin yet yang, Beavis yet Butt-Head.

Bloom actually never gives a straightforward definition of a genius, and this is someone audacious enough to claim that William Shakespeare "invented the human." If he won't do it, then I shouldn't have to either. But it seems to me that a genius is simply someone whose instincts—artistic, intellectual, physical—happen to be valued more than most other people's. In a way, this is pure luck. If you think of it in terms of natural selection, a genius is like a bug that, through a genetic mutation, is born looking like a stick in a stick-rich environment, making its survival more likely. If it looked like a stick in an environment where sticks were the most delicious thing that a bird could ever dream of finding, the bug wouldn't make it. But because it was born the right way in the right place, it thrives, and its fellow bugs would probably say he was pretty amazing. The delicious-stick bug, however, would look pretty stupid.

For humans, being born looking like a stick is only part of the equation. There are plenty of people who are born brilliant and talented but don't rise to the level of genius: Styx, not sticks. What separates the geniuses from the merely above average is a combination of self-confidence, hard work, and individuality. However, the full answer is probably unknowable, which is part of the allure of the genius. So for the purposes of this book, geniuses are people *I* think are so much greater than their peers that they make up a different species.

So what is an Advanced Genius?

This I am obligated to answer. The thought behind the Advanced Genius Theory is basically the opposite of the idea expressed by Sick Boy in the movie *Trainspotting*: "Well, at one time, you've got it, and then you lose it, and it's gone forever. All walks of life: George Best, for example. Had it, lost it. Or David Bowie, or Lou Reed." (Ironically, he told this to Renton, who Advances in the movie by giving up drugs and "choosing life.") The Advanced Theory says that Sick Boy had it all wrong, that Bowie and Reed hadn't mysteriously lost "it," they just changed "it" to something that is harder to appreciate. And since change is scary to most of us, we declare that the problem is with the genius and not us.

Of course it is difficult for anyone to accept that Reed's later work represents artistic progress from *Transformer* or that "All for Love," Sting's collaboration with Bryan Adams and Rod Stewart, could be more Advanced than "Roxanne." (It's difficult for me too. Much more about this later.) But a great artist is great because he challenges himself and his audience rather than doing what is comfortable. Artistically, working on "All for Love" was more exciting for Sting than writing another "Roxanne." And what could be more challenging than doing a song you know your fans will hate just on principle?

Finding those kinds of challenges is essential to Advanced musicians because it is relatively easy for them to write great songs (in the traditional, non-Advanced sense of "great") because it comes naturally to them. But this is not exclusive to musicians; late in his life Leo Tolstoy took to making his own shoes, though he never quite got the hang of it. Still, shoe making gave him more satisfaction at that stage in his life than writing the greatest novel of all time. After all, he did the latter twice. Which leads us to another question:

Are musicians the only ones who can qualify for Advancement?

No, there are Advanced actors, directors, painters, and writers, not to mention boxers, politicians, businessmen, and scientists. While Advancement manifests itself in different ways across media and professions, the general pattern is the same: early innovation that is not immediately appreciated, a lengthy fertile period leading to widespread acceptance, and a long (seemingly) fallow period that eventually sullies their reputations and angers their admirers.

Take George Lucas, for example. Few people in the movie industry gave *Star Wars* much of a chance to succeed, but it and its sequels ended up being among the most successful and beloved movies of all time. However, when Lucas made some computer-generated imagery updates to the original trilogy for theatrical rerelease, the backlash began. And the moment Jar Jar Binks opened his mouth, it was clear that Lucas had lost it. What happened to him? Well, nothing. Both *Star Wars* and *The Phantom Menace* are essentially children's movies, so what you think of them depends on whether you were a kid when you saw them. The fact is, Jar Jar Binks is no better or worse than Chewbacca. Just ask your dad.

The only thing bigger than *Star Wars* in my house was Steve Martin, who is so Advanced that his hair started turning gray when he was in his twenties. Martin combined the wildness he developed at Knott's Berry Farm with the craziness he learned in the California State Long Beach philosophy department to create the most successful comedic persona of all time. Then he just walked away from stand-up to make mainstream Hollywood movies, each one less wild and crazy than the last. It's tempting to explain his change from the jerk to father of the bride as merely a money grab to fund his art collection, and there may be some truth to that. After all, he is paid a lot of money and he does have an incredible art collection. But this misses something fundamental: it's very, very hard to make successful movies, and he has done it consistently for thirty years. The reason he gets those big paychecks is because he is still very good at what he does. Whether he is doing what *you* want him to is immaterial. And even if you don't agree with that, doesn't it seem a little strange to accuse someone of abandoning his art for art's sake?

While every kind of genius can Advance, not every genius can, even if he was once great and then seemingly "lost it." There are prerequisites even to be considered for Advanced status:

1. You must have done great work for more than fifteen years.

The whole premise behind the Theory is that the Advanced are so good, for so long, that they have proven that their judgment is consistently superior to everyone else's and therefore should not be questioned. You can't give that kind of power to an artist with just a few years' worth of greatness, no matter how great that greatness was. For example, John Lennon would not have qualified had he stopped making music after the Beatles broke up because they weren't together long enough. Without his solo work it would still have been tempting to call him Advanced just for marrying Yoko Ono, but that would have been wrong.

A pillar of the Advanced Theory is the idea that genius is not something that is visited upon an artist and suddenly disappears after a few years. If it disappears in a few years, it wasn't genius. I think the key is to separate genius from inspiration. Inspiration can raise the level of someone's art for a while and make it seem as though he is a genius, but the inspiration is external, so if things change—the artist falls in love, leaves his band, gets rich—the "genius" goes away too. I remember reading something to the effect that John Lennon wrote on inspiration while Paul McCartney was more of a craftsman. I don't really believe that (they both relied on both inspiration and craft), but I do think that is the difference between the pretenders and the real-deal Advanced: the former rely on something magical, whereas the latter rely on their talent. It's like Charles Schulz said: writer's block is for amateurs.

The fifteen-year period before the genius becomes Advanced is called the "Overt" stage, because during this period the genius is trying to be innovative (or "weird," in Advanced parlance) in an obvious way. Thought of another way, the Overt are normal weird, whereas the Advanced are weird weird. Over the years, "Overt" has expanded to include people who are not geniuses and has become a sort of catch-all term for closed-mindedness and the voluntary rejection of happiness that is surprisingly common among people who want desperately for you to think they are interesting. There's much more to say about Overtness in the coming chapters.

2. You must have alienated your original fans.

There are plenty of artists out there who do superior work their whole careers, which is admirable, if conventional. To be considered Advanced, though, it's not enough to be great for a long time; you have to be great in a way that alienates people. Unlike the Merely Great—Paul Newman, Bob Newhart, Stephen Hawking—who meet with everyone's approval all the time, the Advanced appear to seek actively the disapproval of their fans, especially the ones who loved them first. They aren't really seeking disapproval, of course, they're just Advancing. The original fans are left the farthest behind because they go back with the artist the longest, so their alienation is the most pronounced. Just as those fans were the first to embrace the artist, so will they be the first to proclaim that the artist has "lost it." The Merely Great never lose it, but they also never Advance.

3. You must be completely unironic.

Those who want to be Advanced but can't quite stomach what it takes to make it there often try irony to protect themselves from the perception that they've lost it. But to Advance, an artist has to truly embrace something that will be perceived as awful. Steve Martin doesn't make family comedies as a way to pull one over on the rubes; he *likes* making family comedies and does what he can to make them as good as possible. However, with an artist like David Johansen, it seems like there is always just a bit of a wink to his work, and there is no winking in Advancement.

4. You must be unpredictable.

The Advanced are unpredictable because they make decisions that are truly unexpected rather than simply the opposite of what is expected. For instance, if Bob Dylan says that he would never feature a sax solo in a song of his, it wouldn't be Advanced for him to change his mind and get David Sanborn to sit in on a session (though the Advanced do like David Sanborn). His doing a Victoria's Secret commercial, however, was Advanced. Extremely Advanced. This is true because in the first example, Dylan fans would be able to explain away the sax solo as just another example of his rebelliousness. But the commercial, as Dylan could have easily predicted, saddened his fans and gave his critics another excuse to mourn the further decline of the Voice of a Generation. In reality, this was not some sort of Galilean recanting but another step in Dylan's own Advanced continuum. Of course, being Advanced, Dylan was going to do the commercial regardless of how it would be perceived.

5. You must "lose it." Spectacularly.

This is similar to point number two, but you can alienate your original fans without losing it (sometimes the original fans move on but are not so disgusted with the artist that they would say the artist has "lost it"). Just as artists who never really had "it" can't qualify for Advancement, neither can artists who start out successful and stay that way. Elton John, for example, has succeeded at just about everything he has done, including having a hit twice with "Candle in the Wind," a distinction he shares with Chubby Checker (though nobody had to die for "The Twist"). He keeps making hit records, Broadway musicals, and film scores, much to the delight of his fans. He's not as successful as he was at his height in the 1970s, of course, but that kind of popularity is unsustainable, and in some ways he is more popular than ever. So though I've always admired that he was capable of being taken seriously while wearing a Donald Duck suit, he's just not Advanced.

These original guidelines were established to define the Advanced Genius, but as the Theory has evolved, it has been necessary to recognize other forms of Advancement. For instance, there are some artists who don't follow the pattern of early struggles followed by success followed by irrelevance. Tom Waits started out writing fairly standard (if great) singer-songwriter tunes but then abandoned that and became some kind of Brechtian jazz weirdo balladeer. It was as if he started out Advanced and then became Overt. It was clear to Britt and me that Waits had to be accommodated by the Theory. We decided that he must have been Overt before anyone had ever heard of him and that his early work was Advanced and the post–*Rain Dogs* era was a stage of Advancement that looked like Overtness.

Another strain of Advancement is the Advanced Overt, including artists like Andy Kaufman, who was so committed to the far reaches of Overtness that he nearly met Advancement from the other side. There is also the Advanced Irritant, or someone who elevates making people mad into an art form. Typically you can't achieve Advanced Irritant status without being truly Advanced—Lenny Bruce was an Advanced Irritant—but I am also tempted to assign the label to someone like Gene Simmons, who is so aggressively irritating that it's awe-inspiring. But Simmons fits more neatly in the Quasi-Advanced category, along with Sylvester Stallone, Alice Cooper, and Dennis Rodman (honorable mention Advanced Irritant). The Quasi class is made up of people who don't quite reach the level of Advanced Genius in their work but are still too uniquely strange not to be included in a discussion of Advancement. However, just because they belong in the conversation does not mean they are truly Advanced. It is important never to lose sight of the fact that Advanced Geniuses are exceptionally rare and the title should not be given without a great deal of circumspection.

Since Chuck's article, I've heard from people all over the globe—Ecuador, Canada, Russia, England, Norway, Japan—who were persuaded that Advancement was the worldview they were looking for or were just curious to learn a little more about the Theory. What I've found is that people are very confused about who is and who isn't Advanced, which I completely understand. As I said before, even I don't understand the Theory sometimes. Like Albert Einstein, who created a constant to explain why the universe doesn't collapse, I've had to put in some placeholders as I grope for completion. Of course Einstein considered the constant a blunder, and I too have made some mistakes. For instance, I declared that it was the other members of the Police who made Sting look so brilliant when he was first starting out. Now I know that Sting is just so Advanced that he makes himself seem awful retrospectively, as if he had passed through some kind of Advanced wormhole. I should add, however, that Einstein's constant never really went away and has experienced something of a renaissance in the last few years.

If it sounds as though the Theory is just about being contrary for the sake of being contrary, it's not. I admit that it did start out that way, at least somewhat. But the more I've studied the Advanced, the more valid the Theory seems to be. Advancement has become a set of deeply held beliefs that happens to go against what almost everyone accepts as true. Which leads us to a problem for critics of the Theory: If you say that Lou Reed's *Mistrial* is a bad album because so many people believe that, you must agree that Celine Dion's "My Heart Will Go On" is a great song because so many people love it. If you say that *Mistrial* is a bad album because you personally don't like it, then that's a subjective judgment that by definition can be neither right nor wrong. So if one has to choose between everyone, a rock critic, or Lou Reed, isn't it kind of stupid not to go with the guy who wrote "Walk on the Wild Side"?

I can't promise you that I'm always right or that I won't sometimes contradict myself. Advancement, in the end, is a personal thing. What is Advanced for you may not be Advanced for me. I've tried to lay down some guidelines to narrow the definition of Advancement to keep out the flash in the pan, the reactionary, the conventionally great, and the actually awful. Beyond that you have to have faith in your judgment, which is why sometimes the Theory seems to break down: reason can't explain matters of faith. But faith without knowledge prevents complete understanding, so you must immerse yourself in the essentials of the Theory, learn about what made the undisputed giants of Advancement—Bob Dylan, Leo Tolstoy, Orson Welles—Advanced, and then you can move on to the Thom Yorkes, Johnny Depps, and Don DeLillos and decide for yourself if they are indeed Advanced. You'll be wrong more often than you are right, but the journey will be among the most liberating experiences of your life.

A Few Words About the Structure of the Book

The book is split into two sections: (1) What is the Advanced Genius Theory? and (2) Who Is, Isn't, Would Have Been, and Might Be an Advanced Genius. The beginning of the first section will provide some alternatives to the "old people suck" theory used to explain why we fall out of love with the people we admire most. Next I will review the stages of Advancement, starting with Overtness, then on to Early, Middle, and Final Advancement.

The second section will explain types of Advancement starting with Musical, or Traditional, Advancement. Then we will explore Advanced actors and directors, other artists, and nonartists (athletes, politicians, businessmen, scientists). We'll also look back on the artists who died too young to Advance and look ahead to who may one day Advance. Finally, I'll show you what you can do for Advancement and, more important, what Advancement can do for you.

Chapter One

Falling Out of Love

Bertrand Russell wrote in *A History of Western Philosophy* that when studying philosophers, particularly the Greeks, "the right attitude is neither reverence nor contempt, but first a kind of hypothetical sympathy, until it is possible to know what it feels like to believe in his theories." He felt that only by abandoning one's opinions could someone truly assess the value of a philosopher. He went on to add, "When an intelligent man expresses a view which seems to us obviously absurd, we should not attempt to prove that it is somehow true, but we should try to understand how it ever came to *seem* true." Advancement combines these two thoughts, rejecting preconceived notions about the life of an artist and embracing the absurdities of geniuses as a means of expanding our thinking about what is good or valuable.

One of the great prejudices one must overcome to appreciate the work of an Advanced Genius is the idea that artists almost always outlive their genius. No matter how great the genius is, the story goes, he's going to lose it eventually. To see why that is completely wrong, it's important to understand why people believe that sucking is the inevitable conclusion to years of brilliance. You have to know what it is that makes us misunderstand genius so badly and furthermore to confuse this misunderstanding with dislike for genuinely inferior work. If you don't believe in Advancement, there is no mystery: artists are good when they are young and then they get bad, so we don't like them anymore. But I believe that the answer is not that the Advanced outlive their genius but that their genius outlives our ability to appreciate it because we reach a sort of saturation point where we've just had enough. It's like your grandmother trying to stuff a third piece of chocolate cake down your throat: the cake is still awesome, but you'll be sick if you have even another bite. The reality is that genius is stronger—and much less fickle—than love.

Before we get into why we end up hating the Advanced, let's take a look at why we love them in the first place:

1. They're great.
   This is the fundamental reason we embrace Advanced Artists, so fundamental that it seems almost too obvious to mention. But greatness is hard to quantify, and it has as many definitions as there are people. The Theory takes this into account, allowing each practitioner to use his own criteria for judging an artist. So if you truly believe an artist is great, then he or she is, no matter what anyone else says. Not necessarily Advanced, but great.

2. They're innovative.
   Whether an artist is innovative is not quite as slippery, though it is still open to interpretation. Though it seems as if some artists just suddenly appear fully

formed and totally unique, the truth is that even the most original artists—including writers, painters, and musicians—are the product of their influences. Let's take Elvis Presley as an example: Before he found his way into a Memphis recording studio he had been exposed to musicians that most people, especially white people, had never seen or heard before. Much of what made Elvis seem so new was lifted from performers like Arthur Crudup and James "Big Chief" Wetherington. But even knowing this, I think he was innovative because he did invent something that no one had ever seen before: Elvis Presley. If you read interviews with people who knew Elvis as a kid, most say that he was not only different from everyone else but differently different because he did not try to hide the parts of his core being that were not like everyone else's. We all have parts of us that are not like anyone else, but few of us—even artists—have the courage to show them to the world. The artists who, like Elvis, have that courage are the only ones capable of true innovation. Though Chuck D. might disagree with me.

3. They're a part of the past.
   Lorne Michaels has said that *Saturday Night Live* is never as bad as people say it is or as great as people say it was. If you actually watch entire episodes from the first season, you can certainly understand what he means. Interspersed among the classic sketches that everyone remembers are painfully unfunny sketches that have thin premises and no ending. In other words, exactly as the show has been in all of its iterations. But that's what happens when you try to put

on a live ninety-minute show that depends on current events and whether the guest host can actually do the job. When you think of it that way, it's amazing that the show is as funny as it is. I should be clear that I'm not saying that the show wasn't great in its first season, just that it's been consistently great since then.

Thanks to nostalgia, we remember only the funny bits of the show we watched thirty years ago, whereas we remember only the unfunny parts of the show we watched last night. Naturally, the best twenty minutes of the Steve Martin show from the first season seems better than the whole ninety minutes of the Shia LaBeouf episode in 2008. Of course, nostalgia is not limited to those who actually experienced what everyone is so nostalgic about in the first place. In fact, we are probably more susceptible to nostalgia for eras we never experienced because we see *nothing but* the good parts. So when it comes to the Advanced, whether you were actually there or just wished you had been, that earlier version will always seem cooler and more vital than the version you see today. Consequently, if an artist makes two works of equal value thirty years apart, the older work will naturally seem better. And because, like *SNL*, the Advanced were so extraordinary when they were new, the esteem for the remembered good parts grows exponentially over the years, widening the gulf between perceived and actual value.

4. You don't understand them.
   You only think you do.

There are myriad other factors why we like the Advanced—you saw *2001: A Space Odyssey* on your first date with your wife, your older brother liked Andy Warhol, you're from Minnesota—but why we like them is far less fertile land than why we end up hating them. So let's start digging.

Man in the Mirror

Before Advancement came into my life, I thought nothing of saying that Bob Dylan had not only lost the ability to make good records somewhere around 1978 but that he had lost the ability to judge whether his own records were good. (Advanced Artists always believe that their most recent work is their best. They are right, of course.) Yet like most people I never thought to turn inward and question *my* ability to judge *him*. Advanced thinking has led me to realize that if it's possible for Bob Dylan to lose his way, it's also possible that I could lose mine. When you stack our accomplishments side by side, it seems likely that I'm the one who doesn't know what he's talking about.

Really, if you compare what he's done with people who are much more accomplished than I, he still seems like the one to bet on when it comes to being able to judge what's good and what's not. That includes music critics, especially those who have never written a song or even played an instrument. It doesn't surprise me that a nonmusician can pass himself off as more of an authority on music than Bob Dylan, but it's somewhat surprising how readily people believe him. You don't have to play an instrument to have an opinion about music, but Bob Dylan has an opinion *and* happens to be one of the greatest songwriters of the last two hundred years. He's got a bit of an edge there.

I don't mean to pick on rock critics, because without them we'd have to decide whether to buy a record without knowing how many stars it deserves. There's nothing worse than thinking that you're listening to a three-and-a-half-star album when it actually merits just three stars. But music critics play a big part in the perceived decline of Advanced musicians because we accept them as authorities, so it's vital to understand that many of them don't really know what they're talking about. This is less true of other types of critics (reviewers of nonfiction, for instance, know what they're talking about because reviews are a form of nonfiction), but they're wrong about the Advanced for other reasons.

The reality is that the Advanced have proven over many years that they are right even when everyone else says they're wrong, and I have no reason to believe that this dynamic should change just because they aren't as good-looking anymore.

Separate Ways

I was part of a tight-knit group of friends at Irmo High School in Columbia, South Carolina. Our bond was made even tighter by our being unpopular, hated even, because of the music we listened to, the clothes we wore, and especially our haircuts. People were so angered by our long bangs that we were called "slingheads" (actually "fucking slingheads" was the full name) because we had to sling our heads to get the hair out of our eyes. You didn't have to have the haircut to be a slinghead, you just had to be generally gay according to the criteria developed in secret by jocks during halftime of the first football game of the year. The nickname turned out to be the best thing that ever happened to us, as it bound a loose confederation of punk rockers, theater geeks, and quiz-team nerds together into a single, powerful entity that ended up being as well known as the jocks. We were even the focus of a segment on the local news, in which I had some unkind words for people who wore stonewashed jeans. I come out looking prescient on that one, you have to admit.

This newfound fame, in addition to getting me punched in the face by a guy who liked stonewashed jeans and was watching TV that night, strengthened our sense that we were a unique group of people and should remain friends forever. But then we went to colleges in other states, met new people, got interested in different things, and started to see one another less and less. When we did get together, it wasn't like it used to be, though it took us a long time to admit it. And while I'm still close with a few of the original slingheads, it's hard to remember what was so remarkable about the rest of them. Of course, just because I don't remember doesn't mean that they weren't remarkable. It's just that we've made thousands of little decisions since then, each one taking us further away from one another.

I know now that this is something that happens to just about every close-knit group of young friends (as a fan of *The Big Chill*, I guess I should have known all along), and I think something similar happens in our relationship to the Advanced, the difference being that they are taking leaps away from us, not steps. Plus, if you can't stay in sync with your closest friends, how likely is it that you would with someone older than you, from a different part of the world, whom you've never met?

Think of it this way: the early work of the Advanced is like the friend you used to get wasted with in college, while the later work is the same friend after he joined AA and got an engineering degree. To everyone else he is undeniably a better person than he was, but you think he's a drag because you still want to get wasted with him. This works in reverse as well, as your friend probably thinks you're a loser because you still like to get wasted so much. Had you not known each other when you were young, you might get along just fine, but you resent the changes in each other—or in your case, the lack of change. So now each friend is depressed by the state of the other and goes off to his new friends as soon as possible.

What I mean to say is that the Advanced are so revered for what they did when they were young, it is impossible for them to change *or* stay the same without seeming to betray the connection you've made with them. They can't win, so they don't even try to play. Meanwhile, you're drinking alone.

The Thrill Is Gone

Of course, growing apart isn't the only reason we stop loving our favorite artists. Growing together is perhaps an even more effective way to kill off the magic. No matter how much artists change their art, they can't change who they are. And let's face it, after a while you're going to get sick of just about anybody, no matter how wonderful they are. In fact, it's the things you like best about a person that end up irritating you the most. (I'll go into more depth about this later.) Chris Rock has a joke about this: no matter how pretty a girl is, there is some guy out there who's tired of fucking her. The fact that the guy is not attracted to her doesn't make her suddenly ugly, just as our lack of interest in the later work of the Advanced doesn't make them suddenly terrible. We just need a change of scenery.

But let's not leave our forlorn beauty just yet, because we can learn a little bit more about Advancement from her. It's a good bet that the guy who is tired of sex with her didn't feel that way when they were first together. They probably did it two or three times a day the first few weeks they were together, staying up until all hours of the night no matter what they had to do the next day. But then he or she had an important meeting one morning, so they took the night off. The next night they had sex twice, subconsciously fighting off the inevitable return to real life, but the spell was still broken. After that things settled down and sex got less and less frequent, until it was an event saved for birthdays, anniversaries, and vacations.

From the outside, this appears to be a tragic story, but it doesn't have to be. If you've ever been in a long-term relationship, you know that the physical stuff gets replaced by a much deeper connection that depends on how good a person your partner is, rather than how good-looking he or she is. That's why Paul McCartney chose to marry a woman like Linda Eastman rather than a trophy bride (not that she wasn't pretty): he could have had any woman he wanted, which made mere beauty meaningless. Instead of going the supermodel route, he chose a woman he could talk to and raise a family with.

When you first discover an Advanced Artist, it's a lot like the early days of a relationship. You listen to the albums over and over, read all the books, or watch the DVDs so much that you can repeat every line. No matter how great a work of art is, it's bound to get old eventually. *Hannah and Her Sisters* is just not as good the fifty-third time (unless you're watching it with someone who has never seen it). Even new Woody Allen movies suffer because you're just burned out on him. You could have a similarly comfortable and satisfying relationship with Allen as Paul McCartney had with Linda, but you don't want to raise a family with Woody Allen, you want to fuck him.

What's He Got That I Ain't Got?

There is a famous exchange in *The Wild One,* so famous that I'm hesitant even to bring it up. But it's instructive for our cause, so here goes: Johnny Strabler (played by Marlon Brando) is asked, "What are you rebelling against?" His response includes the coolest contraction in the history of cinema: "Whadd'ya got?" A big part of the appeal of this line is that we, the moviegoers, are made to feel that Brando is speaking for us and that we would be the exception to his universal rejection of everything. But if you take the line to its logical extension, you can see that if Strabler is rebelling against everything, he'll eventually get around to rebelling against you. In fact, if *The Wild One* had been based on a story by H. G. Wells instead of Frank Rooney, Strabler from the future would rebel against Strabler of the present, the one who said the famous line in the first place.

I don't want this to descend into an argument about the paradoxes of time travel, so I'll get to the point: what we find so appealing about Advanced Artists when they are young—their rebelliousness—is also a major reason why we end up hating them when they are old. The Advanced are much more restless than the average fan, so they are continually working on improving themselves, usually by exploring new avenues of expression that are typically antithetical to what we as fans expect from the artist, like Sting's Super Bowl performance with No Doubt. This goes back to the idea that we are actually to blame for the Advanced Artist's perceived decline, but it's important enough to bear some repetition. We can grow with an artist up to a point, but eventually our image of that artist becomes fixed and we bind ourselves to that image. Usually that image is of certain kind of rebel—a punk rocker, an indie director, a maverick politician—which means that this image will eventually become something for the artist to rebel against. So by rejecting their earlier selves, they're also rejecting you.

Since rebellion is such an essential part of the Advanced Genius Theory, it is important to understand the difference between Overt and Advanced Rebellion. The Overt are purely reactionary, rejecting symbols of authority regardless of those symbols' actual value (whadd'ya got?). The Advanced reject inferior ideas, or, to put it more positively, they put forth only superior ideas. If the H. G. Wells version of Strabler were to Advance, he would still reject the earlier version of himself, not because Future Johnny rebels against everything but because Past Johnny is inferior to the five-years-in-the-future Strabler.

Men Without Hats

Most of us have no idea what it's like to be revered, but almost everyone knows what it's like to be underappreciated. It makes sense, then, that we feel such a strong connection to the Advanced when they were also underappreciated and that the connection would be weaker or even broken after they have gained universal acceptance. For one, Overt-period Advanced Artists write or sing about topics we can relate to—loneliness, lost love, overcoming the dark side of an energy field created by all living things that surrounds and penetrates living beings and binds the galaxy together. But perhaps more important, there's something satisfying about liking an artist that few people know about. Everybody loves the underdog until everybody loves the underdog. But why?

That question was answered for me at the Columbia stop of R.E.M.'s *Lifes Rich Pageant* tour. Having missed the *Fables* concert the year before, I hadn't been as eager to see a concert since the 1976 Kiss show I saw with my brother, father, and mother (who fell asleep). So I was particularly thrilled when a friend of mine in algebra class asked me whether I wanted two free tickets. A relative of his worked at the Township, the venue where the show was going to be, and he knew I was a fan. I half didn't believe that he had access to free tickets, but he delivered a few days before the show.

On the day of the concert I went with friends to the Township about five hours before the show, which paid off because we saw the bands unloading their gear and saw Michael Stipe riding around on a bike. The same bike as on the fuchsia *Fables* tour shirt! Or so we guessed. Anyway, we were among the first to go into the auditorium, and since it was general admission, we took our places right by the stage. While Let's Active (the opening band) played, we still had the pit to ourselves, but between the end of their set and R.E.M.'s appearance, we were displaced by people who didn't care that we were there before them or that we had "discovered" R.E.M. before they had, too.

At some point early in the show, one of the pit crashers took off the cap of a friend of mine and threw it away, then laughed about it with his buddies. I was shocked, having never expected this kind of behavior at an R.E.M. show. After all, this was the band for lonely young boys whose growth spurt didn't come until the summer between ninth and tenth grades. Somebody like that wouldn't steal someone's hat and then laugh. Or have buddies. Then I understood why I'd had the sick feeling in my stomach ever since we had been pushed away from the stage: there were *jocks* in the pit. The barbarians had invaded my sanctuary, and R.E.M. had invited them in.

There is probably an artist—Jerry Garcia, Jack Kerouac, Jean-Claude Van Damme—that you like but are afraid to admit it to your friends or even yourself because you don't want to be associated with the kind of person who likes that artist. But when a hat stealer is among the people who like your favorite band, you can't help but ask yourself, "If an idiot like that is into R.E.M. and I'm into R.E.M., am I an idiot too?" Nobody wants to feel he is on the same plane as a hat stealer, so the question eventually morphs into something a little more palatable: "If an idiot like that is into R.E.M., they probably aren't as good as I thought."

This isn't fair, of course, to R.E.M., you, or even the hat stealer. A lot of people who are not idiots do idiotic things, after all. Maybe that guy who temporarily ruined R.E.M. for me has lain awake at night for the last twenty years wishing that he hadn't been so carried away by "These Days" that he stole that kid's hat. It's more likely, though, that he was just a dick who was there to hear "Superman" and maybe kick someone's ass. In any case, his behavior is in no way a reflection on R.E.M. or me, but I lost some of my respect for them that night, and it wasn't until Advancement came into my life that I could forgive R.E.M. for becoming popular.

Communication Breakdown

As you know from the introduction, the period before an Advanced Artist becomes Advanced, the time when you first fall in love with him, is called the Overt period. During this period, it is clear what the artist is trying to accomplish. In the case of the directors who made up the French New Wave movement (insofar as it could be called a movement), it was clear that they were rejecting conventional movie making as it was understood at the time in favor of a style that was part Jean Renoir and part Alfred Hitchcock, combined with the unique vision of the director. This kind of clarity of purpose makes it easier for the audience to judge whether an artist is successful in achieving the objective of his or her art. We can watch *Breathless* and say with some confidence that it is somewhere between *Le Crime de Monsieur Lange* and *La Grande Illusion,* but it is no *La Règle du Jeu* (especially if, unlike me, you've seen those movies).

There is another advantage to having a clear purpose in your art: consumers can decide whether they believe the purpose itself is worthwhile. Going back to Godard, if in 1960 you felt that movies had grown stale and needed young directors with a new approach to the art form (even if that new approach was new only because it embraced the old), then you were going to appreciate at least the spirit behind *Breathless.* And being human, you were probably going to like it because if you have already been won over by the concept of a movie, you are likely to enjoy the movie itself, if only because the director agrees with you. It's sort of like how we like to read magazines that reinforce our point of view rather than challenge it.

The Advanced have neither advantage because it is almost impossible for anyone to understand what they are doing. We're left unable to judge whether the object of the art has been met or is even worthy of being achieved. So in the absence of some kind of system of measurement for a work of art's quality, we are forced to make up new criteria, and that takes the kind of effort few of us are willing to expend. Instead of trying to understand what the artist is trying to achieve, we fall back on the idea that genius is some mystical force that mysteriously flows into and out of people within a certain age range. If you take the time to try to understand why Sting decided to do a song with Bryan Adams and Rod Stewart, you might judge the outcome differently. (There is an argument to be made that Stewart is Advanced, but I'm not the one to make it. Bryan Adams doesn't qualify because he was never innovative, unless you count the "Heaven" video with all the TVs.) Maybe he was trying to see if it was possible to make a good song with them, and if so, maybe that is a more radical form of experimentalism than, say, John Cage's "4'33"." And finally, if you are someone who values experimentalism, you might appreciate the audacity it took for the guy who wrote "Canary in a Coalmine" to even be pictured with Adams and Stewart, much less sing with them. It could be that he is bad at saying no or was doing a favor for a friend. We don't know the reasons why he worked with Adams and Stewart, but I have to believe that there was something more interesting behind the project than Sting's greed or sudden lack of taste.

You Ain't Got No Alibi

Earlier I talked about how my opinion of R.E.M. was temporarily damaged by their popularity among people I didn't respect. This affected my feelings about not only the music that appealed to the mainstream audience but their earlier music as well. This is not unique to me or even fans of Advanced Artists generally. It is difficult for any of us to avoid allowing later work that we don't like to make us stop liking earlier work. Similar to the hat-stealer formula, if an artist can create something that is genuinely horrible in the latter part of his career, maybe I need to question whether the early stuff is good too. It makes perfect sense, right? It does, but not the way you might think it does.

Advancement merely reverses the hat-stealer formula: instead of judging early work filtered through later work, I propose that we look at later work filtered through early work. We're still on fairly solid and familiar ground here; most people tend to give the benefit of the doubt to their favorite artist, at least for a while. The part of the Advancement formula that causes the most controversy is that it is possible for the early work to be weighted so heavily that it is impossible for the later work to be anything but great. I can understand why people would be reluctant to accept that, and I think that the root of this reluctance can be traced to our relationship to the past and present.

But first, this might be the right time to mention the concept of the Markov chain. Put the only way I can—simply—this is just a way of describing an action that can be predicted solely with the information available in the present. In other words, you don't need to know what happened in the past to know what will happen in the future. Though it sounds like one of those mathematical theories that have no application in the real world, it is, in fact, useful for statistics, biology, and Google's page-ranking system, not to mention gambling. It would be nice if a work of art could fit into a sort of Markov framework, where only the work itself would be judged without knowing an artist's past. In fact, it would be ideal if we could judge art devoid of any context at all, from how it was received by critics to how good-looking the artist is (a frequently unacknowledged factor in our appreciation of art). But we aren't dice, so we should forget about Markov and move on to Bill James.

James, as you probably know from the book *Moneyball*, was a security guard/statistician who wanted to understand how to evaluate baseball players in a way that tested conventional wisdom and subjective observations, which had long ruled professional scouting. What he found was that scouts often discarded a player's past performance if he had the physical attributes scouts deemed important. This meant that players who were tall and strong (and, yes, good-looking) but put up mediocre numbers were valued more than little ugly guys who produced consistently. What James found was that a bigger predictor of a player's success than his height, speed, or arm strength was past performance. If a player is mediocre while in the minor leagues, he will most likely be mediocre in the major leagues, even if he appears to have the potential to be great. Likewise, if a player tears up the minor leagues, there is reason to believe he will do the same in the majors, no matter how little or ugly he is (it's amazing that Lenny Dykstra ever found his way onto the diamond). The Advanced are the littlest, ugliest players around.

Something else James found that relates to Advancement is how a player's value was being judged or, at the time, misjudged. What he realized after breaking down the numbers was that the traditional success metrics—batting average, RBI's, stolen bases—were misleading, while less exciting statistics, such as total on-base percentage, made for a more accurate gauge of a player's worth. Basically, scouts and general managers would discard players who were contributing the most toward winning games for players who only appeared to be contributing. And what's more, sometimes they were getting rid of the truly productive players for mediocre players who looked as if they should be able to put up the big (but deceiving) numbers that seemed so attractive. This was too radical for many to accept, especially for those whose living depended on the conventional wisdom. But when James's theories were actually applied by Billy Beane, the general manager of the Oakland A's, he found that he could put together a very good team without having to pay exorbitant salaries because other teams didn't see the value of the players who fit the James mold and therefore there wasn't as much demand for them. Another disciple of James, Theo Epstein, took these principles to the Boston Red Sox, leading to their first World Series victory in eighty-six years.

Something similar happens when conventional wisdom is applied to Advanced Artists. In the case of rock-'n'-roll musicians, for instance, youth and energy are valued by the average critic more than experience and technique, so the worth of a band like the Killers is inflated simply because they are new on the scene. Conversely, the new work by an artist like David Bowie is undervalued because he has been around for a long time. If it's possible for a scout, someone whose whole life is spent evaluating baseball players, to misjudge how good a player is, even though he has reams of data at his disposal, I think it is probable that we can be wrong about our judgment of art, which is far more subjective than baseball.

He Ain't Heavy

When he was a young man, Albert Einstein used to solve problems with thought experiments rather than by doing actual physical tests. He would often add suggestions to the end of his papers for how to prove what he had written, as if to say, "I know it's true and don't need to test it, but if you don't want to trust me, do this and you'll see I'm right. To do so myself, however, would be beneath me." For instance, he said that an eclipse could prove his general theory of relativity, but he let someone else take care of the actual measurement. Sure enough, once the eclipse came around (actually, the second one) he was proven correct. Now, imagine you were a physicist who was laboring away, trying to solve problems in a more conventional way. You'd probably find Einstein increasingly annoying at each proof of his latest theory. And you would also probably be waiting eagerly for him to finally make a mistake.

Even if you aren't a theoretical physicist, it's natural to resent people who are right all the time, and the Advanced are right pretty much all the time. Subconsciously we feel about them the same way we might about an older brother or parent who always gives good advice. We're irritated by them and want to do the exact opposite of what they advise, out of spite, even though we know they're right. And while there is some value in learning from one's own mistakes, in the end we're just hurting ourselves by not following good advice. If you embrace Advancement, however, you can avoid repeating someone else's mistakes and screw up in ways your big brother never imagined.

As you can see, there are several plausible reasons why you might think that your favorite artists might suck when in fact they don't. But the biggest reason may be that it is simply easier to reject than to accept, to mock than to love, to go than to stay. Such is the human condition, but conditions can change if you want them to.

Chapter Two

Stages of Advancement

The Advanced Genius starts out Overt like all people but then evolves slowly into Advancement by passing through three loosely defined stages. They are loosely defined because for each kind of genius the stages have different elements. A musician is not going to be like a writer, who is not going to be like a painter, who won't be like an athlete, and so on. But generally speaking, all Advanced Geniuses progress from an early stage, characterized by tentative, almost undetectable steps into Advancement, followed by a Middle period featuring bolder, bewildering choices that signal the "decline" of the genius. Finally Advanced Geniuses fully embrace Advancement, in which they become pure expressions of self, though few people care anymore. One thing is true for all types of Advanced Geniuses: the inevitable decline that comes with age is neither inevitable nor a decline.

The Overt Stage

Of all concepts of Advancement, the Overt stage is perhaps the most difficult to comprehend. Many think that to be Overt is to be no good. Others believe that Overtness is the only true period of genius. Neither is the case. But it's confusing because Overtness is incredibly complex, and I've just never found the right words to explain it, though it is a lot like pornography—hard to define, but you know it when you see it. When people have had trouble understanding Overtness in the past, I've often pointed them to Christian Bale's speech about Phil Collins in *American Psycho*: "I've been a big Genesis fan ever since the release of their 1980 album *Duke*," he says to a potential victim. "Before that, I really didn't understand any of their work. Too artsy, too intellectual. It was on *Duke* where Phil Collins's presence became more apparent." Overtness, then, is the artsy, intellectual period the Advanced go through before they are up to the challenge of trying to reach a wider audience.

Targeting a narrow audience is a big part of Overtness, as it is thought that anything with mass appeal cannot be real art. For instance, it was during Richard Linklater's Overt period that he made *Slacker*, a movie that made a huge impression on the tiny fraction of moviegoers he had preselected as his target audience: slackers. Not exactly a big challenge to get slackers to like a movie that ennobles the slacker way of life. It reminds me of that old *SNL* commercial for a movie called *Critic*, which is reviewed ecstatically by critics. Interestingly, even though Linklater has moved on from Overtness, he still makes movies about slackers, only now they teach kids how to rock and play baseball.

Britt and I chose the term "Overt" to describe this early period because it is during this time that the artist's intentions are transparent. Take Woody Allen, Bob Dylan, and Brian Wilson. All three created for themselves a persona that was relatable: Woody, the neurotic nerd with big glasses; Bob, the next Woody Guthrie, writing the topical-song sound track of the civil rights movement; and Brian, the California Golden Boy hit maker (loading up the Woodie). Things got more complicated when Allen stopped being funny and married his girlfriend's daughter; Dylan went electric, then country, then religious, then whatever he was in the '80s; and Wilson stopped touring and became more beached whale than beach boy. In each case, they decided to challenge their fans by abandoning these beloved (and lucrative) caricatures for an image that was much more enigmatic, which led to widespread confusion and resentment. But that's only because their fans didn't recognize Advancement.

While Overt Artists make art that is easy to understand and label, they often achieve their objectives by obscuring the actual content of their work. In fact, obscurity is often used to mask the fact that the artist actually has very little to say. This is an effective tool for connecting with an audience because it allows them to fill the gaps with their own explanations. The artist supplies only enough information for the audience to believe that something interesting is going on and leaves it to them to decide what it is. A great example is the way Michael Stipe used to mumble his lyrics and not print them in the album's liner notes. I never knew what he was saying, but I imagined not only that it was important and great, but also that it had to do with the things I was feeling as a sixteen-year-old. This has the dual effect of empowering the audience as cocreators of the work of art and bringing in personal connections that are not possible in art that has an explicit message. Kurt Cobain mumbled like Stipe but is considered by many to be the voice of his generation, though no one had any idea what he was saying even when you could understand the lyrics. Never mind, indeed!

The Overt do not necessarily mean to be obscure but are often forced into it by time constraints, limited budgets, and other factors that are beyond the artist's control. This is particularly common among young artists who don't have a year to work on a record or the backing of a major studio. So though a director might wish to do a big-budget action-adventure movie laden with special effects, he is forced to work around the fact that it's just not possible to do so. Even Steven Spielberg, who had plenty of money to make *Jaws*, had to figure out a way to make a movie about a killer shark that featured the shark itself as little as possible because of mechanical problems. Spielberg has often said that not having had more scenes with the shark improved the movie, because it created a tension that wouldn't have been there if the shark had constantly been eating people. Using implied menace rather than explicit violence is an effect that Alfred Hitchcock used effectively, but there is a difference between making this choice and having the decision foisted upon you. In the former example, Hitchcock is telling the story exactly as he wants to, giving the audience all the details he thinks are important. In the latter example, Spielberg is making a different movie than he wants, and because he has to leave some details out, the audience members have to supply them with their imagination.

The audience participates in another way that is outside the work itself but still informs our opinion of it. Once we know that a director did not have all the tools he needed, the element of "what might have been" is introduced. This is similar to the Alfred Hitchcock effect, but the difference is that the audience is aware that what they are seeing is not great, and they attribute the lack of greatness to the limitations placed on the artist. What happens then is that the audience imagines what the artist would have done without those limitations, and in place of the actual finished product, we add details that we would personally like to see. In other words, we believe that had the artist been allowed to realize his vision completely, that vision would just happen to mirror our own and, therefore, we'd love it.

The Advanced rarely have to make any concessions, effectively taking the audience out of the equation. Not only do they have all the tools and funds necessary to make art exactly as they want it, they have the confidence to follow through without regard to how the work will be perceived. Going back to the Michael Stipe example, he mumbled not so much because he didn't have anything to say but because he thought that what he had to say wasn't worth saying (or at least understanding). By leaving his lyrics open to interpretation, he could hide what he really felt. Advanced Artists have no need for that because they know that what they are saying is worthwhile. They don't care if you don't agree with them. Stipe, who once described love songs as "odious," later understood that there could be no greater challenge than to write a love song or even a song with clear lyrics describing a genuine emotion. Had he remained committed to Overtness, we would never have had "Everybody Hurts." Unfortunately, he has never been able to cross over to Advancement, which is why the video for that song is so Overt. (I cringe every time I hear the amazed announcer say, "They just got out and walked!" Okay, it was weird. We got it already.)

While there are plenty of Overtly weird comedians, the most widespread form of Overtness in the comedy world—especially online—is going for obvious, mean-spirited jokes. For instance, when I was at VH1's *Best Week Ever* blog, a couple of our writers took the time to tell their readers almost daily that Paris Hilton is a "whore." (That was the whole joke.) I'm not sure why people are so worried about Hilton's promiscuity, but there is no denying that calling her a whore is guaranteed to get a laugh out of a lot of people. But great comedy—Advanced comedy—comes from comedians who are willing to take a risk that people won't laugh.

Andy Kaufman was one such comedian, though his untimely death in 1984 prevented him from fully realizing his Advanced potential. You're probably familiar with his Foreign Man character (also known as Latka Gravas on *Taxi*), whose "act" was a series of increasingly pathetic impressions, making the audience increasingly uncomfortable. Just as this discomfort turned into anger, though, Foreign Man did the best impression of Elvis that anyone had ever seen. (Speaking of which, making fun of Elvis impersonators is Overt, but Kaufman's impersonation was a celebration of Elvis, plus he invented the form. Overtness often depends on context.) The payoff is incredible, even when you know it's coming, so I can only imagine how revelatory it was for those who really thought they were watching an incredibly inept foreign comedian bombing worse than anyone has ever bombed. The perfection of the impression and the affection Kaufman had for Elvis is what took the act beyond the realm of the Overt. I'm not saying that there won't always be a place for the cheap joke, nor that there shouldn't be a place, but it will always be Overt because the joke teller's intentions are clear.

Comedic Overtness of the obvious kind is also very popular among improv comics. For instance, an amazing number of performers believe that the introduction of crack cocaine or sexual situations into a scene always equals laughs, even if it makes absolutely no sense to introduce it. When I was studying at the Upright Citizens Brigade, I often found myself in a scene that revolved around a crack addict mounting me, and though I wanted to just walk off the stage, I had to go along with it because the first thing you learn when studying long-form improvisational comedy is that "Yes" is invariably more productive, and funny, than "No." For example if someone in a scene asks you, "Do you want to clean out the refrigerator?" and you say, "No," the scene has only one direction to go in: two people arguing about cleaning out the refrigerator. But if you say, "Yes," there are endless possibilities for what can happen next. It could be a Lion, Witch, and Wardrobe scenario where a portal to another dimension has been hidden by forgotten leftovers. Or there could just be a lion in there. Even if those particular scenarios are less than hilarious, surely you would agree that they have more comic potential than an argument.

Once you've learned that "Yes" is always funnier, the second thing you learn when studying improv is that your natural inclination is to say "No" to every question. There are exercises to help this habit, such as forming a circle, then someone says an idea and the person next to him has to say, "Yes, and . . ." and add another idea, to which the next person says, "Yes, and . . . ," and so on. But it usually takes being in a few painfully unfunny scenes before it ever really sinks in that you should never, under any circumstances, say "No" onstage, even if someone is humping you while lighting a crack pipe. Saying "Yes" is productive in all forms of art, not just improv comedy (I realize I'm stretching the definition of art), but the Overt make "No" art.

You may understand by now why people think that "Overt" means "bad," so I should make the Advanced position clear. While Overt Artists are definitely inferior to Advanced Artists, this does not necessarily mean they are "bad." It just means they haven't Advanced yet, assuming they have the potential to Advance. No one could ever say *The Jerk* or *Star Wars* was bad, but they were definitely Overt. All Advanced Geniuses go through an Overt period, and it is during this period that they do their groundbreaking, conventionally brilliant work. In other words, the work is great, it's just not Advanced. So when I say that someone like Will Ferrell is Overt, I don't mean that he isn't any good. He is good, maybe even good enough to become Advanced. But if he just keeps making funny movies, he'll have to settle for being another great comedic actor.

Some great artists never evolve beyond the Overt stage, but their Overtness is polished to the point where it seems wrong to lump them into the general Overt category. It is for them that the Refined Overt classification was created. The members of this class are not merely conventionally good artists like Paul Newman or Bruce Springsteen. They are the artists who manage to cultivate their weirdo street cred late into life while somehow managing not to annoy people. David Byrne has been in a prolonged Refined Overt period that has seen him cowrite an opera about Imelda Marcos, turn a building into a musical instrument, and design bike racks for New York City, among many, many other strange but unirritating things.

The differences between the Overt and the Overt Refined David Byrne are subtle but significant. Take his movie *True Stories*. In it, he takes an ironic but still loving look at a town in Texas, marveling at its inhabitants' lives as if he were a benevolent visitor from outer space whose culture is vastly superior to theirs. I love the movie, but the condescending tone is pure Overtness. The later, gray-haired version of David Byrne is still a visitor from outer space, but he can see that there is much to learn from the earthlings. He could even learn from Whitney Houston, whose "I Wanna Dance with Somebody" he covered with a hint of a Latin vibe but without irony. To do a song with Whitney Houston or, better yet, Bobby Brown, would have been the Advanced thing to do, but Byrne has never made the final step required of him to move into that realm. The Advanced world would welcome him and other Refined Overt Artists—Brian Eno, Steve Buscemi, Don DeLillo—but they remain content to straddle Advancement and Overtness.

One final thing about Artistic Overtness: there are plenty of Overt Artists, but just because you're Overt doesn't mean you can become Advanced. You have to be Overt and great too, and for at least fifteen years. Karen Oh of the Yeah Yeah Yeahs could make music for fifty years and never be Advanced because her band just isn't good enough (plus she misbehaved at my karaoke show).

Early Advancement

There is a very good explanation for why so many superior minds remain Overt: it's easier. Everyone, the Advanced included, wants to be accepted and liked by as many people as possible, especially as a young person. If a genius has done all the hard work necessary for gaining acceptance, naturally that genius would find it attractive to continue down the same path. Advancing, though, requires that the genius put aside everything that brought success and go down a solitary path, one that will cost him his fans, fortune, and reputation. But few artists have the courage to face their followers and say, suddenly, "I'm going to be who I am. You can come along if you want, but it doesn't matter to me if you don't." So typically, instead of just completely embracing Advancement in one step, the genius's first move into Advancement is so subtle that it appears to be no more than an extension of his Overtness.

The most famous example of Early Advancement was Bob Dylan's decision to go electric at the Newport Folk Festival. Dylan made it very clear to all that he was not content to be merely the topical songwriter/protest singer the folk crowd wanted him to be. There was no better way to do that than to plug in and no better place to do it than at Newport. Bold as this was, though, he was still convinced to play an acoustic set after it became clear that the fans were unhappy with the electric one. (Why they were unhappy is a matter of some contention. It might have had more to do with the shortness of the set rather than the wattage.) That Dylan would back down, even a bit, shows how difficult it is to Advance too far, too soon. Still, his decision to go electric is the most emphatic declaration of impending Advancement of all time, which makes sense considering how Advanced he would become.

Nicolas Cage's Early Advancement was more typical. Cage was everybody's favorite quirky actor who, with his bulging, sad eyes, crooked smile, and rat's nest hair, perfected the art of innocent bewilderment in movies like *Valley Girl* and *Raising Arizona*. In *Wild at Heart,* he added an element of rage to the "Nicolas Cage" character we had come to love, but it was still a comic, fairy-tale menace that didn't threaten our understanding of him as actor.

Then he won an Oscar playing the suicidal, drunk version of "Nicolas Cage" in *Leaving Las Vegas*, putting him in the position to make whatever movie he wanted. That movie was *The Rock*.

I admit that I was confused when I saw he was doing *The Rock*, but like most of his original, Overt fans, I figured he was doing it as a goof or maybe a quick grab for money. Great actors do it all the time, and it made sense for him to cash in while he was hot because surely that wouldn't last. Plus, Sean Connery was in the movie, and though it is Overt to say that he is the best James Bond ever (it's also Overt to say that Timothy Dalton is the best), he is still pretty great. It came to pass that *The Rock* was by far the biggest hit of Cage's career, but we had every reason to expect Cage to cash his check and go back to the movies we loved him for. We did not expect *Con Air*.

Like *The Rock, Con Air* had a good cast (John Cusack, John Malkovich, and Steve Buscemi, the man who would take over for Cage as the go-to quirky, bug-eyed actor), but it was certainly not a Coen brothers movie. Something was surely wrong, but it was still possible that he would go back to doing "Nicolas Cage" roles. After that came *Face/Off*, which was so ridiculous that it made you kind of wonder if someone might have stolen Cage's face. His choices would get ever more ridiculous with *City of Angels, Snake Eyes, Gone in 60 Seconds*, and the *National Treasure* movies. In retrospect *The Rock* was both the height of his popularity and the beginning of his (supposed) slide into terribleness. But he wasn't jumping the shark, he was stepping into Advancement.

Some Advanced Geniuses choose to begin their journey into Advancement by dabbling in another means of expression besides the one they are famous for. Often this means an actor taking up painting or a singer trying acting or a comedian appearing in a vampire movie, like Eddie Murphy in *Vampire in Brooklyn*. Painting actors or acting singers will usually talk disparagingly about their talent in their new medium, dismissing it as just a hobby.

They are right to do so in most cases. However, trying something that they aren't supposed to be great at gives them a new kind of freedom: the freedom to fail. Few of us can understand what it must be like for someone like John Lennon, whose next song, whatever it was, was expected to be the greatest song of all time. Though he was capable of satisfying that expectation, he was in a no-win situation: if he wrote another "Strawberry Fields," it would have been no big deal because that's what he was supposed to do. But if the next song was not up to that level, people would have been disappointed and maybe even angry. As a response, he wrote a couple of books and went to Spain to shoot a non-Beatles movie, *How I Won the War.* (Incidentally, it was on the set of that movie that he wrote the actual "Strawberry Fields.") Whether he was good in that role was beside the point. He just needed some time to be something other than one half of the greatest songwriting duo of the second half of the twentieth century. At that point in his career, he had convinced the world that he was the genius he had always thought himself to be. He was still Overt, so his ego would not allow him to make music that some people might not like. He needed to get bad reviews for something besides music to prepare for the eventual criticism that would come with Musical Advancement. It would take a few more years and involvement with a certain Japanese avant-garde artist before he would get there.

Sting is among the more complex Advanced Geniuses. In fact, I've hypothesized that he is Super-Advanced because he seems so awful. But his Early Advancement was pretty straightforward: like Cage, he explored a new direction in his art that was just different enough to be a challenge but still palatable enough not to shock his fans. And, like Lennon, he tried acting to allow himself to fail, but he was actually pretty good at it, especially in *Brimstone and Treacle.* (He also took the Eddie Murphy route, though opting for Frankenstein rather than Dracula.) But it was his solo performance at the Secret Policeman's Ball that was his most obvious statement that he intended to Advance, whatever the cost. Among the songs he did was a sort of reggaeish/all-star jam version of the Bob Dylan song "I Shall Be Released," which is quite Advanced. But his rendition of "Message in a Bottle" was his statement of principles, his *Infanterie greift an.* This version was slower, softer, and jazzier, which is exactly what his music would eventually sound like. Plus, he was alone on the stage with the spotlight shining on him, which also presaged his preferred treatment. Really everything that he was to become was evident during the song, but because he hadn't yet fully embraced Advancement, it was a coded message.

The Middle Advanced Stage

The codes are left behind when Advanced Geniuses enter the Middle Advanced stage, when they have become confident enough in their ability that they no longer need the approbation of critics or fans. Predictably, this is when fans start to turn on them and critics decide that the genius is no longer relevant. ("Relevance" is a term critics have made up that means "It's interesting to me.") This is also the time when the Advanced Genius embraces new technology and multiculturalism and proclaims the greatness of seemingly mediocre new talent.

In his Overt period, Miles Davis played a major role in moving traditional jazz forward. But it was in his Middle Advanced period in the late 1960s and '70s when he decided to go electric, add several musicians to his band, and fuse jazz with rock 'n' roll. He also toured with the Steve Miller Band, which speaks as much to Miller's Advancement as Davis's. Though jazz aficionados and rockers hate his fusion work equally, it was actually well received in its time. (Aficionados are almost always behind the public.) At some point in his Middle Advanced period he started to wear leather coats, grew his hair long in the back, and was always in sunglasses. Unfortunately his Advancement was stunted by heroin use, so he never actually left the Middle period. But he did make a Honda scooter commercial (just like Lou Reed and Devo), appeared in *Scrooged*, and made a rap record featuring all the latest sampling technology.

Middle Advanced Geniuses have the ability to be so bold because they have established themselves as successful artists who can be trusted with control over the projects. Or they are powerful enough to insist on that control. Whatever the reason, during Middle Advancement the genius is, for the first time, unrestrained by budget, time, or need for approval. Ideally, at this point the artist could change identities, not like John Cougar becoming John Mellencamp but more like when Bill Pullman wakes up as someone else in *Lost Highway*. They could then go off somewhere and find out the identity of this person they have become, and then, after they finish their search away from the eyes of the world, they would reemerge as themselves. Instead they have to go out in front of the public, grappling with the power of being able to express themselves completely for the first time. It is in the Middle Advanced period when the critics, who have been waiting for the Advanced Genius to slip up, come out in full force to declare the formerly great person "self-indulgent."

Let's examine that phrase for a moment. Whom should artists indulge if not themselves? Critics? The public? Both avenues lead to paralyzing self-consciousness, not to mention bland art. One of the goals of art is to reveal truth, and truth isn't found by worrying about whether Robert Christgau is going to disagree with your decision to make a gospel record. One of the ways we benefit from art is by observing another person's truth and learning from it. Nothing is to be gained from an artist's trying to guess what my truth is. Almost all geniuses are self-indulgent, which, paradoxically, is exactly why they appeal to so many people because their truth, by some great stroke of luck, is universal. To pander to others whose truth is less than universal would destroy the power of their work. Don't worry, I don't think the Advanced approach the status of gods. They still screw up and make bad art from time to time, but their mistakes are at the very least interesting and serve their evolution as Advanced Geniuses.

Speaking of God, it is during Middle Advancement that many Advanced Geniuses find Him, Her, or Them. Elvis, the Beatles, and Mike Love gravitated toward exotic religions with an Eastern flavor, with various levels of commitment. Madonna has stuck with Hollywood Kabbalah for some time. Beck didn't find Scientology, his parents did, but he seems to have stuck with it, which is impressive given how little respect your average Beck fan has for the religion. Tolstoy stopped writing novels to proselytize a new version of Christianity that emphasized living as did Jesus, or at least Tolstoy's interpretation of Jesus. Most impressive to me are Muhammad Ali's commitment to the Muslim faith because it cost him so much and Bob Dylan's conversion to Christianity because he not only embraced it in his life but gave his art over to it as well. Of course, he was crucified for it.

The Overt view of religion is seen clearly in Christopher Hitchens's imaginatively titled book *God Is Not Great*. Clearly this is a man dealing in opposites, one of the great hallmarks of Overtness. His argument, as near as I can figure, is that religion is at best superstition and at worst the cause of basically all the bloodshed over the last twenty centuries or so. He's welcome to that opinion, of course. However, it doesn't add anything interesting to our understanding of man's quest to comprehend what science has not yet been able to explain or what is hard to accept when science has explained it (I'm looking at you, intelligent designers).

The Overt find faith in a Christian or Muslim God to be absurd, though they frequently believe in other kinds of spirituality such as yoga or quasi Buddhism that don't prohibit believers from getting drunk or having sex before being married. What is interesting is that Overt people typically find religious people closed-minded and intolerant, but they too have a very specific set of rules about what makes a person acceptable or unacceptable. And someone like Hitchens is so confident in his correctness that he wouldn't be persuaded that the Christians might be onto something if Jesus himself came down from the heavens and gave him a bottle of Scotch.

You may wonder why rational, brilliant people would allow themselves to be seduced by the divine. Maybe it's possible that the hundreds of millions of people who believe in some form of God know something that the editorial staff of *The Atlantic* doesn't. Advanced Geniuses are open to all possibilities, which allows them to make use of the best parts of all belief systems. Advanced Artists seek out a personal truth (the only truth that is really possible) and get closer to it than Overt Artists because they look everywhere instead of limiting themselves to the places that reinforce their preconceptions of what the truth should be. Many Advanced Artists move on from their periods of religious observance, but they are better artists for their time in the Light.

Less profound but just as troublesome as finding religion is the unembarrassed embrace of technology, another sign of Middle Advancement. We will study this in depth for musicians who leave their real pianos behind for synthesizers and their drummers behind for the latest Dr. Beat, but it happens to all Advanced Geniuses. In Einstein's case, he was less interested in technology than in math, but I think we're still in the same neighborhood. Early in his career he depended on pure thought experiments to arrive at truth, almost reveling in his lack of mathematical ability. But it was a mathematician friend of his who helped him make necessary breakthroughs in his early work. As a result, in his Middle period he began to see that the thought experiments weren't going to get him to the breakthrough he was seeking. The early

Einstein would have mocked the middle version, and he would have been quite Overt to do so.

In Andy Warhol's Middle period, he used silk screening not because he couldn't draw or use a paintbrush but because it produced an effect that no one had seen before. (Silk screening wasn't new, even among painters, but what he did with it was new and feels new even today.) The Middle Advanced George Lucas was among the first filmmakers to leave behind film for digital. Just as music snobs complained that CDs were somehow less "warm" than vinyl, movie snobs imagine that film is superior to digital. But the music snobs don't really take into account that most people had crappy record players and didn't take care of their records obsessively, so the vinyl experience was not so much warm as wool but twice as scratchy. The movie snobs forget that most prints that are shown in the average movie theaters are degraded. For music and film, digital gives a greater percentage of people a superior experience because it doesn't degrade with use and it doesn't need to be taken care of.

For Advanced Artists, technology is often a means to achieving their objective, namely, portraying their vision of truth as precisely as possible. When thinking about this issue, I always point to Merce Cunningham. Cunningham, whose choreography required a high level of athleticism and technique, stopped being able to dance in his later years and consequently found his choreography limited. He started using a computer program that allowed him to show his assistants what he wanted, and this allowed him to continue making dance for several years. To imagine that a new form of technology is somehow worse than the old way of doing things is stultifying to a true artist and just plain undemocratic.

Finally, the Middle Advanced period is a time of cameos in movies and television for musicians, albums by actors, movies by painters, and explorations of rapping by everyone. It is a time of breakups with longtime collaborators, greatest-hits records, sequels, and directors' cuts. In Middle Advancement, old singers team up with younger musicians, rock musicians make country records, serious actors take on comedic roles, comedians take on serious acting roles, and indie directors date movie stars. In short, this is when they sever all ties to their old Overt selves, leaving a series of bad reviews, hurt feelings, and ex-wives in their wake. By the end of the Middle Advanced period, only the hearty few care about their work.

And that's when it gets really interesting.

The Final Advanced Stage

The Final Advanced stage is the fallow period discussed earlier when the Advanced are relegated to the status of celebrity emeritus, being trotted out occasionally for an award but otherwise forgotten. The problem is that, like a ponytail, what looked great on the Advanced when they were young—independence, originality, eccentricity, vision—appears ridiculous when they are old. Young people don't want to hear what the old have to say because it reminds them that they will be old themselves, and old people don't want to hear it because it reminds them that they are indeed old. But the Advanced keep working, often destroying whatever reputation they have left.

Fully Advanced Geniuses are considered pitiful, if they are considered at all. What is especially pitiful to the average person is that the "washed-up" geniuses are the only ones who don't recognize that they are washed up. On the contrary, they'll tell you that they have never been more in command of their abilities, which they typically employ in the service of a vision that seems ridiculous. For instance, Orson Welles did all manner of commercials (I didn't even know he was a director until I was a teenager) in an effort to fund movies that were never going to be made and/or watched. Albert Einstein spent the last part of his career in the vain pursuit of a unified theory that would serve as an alternative to quantum mechanics, which existed only due to his work in the first part of his career. And Lou Reed has talked for years about his efforts to play the perfect D chord, which is one of the first three chords most beginning guitarists learn. It is seriously the equivalent of subject-verb agreement. I've seen him demonstrate this amazing chord, and even I have absolutely no idea what he's talking about.

This fantasy D chord, along with Welles's movies and Einstein's theory, is an example of a phenomenon called Quixotic Advancement. The traditional sense of *quixotic* is pejorative, as reflected in the Merriam-Webster dictionary's definition: "foolishly impractical especially in the pursuit of ideals." But I don't think that the actual Don Quixote was foolishly impractical at all. I have to turn back to Harold Bloom to help me out here. In his review of a new translation of *Don Quixote* that appeared in *The Guardian,* he noted:

> The aesthetic truth of *Don Quixote* is that, again like Dante and Shakespeare, it makes us confront greatness directly. If we have difficulty fully understanding Don Quixote's quest, its motives and desired ends, that is because we confront a reflecting mirror that awes us even while we yield to delight. Cervantes is always out ahead of us, and we can never quite catch up.

It sounds as though Bloom is arguing that Cervantes was one of the first Advanced Artists (Shakespeare probably was too; his father did own a leather shop, and leather is the most Advanced fabric), but Don Quixote the character was Advanced as well. He may have seemed ludicrous, but at worst he was deluding himself so that he would not succumb to the deficiencies of the age in which he was living. At best he knew exactly what he was doing and had the very sensible purpose of living life on a plane of existence that was unrestrained by conventional views of reality. Only by doing so could he arrive at new forms of truth and beauty. I believe the latter explanation is true, and I think this applies to late-stage Advanced Artists as well. Had Einstein not rejected what the younger generation of physicists was advocating, he likely would have added very little. But by going in his own direction, he forced the new generation of scientists to be even more rigorous in proving their theories. That is not to say that he didn't believe that he would one day achieve his aim. He honestly did believe that God didn't play dice with the universe. (Considering that Einstein was more or less an atheist, one wonders why he was so sure what God did or didn't play or why it would have an impact on physics. But that's late-stage Advancement.) It's just that everybody benefited from his quixotic pursuit of the theory in a way that would not have happened if he had simply acquiesced.

If the Advanced are self-indulgent in their Middle period, which we know now is not a bad thing, it's hard to figure out whom they are indulging in the Late period. For instance, Marlon Brando's final performance was for a video game version of *The Godfather*. It's possible he was doing this for a grandchild or perhaps the shingles on the hotel on his island needed replacing, but it seems just as possible that he was a huge fan of video games and believed that they would eventually take the place of traditional movies. That may seem ridiculous, but don't be surprised if it comes to pass. Don't be surprised if it doesn't, either, because one thing is for certain: he didn't give a moment's thought to how he would be perceived when he signed on to the project, even before he knew he would be dead.

Had he not died, he would have been called a sellout. For the Overt it is better to starve than to make money in ways that are impure. An actor shouldn't endorse a product. Songwriters should not allow their songs to appear in commercials. If you started out directing independent movies, you can't be taken seriously anymore if you move on to making big studio pictures. Interestingly, this is a sort of aristocratic take on what an artist should be, coming from a line of thinking that began in pre-Socratic Greece. At the time, many philosophers believed that to truly think, one had to avoid doing any real work. This ideal was fine as long as your parents were rich, but not so much if you were a helot. So out of this worship of trust-fund kids came the idea that an artist should be purer than other people and that to make money on one's art somehow defiles it. What's key to this is that the Overt take it for granted that it is appropriate for certain people to be consumers of art in certain contexts but the rest should be deprived of this content if they don't meet Overt standards. It is okay to associate songs with memories of driving in your father's Oldsmobile, but it is not okay for Led Zeppelin to associate their songs with Cadillac. As is so often the case, the Overt insist that they know better what is best for artists than do the artists themselves. As you will see next, they are wrong, as is so often the case, and the whole idea of selling out is completely illogical.

To the Advanced Artist, there is no such thing as selling out. If you are an artist and you make money for your art, you have already sold out and it's silly trying to draw some arbitrary line across which lies an unacceptable means of making money. For instance, the Overt would approve of a band's playing at local clubs and never signing a big record deal for the sake of their "integrity." (Though often these same people deride the music industry for not recognizing the truly great bands.) The problem is, there is no guarantee that the local club owner is a good guy; if you played any shows in Columbia, South Carolina, it was guaranteed that the club owner was decidedly not good. Also, a band in that situation has to endure countless indignities to play shows: bad soundmen, driving all night from New York to Atlanta because you can't book two shows anywhere in between, playing empty rooms, trying to sell your shirts at a table set up at the front of the club, breaking down your equipment at 3 A.M., getting ripped off by the club owners, sleeping in a filthy van, and being forced to use toilets straight out of *Trainspotting*. Meanwhile, you've still sold out because you're getting paid. You're just dumb for not getting paid more.

The Overt can sometimes accept a band's signing with a big label, but if that band allows one of its songs to be used in a commercial, the band should written off forever. The idea being, I suppose, that making money for a record company is totally fine but making money for a car company is not. This is ridiculous on several levels, but let's stick with two: record companies are run by evil people who hate musicians, music, and the people who listen to it. There are a few exceptions, of course, but not many. The second reason is that if you make records, they are played on the radio (if you're lucky). The radio industry is even worse than the record companies, plus they make their money on ad revenue, which they are able to collect because they are playing music. The songs a radio station plays are essentially an advertisement for the radio station. So the distinction between making the music featured in a commercial and the music played between commercials is that in the former, you're paid a lot for it. Ironically, for an older artist like Sting, his music is more likely to be played on the radio if it first gets exposure in a commercial. So he gets the commercial money *and* the royalties from radio play. The Overt may not like that strategy, but they aren't the ones who have to pack up the equipment at 3 A.M. It's pretty easy to question someone's integrity when you leave the club after the encore and go home to a clean bed.

The good news is that after becoming Fully Advanced, the genius is eventually accepted again, usually by a new generation that is curious about what all the fuss was about in the first place. I've tried to graph this out, though I think it requires someone with some knowledge of linear algebra. Here's an illustration: Think of three people born in, say, 1945. By 1963 the future Advanced Genius will be even with the Overt person and slightly ahead of the public. As the years go by, the Overt stay essentially on the same line, while the Advanced Genius progresses at a slow rate, allowing the public to catch up with him or her. At that point, though, the Advanced Genius picks up speed as he or she enters Middle Advancement, while the Overt and the public keep on the same trajectory. This would explain why the Fully Advanced Genius would have completely alienated everyone until a new generation born in, say, 1971, comes along to appreciate the genius's Middle period, because that's what they hear first, and the Late period, because they aren't too enamored with the genius's Overt period.

The problem stems from the original, Overt fans, who finally embrace the Advanced Genius once they've had enough time to work out their anger and disappointment, allowing them to judge the Middle period more honestly. Plus by that time the Middle period stuff is old enough to have gained legitimacy. Helping matters is that the Late period genius typically produces a project that is regarded as a "return to form," which gives the original fan the coverage necessary to rethink the Middle period. But how does the Overt person suddenly jump levels of consciousness, which is just as unlikely as a genius suddenly sucking? I think the answer is that Overt people don't really believe anything, so they are everywhere and nowhere at the same time. They arbitrarily pop up along the continuum, sometimes ahead of and sometimes behind the public, and sometimes nearly even with—but never ahead of—the Advanced. In other words, God does play dice with the Overt.

Chapter Three

Advanced Musicians

Musicians were long the sole focus of the Advanced Genius Theory, so there is more known about what makes a musician Advanced than any other type of genius. It may be more accurate to say that we know more about the outward signs that suggest Advancement because we can't really *know* what makes someone Advanced. That's part of why the Advanced are Advanced. But years of study reveal that there are patterns across many Advanced musicians that occur too frequently to dismiss as coincidence. It starts with these: black leather jacket, long hair in the back, and dark sunglasses.

The Look of Advancement

For a long time, Britt and I believed that Advancement was limited to Lou Reed and Bob Dylan. There weren't many musicians we could point to who had achieved so much and fallen so far in the estimation of critics and their fans—including us. For a while we weren't even sure if those two were connected, until Britt saw an article describing a period in Dylan's life when he had long, frizzy hair and always wore black leather and sunglasses. This was significant because we had noticed that Lou Reed's look—black leather jacket, long hair in the back (a pre-irony mullet), dark sunglasses—had to be a part of his Advancement because it seemed so out of character for an artist with such an original mind. Black leather had been a sign of rebelliousness so long that by the mid-'80s it meant about as much as a tattoo does now, maybe less. The same goes for the dark sunglasses, which are the world's most obvious way to look cool and mysterious. Throw in a mullet, which even twenty years ago was not highly respected, and what you have is a pretty dumb-looking guy. But if Lou Reed chose to look that way, there must be something more to it. And if Bob Dylan did too, so we thought, then maybe something really interesting was happening.

As we dug deeper, we realized that an astounding number of musicians we admired had embraced this look at one time or another, including David Bowie, Miles Davis, and Michael Jackson, among others. The combination of jacket, hair, and glasses was so common among Advanced musicians that it became known as the Advanced Trinity. What was particularly interesting to me was that non-Advanced artists such as Alice Cooper and Billy Joel seemed to understand that one had to embrace the Trinity to enter the Advanced club; it was like some kind of secret handshake for geniuses. Joel sported the look in the "We Didn't Start the Fire" era (a song that was an homage to Dylan's "Subterranean Homesick Blues," I might add), insisting on wearing sunglasses during all his interviews. Joel doesn't quite rise to the level of artistic genius and therefore can't qualify for Advancement, but it was a good try nevertheless.

Bono, as we'll see a bit later, never officially joined the club, but he certainly visited enough to know the secret handshake. In one of the many videos for "One," he is shown drinking a beer and smoking a cigarette from time to time, without sunglasses. At the very end he puts on his sunglasses, which made those of us who knew about Advancement think he was making a statement: I am ready to Advance. But it wasn't to be—even though his character the Fly sported the perfect Advanced look, there was an element of irony in it. It's not too late for Bono, but it's going to take a lot for us to believe that he has honestly embraced the look.

Bono also had Advanced hair, but he made fun of himself for it, describing the style as being "business up front, party in the back." This is the way people refer to mullets now, and it saddens me that Bono would accept that view. It's Overt, of course, to make fun of mullets, as having one really is no dumber than expressing oneself by sporting other, more highly respected haircuts, such as a green spiked Mohawk. And while the mullet is thought of as a modern hairstyle, it has been around for centuries and has been fascinating people the entire time. For example, Marcel Proust wrote about the mullet's mysterious power (and practicality) in *Swann's Way*. Einstein had a bit of a mullet himself for a while, plus he loved wearing leather jackets, and though I don't have any record of his wearing dark sunglasses, he did spend his last twenty-two years at the Institute for Advanced Studies.

Rock 'n' Roll

Just as the Advanced Trinity seems to be an outdated expression of rebellion, so does the Advanced musician's love of rock 'n' roll. Rock at one time may have scared old people and closeted homosexuals masquerading as defenders of the nation's children, but now it's the music of grandparents, as safe as Benny Goodman or Bach. But that doesn't matter to the first generation of Advanced musicians, who worship rock 'n' roll because when they were young it was at the heart of a revolution that gave them the freedom to express themselves.

Though Advanced musicians share a love of Chuck Berry, Fats Domino, and especially Elvis Presley, in their early careers they made music antithetical to the accepted idea of what rock 'n' roll was supposed to be. That was on purpose, but it wasn't because they didn't respect rock 'n' roll. They just didn't have the courage to do it because straightforward rock 'n' roll was already beginning to seem old-fashioned. But as that generation of Advanced musicians became more comfortable with themselves, they could speak more openly about their affection for rock 'n' roll, regardless of its status. You can see this very clearly in Lou Reed's career, as he distanced himself slowly but surely from the spooky, droning music about S&M of his early days, moving toward pure rock music. In case anyone wasn't quite clear what he was up to, he wrote a song called "Rock 'n' Roll" for the last VU album just to make sure everyone knew where his allegiance lay.

But what is rock 'n' roll anyway?

I grew up in the 1970s and '80s listening to my dad's music (Buddy Holly and the Crickets, Led Zeppelin, the Doors, Rolling Stones, ZZ Top), which I just thought of as "rock 'n' roll" and still do. But when I look back at the style of music each of them played, there is almost no real connection. It occurs to me now that there never really was such music as rock 'n' roll. Even the King of Rock 'n' Roll was singing ballads, gospel, country, and other types of music as early as his first recording session. Surely it dawned on Lou Reed by the time he was ready to leave Velvet Underground that rock 'n' roll was really just a random label, as meaningless as most labels for movements, like postmodernism or surrealism. The only thing real about rock 'n' roll is the attitude, but not the attitude you're thinking about.

At some point in the 1960s rock 'n' roll got linked to sex and drugs, and an appealing but destructive stereotype was born. Appealing because it's a lot of fun to do drugs and have sex, destructive because doing those things can kill you. It's also destructive to one's development as an artist because it's hard to be original when you are a living cliché (even a cool one). And it's not even a rock cliché: jazz musicians discovered heroin long before rock 'n' roll existed.

Of course, many Advanced musicians started out using drugs, and there is no doubt that they made interesting music while they were using. However, most will say that they never touched drugs while actually recording or that nothing ever came of the sessions they did while high (with a few exceptions). After a while they realize that they can make more interesting music without drugs and also that not feeling bad helps you write interesting music. Most important is that they realized that rock music had nothing to do with the so-called rock-'n'-roll lifestyle and that it is impossible to Advance if you are hooked on drugs. Rock 'n' roll is about heightening your senses, not dulling them. When Elvis walked into the Sun studio, he wasn't on heroin, and Scotty Moore wasn't doing coke in the bathroom between takes, but no one has ever rocked harder than those guys did that night.

What is ironic is that casual sex and drug abuse are exactly what the preachers and politicians (who are portrayed as so ridiculous in every rock-history documentary) predicted rock 'n' roll would lead to. And the fascination with the stereotype, especially with the drug part, has stunted the artistic growth, not to mention killed, so many of rock's greatest practitioners. We've been essentially killing our own for forty years now, and there is no sign of it stopping (Amy Winehouse, Pete Doherty, and so on).

Professionalism

Another takeaway from the Sun sessions is that those guys could really play. Not only did they get a lot of sound from a three-piece, but they understood when to play a lot and, more important, when not to play a lot. But, as with the drugs myth, people became persuaded that rock music not only *can* be played by people who barely know how to play their instruments but that it *should* be. Even though most early rock music was played by seasoned musicians (Little Richard, Chuck Berry, Booker T and the MGs, James Brown) who were well versed in the history of music and could play in a variety of styles, sophistication was no longer allowed. That's why you think you don't like Steely Dan.

The reason the idea that you can be a rock musician without knowing how to play is so powerful is that people are generally lazy, preferring get-rich-quick schemes to saving their pennies. It takes a lot of practice to become a good musician, and that can be incredibly tedious. So if you simply decree that it is not necessary to be a good musician to make good music, the hard work is also not necessary. Not only that, anyone who makes the effort to become good is to be ostracized, like the kid who starts working on his science-fair project the day it's assigned rather than the night before it's due. He may seem like a dork at the time, but he's going to be the interesting one once he goes to college. And his project will be a lot better than everyone else's.

By now you're probably thinking that there have been plenty of bands that have made great records but "couldn't play." The musicians themselves often claim this. But in almost every case, they are exaggerating and are comparing how they played when they started with how they played later in life. The bands that actually can't play are all crappy punk bands you've never heard of. But the great ones all understood that if you really want to make good music, even punk music, you've got to work at it, practicing relentlessly and playing as many shows as possible to perfect your onstage act. No one understood this better than the ultimate punk band, the Ramones.

In the documentary *End of the Century* you learn that from the start the Ramones were a business, but ultimately an unsuccessful one. Unsuccessful because like all musicians who bother to form a band, they wanted to write hits but never could manage to do it. So they were stuck on the margins, where their hard-core fans wanted them anyway because it allowed those fans to feel better about their own failures in life. But that certainly wasn't for lack of trying. As far back as their CBGB days, they were selling an image, hiring an art director, dressing in matching outfits, and changing their names. Plus they wrote incredibly catchy (and short) tunes that were as infectious as any pop song. None of it would have made any difference, though, had they been from Topeka, Kansas, or Kankakee, Illinois. As much as people marvel at the unlikelihood that a bar like CBGB would be the center of the music scene, the reality is that there are bars like that all over America, they just aren't down the street from the center of the media universe.

However, the advantage of living in Kankakee is that you can suck for years while you work on your act and it doesn't matter because no one is really watching. If the Ramones hadn't worked as hard as they did to prepare themselves, they would have been destroyed before they began because of the intense competition from bands like Blondie, Television, and Talking Heads, which were all made up of accomplished musicians and songwriters. One of the ways the Ramones set themselves apart was by sticking exclusively to incredibly fast, incredibly short songs, which they played one after another with little more than a "one-two-three-four!" between songs. That sounds easy, but to pull it off, you have to practice the set—all the songs, in order, with count-offs between songs—beforehand. A lot of bands practice their songs in whatever order they feel like and then come up with set lists right before they go on, but that doesn't work if you want to put together a seamless performance. Needless to say, practicing the same songs the same way over and over is not much fun, but the ones who can't hack it don't become legends, and they absolutely don't Advance.

Almost everyone's first band is like the Ramones, just a bunch of guys who live in the same neighborhood. Usually they don't even know how to play instruments, but their parents are friends, they like the same records, and they like hanging out together. So each of them picks an instrument to play (short straw plays bass) and declare themselves a band. The band may develop chemistry through the years, but it will always be limited technically because the chance that a single neighborhood will produce a number of musical geniuses is extremely small (unless you grow up in Liverpool, Dublin, or various small towns in Georgia). This technical limitation is the reason that eventually Advanced musicians must go solo and find musicians who have the skill to help them realize their vision. This usually means session musicians, who can play anything you need and will play it the same way every take. Session musicians are mocked in the Overt world because they wear uncool clothes and play on uncool records, plus they can read music. (Reading music is inconsistent with the rock-'n'-roll aesthetic.) But Advanced Artists are looking for a sound, one that no one has made before, and they are going to chase it even if it means firing a friend because he can't keep perfect time. That is what a real artist, an Advanced Artist, does.

Technology

The Advanced are by definition innovative, so it follows that they will embrace technology. Musicians, especially rock musicians, who have long careers typically see a great deal of technological innovation, which makes the music they make early in their careers sound very different from their later work. Advanced musicians are thrilled to be able to record music that sounds more like what they have in their heads, so they welcome the clarity that modern recording techniques afford them. But since we are nostalgic by nature, the newer music suffers by comparison. We prefer the gritty sound of a song like "Street Fighting Man" to the more pristine "Love Is Strong." But it would be nothing less than dishonest and a bit pathetic if the Stones tried to make a song in 2008 that sounded like 1968. There are "lo-fi" bands that try to do this, but they either don't have the money to be hi-fi or they are just being Overt. Robert Pollard can pull it off, but that's only because he doesn't really belong to any time that I can identify. Plus, when you record six albums a year, who has time for mastering?

Part of the Overt ethos is a sort of selective Ludditeism, where technology is okay up to a certain point, but innovation afterward is evil. It's like the Unabomber typing his manifesto decrying the evils of technology. Never mind that the typewriter he used was the Internet of its day. Never mind that he used bombs. Forget about the tools he used to build his shack. And the paper he typed on. And language. Those were fine inventions, but after some arbitrary point, new things started to be bad for society. I'm not likening the Overt to the Unabomber—after all, he was really smart and had a good work ethic—but they do have arbitrary cutoff points for when things were acceptable. When the Stones were recording "Street Fighting Man," they were using the modern techniques of the day, so nothing has changed for them. But the Overt think that music by old people should sound old, with most of the actual music being left to the imagination, and, as previously discussed, people almost always prefer what might have been rather than what is.

The World Beat

When I speak of the "world beat" in reference to Advanced musicians, I mean only that they are open to all cultures, but with a particular fondness for African and island nations. Not only do the Advanced listen to music from around the world, they incorporate elements of it in their own music or at least have a Brazilian bassist and maybe a Nigerian percussionist in their band. The Overt, on the other hand, typically limit themselves geographically and sonically, usually under the guise of keeping their style of music "pure." As Henry Rollins has noted in numerous VH1 and VH1 Classic documentaries, pure punk rockers are really just pure conformists who can't think for themselves.

There's really not that big a leap from rock to world music, because it is influenced by rock 'n' roll, just as rock 'n' roll was rooted in music that came from cultures too numerous to count. I believe this is the reason rock 'n' roll is pervasive around the world: it is the best bits of all cultures distilled into catchy three-minute songs. Sam Phillips, the Advanced producer/label owner who discovered Elvis Presley (though it might be more accurate to say that Elvis delivered himself to Phillips), understood that it would take someone like Elvis (white) to get the Overt public to embrace music that had come to them by way of an around-the-world cruise. To allow themselves to accept exotic music, the Overt of the time needed it to look local, and that's what Phillips gave them.

One particular style of World Beat music that is beloved by all Advanced musicians (and sorority girls) is reggae. Willie Nelson, Paul McCartney, the Pixies, the Police, the Clash, Blondie, and countless others have all written reggae songs or played around with the reggae style. But I have to confess that I have the same opinion of reggae that I do of the Grateful Dead: I don't understand what all the fuss is about. And I always feel a bit embarrassed when a nonreggae band such as, say, Guns N' Roses goes into a reggae beat. I'm thinking particularly of the reggae part it added to its cover of "Knockin' on Heaven's Door" at the Freddie Mercury tribute concert. What got me was that Bob Dylan has written actual reggae songs, so if GN'R really wanted to do a Dylan reggae song, why not do one of them instead? At the very least it could have played "I and I" from *Infidels*. But the crowd loved it, so I guess I'm just being Overt. My personal feelings aside, there is something about reggae that inspires Advanced musicians. In this case, I'll have to just record this fact rather than explain it.

Rap Music

In the Advanced world, rap lies somewhere between rock and reggae. Like reggae, Advanced musicians not only love it, they think they should do it themselves. This has produced some of the most Advanced moments in the history of music. Debbie Harry kicked things off with "Rapture," the first rap number one. That wasn't the only rap that sprang from CBGB: Dee Dee Ramone quit the Ramones to fulfill his destiny as the rapper Dee Dee King, producing the Advanced classic "Funky Man." Do not listen to this song until you are in a completely Advanced state of mind. KRS-One's appearance on R.E.M.'s "Radio Song" was Advanced of him, not of R.E.M. He had the most to lose, after all. The same goes for Chuck D., who appeared on Sonic Youth's "Kool Thing." I have to give Sonic Youth some credit, though, as I can't think of a better way to annoy their core fan base than to have a guest rapper on their first single on a major label. Of course there was the pairing of Run-DMC and Aerosmith, but that's something we'll have to get back to a little later.

The post–Brian Wilson Beach Boys dabbled in rap, teaming up with the Fat Boys to make "Wipeout." My favorite aspect of this song is that "Wipeout" was not a Beach Boys song. Wilson himself tried his hand at rap, and it is perhaps the most Advanced thing I've ever had the pleasure of listening to. Words cannot describe this effort, but I can give you some context. The song was featured on the album *Sweet Insanity* (which was rejected by Wilson's label), recorded while he was under the spell of his psychologist, Eugene Landy. In addition to having Landy as coproducer, *Sweet Insan-*

ity included performances by Weird Al Yankovic and Bob Dylan. Even without the rap, this is dangerously Advanced. But alas, the rap does exist, and it's called "Smart Girls."

The rap is about Wilson's infatuation with intelligent women and includes bits of old Beach Boys songs intended to illustrate that this was not always the case. Wilson combines lyrics from songs that show only a superficial appreciation for women—"Help Me, Rhonda," "Wouldn't It Be Nice," and "God Only Knows"— with lines that show his more mature point of view, such as "strokin' me with hypotheses" and "intelligence is an aphrodisiac." You owe it to yourself to listen to the song.

The only issue I have with it is that, as the album title implies, Brian Wilson was a bit crazy when he was making this song. Just as drug use can mute Advancement, so can mental illness, and he was clearly not stable around that time. However, he was unstable when he was writing most of the great Beach Boys songs, so there may be nothing crazier about "Smart Girls" than there was about most of the *Smile* project. Certainly the lyrics are no more ridiculous, but that was the part he was least responsible for. While the results may be substandard as a rap song, it is laudable that Wilson had the courage to put himself out there so boldly. What is important is that Wilson was embracing rap when many older rockers thought that rap wasn't real music. As ridiculous as "Smart Girls" may seem to you today, at the very least, Brian Wilson was on the right side of history.

While rockers who rap are often Advanced, it's hard for me to tell when a rapper is Advanced. I'd like to say that rappers who rock, like Run-DMC and Ice-T, are Advanced, but it's not that easy. The rap culture is very different from the avant-garde rock scene, so whereas the singer of Modest Mouse might be reluctant to reveal how much money he has made through his music, a typical rapper might be reluctant *not* to. But if the rapper is Advanced, he can't simply reject materialism (that is, do the opposite of what is expected); he would have to do something that is original. Maybe that would be something like Snoop Dogg's becoming a producer of pornography and coaching a kids' football team. Or maybe it would be Ice Cube's appearance in the *Are We There Yet?* franchise. I really don't know. But the biggest reason I can't identify Advanced rappers with any certainty is that I just don't know enough about the music to judge accurately. It's like asking an American with two years of high school German to critique a German comic's performance. The Wu-Tang Clan, though, has embraced Chinese culture, made movies, rapped from jail by phone, been investigated by the FBI, appeared in video games, had a clothing line, gone solo, and reunited. This is Advancement in any language.

There are other minor hallmarks of Advancement—writing songs about sports, featuring unflattering pictures of oneself on album covers, reuniting with band members, hosting satellite radio shows, playing the Super Bowl halftime show, saying "baby" in songs—but even the major hallmarks already discussed are superficial and not even exclusively for the Advanced. So to deepen our understanding of Advanced musicians, it is essential to look at what makes their art Advanced, rather than the package that art may be wrapped in. Even if it's wrapped in black leather.

Chapter Four

The Most Advanced
Musicians Ever

I n 1970 Bob Dylan released a double album of covers, instrumentals, and live tunes called *Self Portrait*. In his now famous review of the album for *Rolling Stone*, Greil Marcus asked, "What is this shit?!" Five years later, Lou Reed recorded a double album of feedback called *Metal Machine Music*, and when it came time for James Wolcott to review it, the only album he could compare it to was *Self Portrait*. (To paraphrase, he asked, "What is this shit?! *Self Portrait*?") The albums sound nothing alike, but Wolcott was exactly correct to compare them, even though, like Marcus, everything he wrote in his review was wrong. The connection is that they both represent the end of the Overt period for the two most Advanced musicians ever.

Dylan and Lou Reed are both credited with bringing a new kind of poetry to rock 'n' roll, though I think their introduction of prose to rock 'n' roll was more significant. Each brought novelistic elements to songwriting that required a completely new kind of music, beyond just throwing away the traditional three-minute song with verse-chorus-verse structure. Not only were the words different from anything anyone had done before, they were delivered in a new way. Both are thought to have limited, if not downright bad, vocal ability, but if you've ever heard someone who can "really sing" do their songs, you hear how much is lost. The truth is that they are both fantastic singers and are not nearly as limited as people think. On *Self Portrait* alone, Dylan uses at least four completely different singing styles (I'm partial to the country-crooner style made famous in "Lay Lady Lay"), and when I saw Lou Reed live a few years back, he occasionally put aside the talky, weirdly arrhythmic style he's used the last fifteen years or so in favor of a tuneful, even beautiful delivery. And they came alive in New York City and shared an affinity for black leather, bad haircuts, and sunglasses (of course). Yet if they are so similar, why does it feel as if they, or at least the idea of them, reside in completely different parts of our collective brain?

I've come up with a couple of possible answers. One is that they have used similar means but for totally different ends. Dylan is raw while Reed is polished, Dylan is emotional while Reed is cerebral, Dylan is in love with a woman while Reed is in love with his guitar. After immersing myself in the Advanced work of both for the last several months, it strikes me that Dylan is inspired most when he is on the move, but he has no ultimate destination. (I'm not going to say he has no direction home, but it would be true were I to do so.) Lou Reed, however, appears to be leading up to a fixed point in the distance that only he can see. While artistically Dylan is essentially the same guy who copied Woody Guthrie as a college freshman in Minnesota, Reed has become an ever more refined version of himself. Dylan keeps adding layers while Reed is perpetually shedding them. You might say that Dylan is Pablo Picasso to Lou Reed's Piet Mondrian.

The other explanation for why Bob Dylan and Lou Reed are in different parts of our brain is that they are so Advanced, our heads would explode were they too close together. To be on the safe side, we'll look at them both in greater detail, but separately.

Lou Reed

As you know, Lou Reed was the inspiration for the Advanced Genius Theory, as Britt and I tried to figure out what makes a guy go from singing about heroin to rapping about waffles. Like most people, we had trouble following him down this difficult path. In fact, if it weren't for the Theory, the work between his initial success as a solo artist and his so-called return to form with *New York* might have been lost. Certainly that music would not have been considered evidence of artistic growth.

But let's go back to pre-Advancement Lou Reed to examine exactly why he qualified in the first place. When he was in the Velvet Underground, he wrote great songs about bondage and waiting for drug dealers, offering an alternative to the hippie peppermint-lollipop stuff that characterized much of the '60s. In addition to the weird lyrics, VU used unconventional instruments like the viola, had a girl drummer who turned her kick drum on its side, and employed a German chanteuse with a thick accent. Plus it had Andy Warhol's endorsement and looked extremely cool. It was this combination of factors that made them stand out from their contemporaries. Of course, standing out is often a recipe for failure, and so it was for VU.

You don't need to be told by now that his time with the Velvet Underground was Lou Reed's Overt period. While it took guts to go against the prevailing tastes at the time—a decision that nearly destroyed his career before it started—his work was still defined by his reaction to the art of others, rather than an intrinsic expression. Clearly, being innovative was a central motivation of songs like "Venus in Furs" and others, and he wore that motivation as

Overtly as possible. But even his style of Overtness had a touch of Advancement. As early as the first VU record, *The Velvet Underground & Nico* (the one with the Andy Warhol banana on it), he was challenging people's expectations, selecting the genuinely lovely "Sunday Morning" as the opening track. This was a song that was supposed to be Nico's but Reed sang it instead, just to prove that he could be beautiful when he felt like it. Before they were signed to a record label, the band was known for being, basically, freaks who made a lot of noise, so opening the record with a nice song like "Sunday Morning" was an interesting decision. Overt, but still interesting.

Each new record after *Nico* sounded completely different from the last one, yet they always managed to sound like the Velvet Underground. *White Light/White Heat* was the assault on the senses one might have expected from their first record. It included "Sister Ray," a twelve-and-a-half-hour song that takes a dig at the climate of the Carolinas (among other things). On *The Velvet Underground*, the group's third album, Reed's songwriting showed a completely different character than what the few people who had been listening to the band's records had come to expect. Lester Bangs described this new style in a review for *Rolling Stone*, saying that Reed combined "almost overpowering musical lyricism with deeply yearning, compassionate lyrics." (This was the album that featured "Jesus," another early indicator of Reed's impending Advancement.) While Bangs was pleased, he was in a very select group, and VU sold relatively few records. But that's what happens when you appeal to just a few people in the first place and then change your sound so much that you turn them off too. At the time, it might have appeared to be career suicide, but Reed was interested in something more than just selling records, though I'm not sure if even he knew what that something was.

He left the band before finishing VU's last real record, *Loaded*, though not before channeling the Marshall Tucker Band in "Oh,

Sweet Nothing" and contributing what would later become one of his signature tunes, "Sweet Jane." (He apparently was not a fan of the introduction in the final version of the album, so he fixed it up on the live album *Rock 'n' Roll Animal*. More on that record later.) Of course, the song "Rock and Roll" was Reed's strongest statement to date that he would be an Advanced Artist, declaring that a life could be saved by rock 'n' roll. Though a line like that could be easily misinterpreted as cheekiness, he later told Elvis Costello on his show *Spectacle* that he was living proof of rock's power to save.

Despite all the hints of Advancement, Reed's entire history in the Velvet Underground—except for the reunion—is a story of Overtness. While you have to give him some credit for making such bold artistic choices, he was still dealing mostly with opposites. He was the antihippie who challenged expectations by oscillating between loud and quiet, sweet and harsh. His first solo record was more or less a continuation along the same path, as it was a collection of songs that didn't make it onto official VU albums. It flopped as spectacularly as an album that no one cared too much about can. Yet the record company stuck with him and allowed him to make 1972's *Transformer*, which would yield his biggest hit, "Walk on the Wild Side." There's a lot to say about this album and that song in particular, starting with the choice of producer: David Bowie.

David Bowie is one of those rare artists, like Dolly Parton and Milton Berle, who manage to be very strange but still loved by everyone. Bowie also happened to be a big fan of Reed, and he wanted other people to see why they should be fans too. So two of the greatest artists of the last fifty years got together to make one of the greatest albums in rock history. But all the Velvet Underground records were great too, so what was it that made *Transformer* so much more palatable to a wider audience? There wasn't a thematic shift in Reed's songs, as the album is filled with songs about the weirdos he had encountered in his life doing the weird things they did, including aberrant sex and drug use. And his voice certainly didn't change. If anything, his delivery had become even flatter and more deadpan than it had been in the previous records. I think the success of the album came down to Advancement.

The first sign that Reed was ready to begin Advancing was that he and Bowie decided to use highly trained studio musicians. His decision to hire musicians (including the oompah band featured on "Goodnight Ladies") who were paid for their time in the studio, rather than forming a new band with some friends, paid off in other ways besides just helping him raise the level of musicianship on his album. Specifically, had the bass player not found out that he could get paid twice as much if he played one bass part and then overdubbed another on top of it (his union stipulated that players be paid by the track, not by the song), we might never have heard what might be the most recognizable bass part in the history of rock music, and "Walk on the Wild Side" might never have made it onto the radio. Sure, Reed got lucky that he happened to choose a highly entrepreneurial bassist, but had he chosen to play with people he knew well and not gone outside his comfort zone, the happy accident wouldn't have happened. It helped, too, that he had written such an amazing song that it would inspire a session player to make up something so remarkable rather than just going through the motions and getting his check(s).

Transformer also marks the introduction of highly trained African-American women backup singers to the Lou Reed oeuvre. The only acceptable way to have backup singing in the world of weirdo music is to sing with your bandmates (Modest Mouse is a good example), but again, if you have a sound in your head that requires just the right note hit in just the right way, your chain-smoking lead guitarist might not necessarily have what it takes to get the job done. Even though I have written about the Theory for so many years, I still don't get the appeal of professional backup singers, but that's obviously my shortcoming because all the greats have used them. Reed not only used them but boldly announced that he was using them in the lyrics of "Walk on the Wild Side." That was Advanced, but it was even more Advanced when he revised himself in a later reworking of the song, taking out the reference to "colored girls." A lesser artist would not have changed his lyrics for the sake of cultural sensitivity, but Reed knows there are more interesting ways to rebel than to use inconsiderate language.

At the time of the making of *Transformer*, he was still Overt enough for his vision to include making hit records, and since for the first time he had finally assembled the right producer and musicians to help him realize that vision, that's exactly what happened. "Walk on the Wild Side" seems like an obvious hit in retrospect, but just think how many hit songs there were before Reed came along that featured a transvestite giving blow jobs, not to mention rhyming "head" with "head." As when he showed that he could sing in a conventionally beautiful way, Reed proved that he could do anything he wanted to, no matter how impossible it might have seemed before he did it. But Reed is not the kind of artist who wants to do the same thing twice, so after having his hit, it was time to move on. The result was the biggest bummer of 1973 (and maybe all time): *Berlin*.

For many listeners, the album is incredibly depressing, but not just because of the tragic subject matter—more junkies, this time with kids thrown in to raise the emotional stakes—but because the work was heavily orchestral thanks to the producer, Bob Ezrin, who was famous for his collaboration with Alice Cooper and who would later work his magic on Kiss's *Destroyer*. For some reason, people just couldn't stomach the idea of a Lou Reed album featuring a horn section and a choir. Some were angered to the point that they forgot that they'd never thrown a punch in their lives: Stephen Davis of *Rolling Stone* wrote of *Berlin*, "There are certain records that are so patently offensive that one wishes to take some kind of physical vengeance on the artists that perpetrate them." Surely Lou Reed shook in his (black leather) boots at the thought of the terrible physical vengeance a rock critic might take. After his terrifying threat, Davis added, presciently, "Goodbye, Lou." After this devastating review, Reed would make only about twenty more albums, and *Berlin* would rank a mere 344 on *Rolling Stone*'s list of the 500 greatest albums of all time.

The next stage in Lou Reed's Advancement was the live album from 1974, *Rock 'n' Roll Animal*, which, along with 1986's *Mistrial*, was the catalyst of the creation of the Advanced Genius Theory. When I first heard this record, I was completely horrified. In high school, Britt and I listened to *Rock 'n' Roll Animal*, purely for laughs because we could not believe how terrible it was. Not terrible, actually, just ridiculous. In particular, "White Light/White Heat," with its thumping bass and Guitar Center–salesmen solos, was just over-the-top stupid. Or so I thought. I was conditioned to expect the Velvet Underground version of Lou Reed, so I couldn't relate at all to what he was trying to do in *Rock 'n' Roll Animal* and rejected it as cheesy. Later, however, I absolutely loved it, but ironically. I thought that he knew how ridiculous it was to jazz it up with fancy musicians and Southern Rock riffs, so he did it as a trick on the ignorant or just to make people mad. Now I understand that it isn't ridiculous at all and that the *Rock 'n' Roll Animal* version of "White Light/White Heat" is much more interesting than if he had tried to reproduce the Velvet Underground version. This is how it works with the music of Advanced musicians: you hate it and feel betrayed, you think it's a joke, then later (usually much later), you love it and wish the stuff the musician was doing today sounded more like the stuff that you originally hated. And the cycle continues.

Sally Can't Dance came next, and I'm not quite sure what to make of it. The record was a hit, but he denounced it, claiming that he was just doing what people told him to. He also said, "It seems like the less I'm involved with a record, the bigger a hit it becomes. If I weren't on the record at all next time around, it might go to number one." Perhaps it was that thought that inspired him to make *Metal Machine Music,* which may be his most misunderstood offering. This was the work of an Overt Artist in transition, but it is not the Advanced Irritant that many thought it to be. (Reed contributed to this misperception, writing in the liner notes that he had never listened to it all the way through.) Some appreciated the audacity of the (double) album because it certainly takes guts to make something that is sure to please almost no one. In fact, for thirty years just about everyone but Lester Bangs believed that Reed made *MMM* for the sole purpose of displeasing people. It was thought that it was merely Reed's attempt to sabotage his own career after becoming disenchanted with success. But in the last few years the album was revived by the German new-music ensemble Zeitkratzer, which has been praised by critics and Reed himself. (Advanced Artists always love other people's versions of their music, usually insisting that the cover is better than the original.) The gradual acceptance of *Metal Machine Music*'s greatness is yet another example of an Advanced Artist being years ahead of everyone, even though he was himself Overt at the time. Liking the album immediately was also quite an Advanced feather in Lester Bangs's cap.

In my search for other real-time reviews of *Metal Machine Music* and the rest of Lou Reed's solo works, I found that no consensus on his career emerges. Either he was too serious or too unserious, too commercial or too noncommercial, a great singer or a terrible singer, and countless other conflicting opinions. The only thing that journalists agree on, whether they love him or hate him, is that he is a jerk. (Even Lester Bangs said that, but lovingly.) There are endless accounts of Lou Reed's mistreatment of writers assigned to interviewing him, and, in their defense, they were just doing their jobs. However in his defense, most of the stories come from journalists who were just doing their jobs badly. Of course, it's the journalists who get the last word because they write about the experience, so no matter how unprepared they were or inane their questions, he's always going to be the asshole.

Luckily for Lou Reed, we like it when old people are assholes, which is probably why critics decided to praise *New York*, even though it sounded pretty much like all the rest of his albums, though maybe with a little less panache. I would guess also that the record company rep assigned to promoting the record was better at his/her job than the ones who had done the previous records. You'd be surprised at how much difference that can make in the critical reception and "buzz" around an album. It is a great record—it is by Lou Reed, after all—but that is often of secondary importance in terms of how a record by an older artist is perceived, especially one who hates journalists so much.

I had an initial reaction to *Mistrial* similar to the one I had to *Rock 'n' Roll Animal* (sadness, confusion, hurt feelings) but now I understand that any cut on *Mistrial* is as good as "Sister Ray," plus much weirder. Anyone can make a lot of noise and sing obscure lyrics, but it takes someone truly weird to make a song like "Original Wrapper," where he sings about watching TV, waffles, and pitchers and batters. This was also the time when he became completely committed to the Advanced Trinity. (Just check out the album cover.) When Lou Reed's hair was short on top and long in the back, there were no mullet.coms. There was no ironic attention paid to that hairstyle. Reed's appearance was much weirder than the look he cultivated in VU because almost no one would appreciate it. In VU, he at least had the transvestites and pushers on his side. And the music on *Mistrial*, with its drum machines and generally synthetic production qualities, was the sonic equivalent of the mullet.

Like your hairstyle, glasses, and jacket, the type of guitar you play can say a lot about how Advanced you are. The Overt typically use Fenders and Gibsons in the classic shapes (Telecaster, Gibson Les Paul, Mustang), semiobscure guitars in weird shapes (Danelectro, Supro, National), or ironic guitars (flying V, double-neck). This is because they are comfortable sounding like other musicians and they want to look cool. But since the Advanced chase new sounds, love technology, and are never afraid of looking terrible, Lou Reed leans toward guitars with a little less pedigree and even less aesthetic appeal. The most Advanced of all his choices was the guitar he used during the Velvet Underground reunion. It had no headstock and the body was barely wider than the neck. If you don't know much about guitars, think of it this way: if the flying V is the mullet of guitars (which it is), Lou Reed's guitar is the haircut people who have mullets make fun of.

Earlier I mentioned that one of the minor signs of Advancement is featuring pictures of yourself on your album covers. Lou Reed's album covers, however, are majorly Advanced. *Transformer* is the beginning of his long tradition of featuring himself on the cover. Since it is an early work, it's a pretty artsy shot, with his features washed out to the point of making him seem positively pretty. *Berlin* too is artsy, and it is a step back as far as Advancement is concerned because there are other people besides Reed in the picture. This is against the Advanced Code, and Reed quickly rectified his mistake with *Sally Can't Dance.* We're still in somewhat washed-out, artsy territory here, but his hair is blond, and he looks a bit like a flirting Dr. Zaius.

Metal Machine Music represented a step toward Advancement visually even as it was Overt sonically. He is sporting the Trilogy look, except his hair is a little too short. Also, he is not looking directly at the camera, which is an Overt touch. He is dressed like Joel Grey for *Coney Island Baby,* and he's a blue flame for *Rock and Roll Heart* (highly Advanced title). I love those covers, but they aren't quite Advanced, at least not as much as *Street Hassle,* where we see a glimpse of what appears to be a satiny black blouse while the shimmering light of Advancement reflects off his sunglasses. *Mistrial* is pure, no-frills Advancement, just Lou, his leather, and his guitar, while *New Sensations* is notable for showing him twice: once inside a TV and once holding a joystick, presumably controlling himself on that TV. But my personal favorite is *Legendary Hearts,* which I thought violated the album-cover rule because it shows a motorcycle helmet and two black gloves but no Lou Reed. Except if you look closely, you'll find a faint reflection of him in the helmet. Now just try to tell me he doesn't know he's Advanced.

Even after Advancement came to me, I have had moments of doubt and believed that he had indeed outlived his genius. I was particularly concerned about the music he did for a piece of theater called *Time Rocker* (though I never doubted that the title was Advanced) and the concept album he recorded based on the works of Edgar Allan Poe, called *The Raven* (the album cover features a raven in a black leather jacket). The latter especially shook my confidence because not only is Poe a darling of the Overt, but the music was simply not good. I didn't think I could ever like it. But then I went with my mom to see him live in 2005, and the best songs of the night were all from *The Raven,* except for "The Blue Mask." It made me go back for another listen, and unsurprisingly, it has some truly amazing songs that I just didn't get at the time of the album's release. However, there are some turkeys in *The Raven* that I still think are no good. So what does that mean for the Theory? Advanced Geniuses are not infallible, they are just right more often than everyone else, no matter how many people disagree with them. Lou Reed has been right about just about everything he has done artistically, but because he is willing to experiment, he occasionally fails. On the other hand, maybe he doesn't fail at all and I'm just not Advanced enough to recognize the experiment, much less judge its outcome.

Bob Dylan

The story of Bob Dylan's rise from Minnesota kid to Greenwich Village open-mic-night regular to Voice of His Generation is one that is known in great detail, but things get pretty hazy after that, around the time he had his motorcycle accident (even the details of that accident are hazy). Dylan, who like most Advanced Geniuses enjoys making up things about his past when talking to journalists, helped build the mystery surrounding himself. Mystery is good for business, but keeping one's true identity a secret is often self-defense. Even if you tell journalists the truth, they can get the story wrong (sometimes on purpose), so you might as well get the facts wrong yourself. Perhaps Dylan felt that if he was a little left of factual, the journalists would miss to the right and the true story would be told.

Whatever his reasons, Dylan allowed people to believe anything they wanted as long as they left him alone with his wife and kids. In this vacuum a perception was formed, and then hardened, that he had lost it. By the late 1980s, the view of Dylan was that he had become a mumbling caricature of a once-great musician who needed, for the good of the baby boomers, just to stop. But then came *Time Out of Mind,* and all of a sudden he was great again and even speaking coherently, most notably during his acceptance speech at the 1999 Oscar awards for his song "Things Have Changed" from *Wonder Boys.* Things had changed, but Dylan hadn't. As Dave Van Ronk says, he was exactly the same guy in his later years as he was when he came to New York the first time, looking for Woody Guthrie. The same but Advanced, I should add.

In those early days as now, Dylan was open to everything— pop, rock, folk, Tiny Tim—but that wasn't evident in his music. His entire career, like Picasso's, is made up of phases where he completely scraps what he was working on before for something new until the new style no longer inspires him, and then it's on to the next thing. In the early '60s, he just happened to be inspired by folk music, which, according to his autobiography, seemed more timely than anything else going on at the time. But even then, when he was young and Overt, he admired boxers and military men and was comforted by an approving glance from the wrestler Gorgeous George. (The Advanced love Gorgeous George.) Plus, though he played only folk music, he says that he loved all music and that "there are no bad songs," even the most sugary pop songs. So, like Lou Reed, his art was Overt but he was Advanced in spirit.

I can't leave out something about the "going electric" business because it is essential to the story of Dylan's Advancement. I don't think he thought it was such a huge deal at the time, though he certainly heard the boos at Newport and as he toured around with the new electric material. Even today, Bob Dylan seems unable to understand why people get so worked up about what he does. What is easy to understand is why he felt so hemmed in by the folk scene. First of all, just as Advanced musicians must go solo, they can also never really be a part of a scene because it's too restricting artistically. To be a member in good standing in any scene demands conformity, which leads to mediocrity because the rules are made by the least of its members. For Dylan to be acceptable to the folk scene, he had to stick to doing topical songs, alone, with an acoustic guitar and a harmonica. Of course, the true artists within the folk scene were not that offended at Dylan's turn to rock 'n' roll. Pete Seeger, who was supposedly so offended by Dylan's electric set that he tried to find an ax with which to chop up the power cords, was actually just upset that he couldn't hear the words. It was the common folkies who called Dylan "Judas," not the royalty.

The queen of the folk scene, Joan Baez, seems to have the best take on Dylan's early years and his subsequent development. Despite her reputation for being humorless (see *SNL*'s sketch "Make Joan Baez Laugh"), she's actually pretty funny, including doing a super impersonation of Dylan, whom she calls "Bobby." She knew early on that he wasn't like her. She really believed in the causes she was fighting for, while he was just following whatever inspired him at the time, whether it was the murder of Medgar Evers or brass beds.

When Baez talks about "Bobby" these days, she sounds like a proud mother whose child has grown up to be a happy, successful adult, but the pride is diminished somewhat because he didn't go down the path she would have chosen. On a larger scale, the fans of the Advanced are also like parents, but unlike Baez, who achieved everything she wanted, the fans are disappointed because their "child" (the Advanced Artist) chose not to live out their unfulfilled dreams. They look to artists to make the sacrifices that they are afraid to make themselves. In Dylan's case, he was expected to be loyal to a style of music so a bunch of white college kids could feel as if they were making a difference. One of the differences between Lou Reed and Dylan is that in Dylan's Overt days he was singing to people who were pretending to care about what was going on in the world while Reed's audience was pretending *not* to care about what was going on in the world. In both cases, staying on the same course led nowhere, and Dylan was Advanced enough to see that if he didn't break free, he was going to end up doing fund-raisers for PBS like Peter, Paul and Mary.

After leaving the PBS track behind, Dylan burned through folk, rock, and country, then released *Self Portrait*, which, as I wrote in the introduction to this chapter, was an eclectic collection of some original material, covers, standards, instrumentals, and live performances. Even though it has a reputation for being a piece of junk created by Dylan to put off his followers, *Self Portrait* is probably his most interesting and satisfying record. But it's easy to see why critics and fans thought of it as a joke that only Dylan got, because not only did it feature covers that were seemingly out of character for Dylan ("The Boxer"? "Blue Moon"?) but it was a *double* album of covers that were seemingly out of character that he called *Self Portrait*. However, this was not merely an example of

Dylan's being an Advanced Irritant, even though he likely enjoyed making a record he knew people would reject. There is a vast difference between making music for people to hate and making music you like even though you know other people will hate it. The former is what Overt Artists do, but Dylan seems to have been up to the latter.

If you take the time to become intimate with *Self Portrait,* you'll find that it is less like *Metal Machine Music* and more like another, more celebrated, double album: *The Beatles* or, as it is known by people who aren't Overt, the White Album. Like the White Album, it's filled with songs of different genres, voices, mining songs, and half-finished-sounding miscellany held together only by the audacity of an artist so sure of himself that he knows his throwaways are better than the best work of many of his rivals. In addition to featuring some truly fascinating interpretations of songs you'd never expect to hear Dylan sing, the album is compelling because it shows an artist in the process of becoming Advanced: many of the tracks were recordings of his *Nashville Skyline* band trying to find the sound of the room. In this way, the album is like the series of studies a painter does in preparation for the final product. This is not to say that the product itself isn't great, but at the very least, one can get the satisfaction of hearing an artist being himself, even if he is singing someone else's songs. That's why *Self Portrait* is such an appropriate title.

Of course, as Cate Blanchett could tell you, Dylan has had many selves. On *Self Portrait,* he sings in several different voices, and that habit has lasted throughout his career. Most singers' voices change as they get older: for most rock singers the upper range goes, which is why so many older bands require female backup singers to take over the high parts. A few voices, such as Elvis Costello's, become more nuanced and powerful with age. But Dylan, like Lou Reed, is in a category by himself. If you listen to his entire discography on shuffle, it is astounding how his voice has changed over the years.

If you didn't know who you were listening to, you could easily be convinced that you were hearing five or six different singers. Other singers, such as Morrissey and Bono, add little tricks like growling and singing falsetto to their repertoire, but Dylan completely changes everything about the way he sounds. He has gone through several phases, each with its own voice, including (in roughly chronological order):

- Fake Woody Guthrie Bob
- Voice of a Generation Bob
- Electric Bob
- Country Bob
- Angry Bob
- Faithful Bob
- Marianne Faithfull Bob
- Grateful Bob
- Not Dark Bob

Not only has he changed the sound of his voice, he has also changed the intonation of his lyrics to the point where you can be listening to a live performance and not realize that you've been listening to one of your favorite songs. And just when you think you've got him figured out, he changes again. It would not surprise me in the least to hear him sing like Linda Ronstadt on his next record.

Of all the phases Bob Dylan has passed through over the years, the most fascinating to me is his Christian period. Analyzing his motives is probably a waste of time, so let's stick to the music and the reaction to it. The first two albums of the period, *Slow Train Coming* and *Saved*, were purely religious, while he included some secular touches on the third, *Shot of Love*. Interestingly, *Rolling Stone* founder Jann Wenner was immediately a fan of *Slow Train Coming*, which makes me wonder why he had so many Overt people working for him. One of those people, Kurt Loder, wrote that the album "affected a faceless R&B ambiance," even though it was produced by Jerry Wexler, who knew more about creating an R&B sound than just about anyone in the world. But Loder seems to have been put off by the inclusion of religious themes in a Dylan record (you might say that Loder preferred faithless R&B ambiance), so he was unlikely to have positive feelings toward the record regardless of the execution, and we probably shouldn't take his opinion too seriously. Yet, because of Overt, God-fearing (not the good kind) reviewers like Loder, *Slow Train Coming* and the other religious records aren't taken seriously. Hopefully I can help these records be born again.

If "Precious Angel," "In the Garden," and "Property of Jesus" were called "Filthy Statue," "At the Party," and "Property of Ginsberg," all three would be considered among Dylan's finest. As it is, I feel self-conscious listening to them in my car with my windows down, especially in a hip neighborhood. It isn't necessarily the explicit religiosity of these songs that makes it so difficult for us to like them but that it's Bob Dylan writing them. The confusing thing for me is that his message isn't all that different from that of his earlier songs. He always knew better than everyone else ("Masters of War," "Positively 4th Street"), it's just that his self-confidence came from a different source during this period: God. The Overt people were thrilled when Dylan was attacking the industrial military complex or tearing apart ex-lovers, but not so much when he turned his pen against them.

On *Shot of Love*, Dylan sang as much about how everyone else is damned (and damned stupid besides) as how he is saved. Plenty of Advanced Artists have told their fans that they can go to Hell, but Dylan is the only one to have meant it literally. Many critics have complained that in *Shot of Love* Dylan wallows in self-pity, whining about how misunderstood his devotion to Jesus is. But if we were to disallow self-pity as a topic for songwriting, we wouldn't have many songs left (and Morrissey would have to find a different line of work). Other critics have asserted that *Shot of Love* is just plain bad and marks the beginning of a lost decade. (*Saved* came out in 1980, but God, not the calendar, is blamed for its badness.) If you are like most people, you've never even bothered to listen to the record because it is practically forgotten. I'm begging you to buy it. Don't worry, I guarantee it will be on sale.

I first heard *Shot of Love* as a teenager and thought it was just cheesy, overproduced rock 'n' roll like all '80s-era Dylan. With the help of Advancement, I rediscovered it in the last couple of years, and I think it is among his five best records. There are some clichéd rock licks and some dated studio tricks, but look beyond that and you will find some truly Advanced music: professional backup singers, session players, reggae, rock licks, fancy production, it's all there, and right from the first moments of the title track (except for the reggae, which he takes a while to get to). The second song, "Heart of Mine," is a lovely, piano-heavy tune that shows off Dylan's ability to sing in a conventional style when called upon to do so. He's positively vulnerable in his portrayal of a man's losing battle with his desire for love from the wrong source. "Property of Jesus," which I mentioned before, is proof that Christian rock is indeed possible. "Lenny Bruce" is probably the most Advanced song on the record because I don't get it, though I do love the line "He never did get any Golden Globe award." One day I'm sure the song will make me cry, but I'm not there yet.

"Dead Man" is a haunting little reggae number, "Watered-Down Love" sounds like a song you'd hear on the radio and not change the channel, and "In the Summertime" sounds like a Bob Dylan song. But there is no better rock song, by Dylan or anyone else, than "The Groom's Still Waiting at the Altar." Backed by musicians playing like the most psychotic bar band in history, Dylan sounds like a mix between Jonathan Edwards and Johnny Rotten. And the lyrics are sublime, scary, and hilarious. Every line is worth recounting, but I'm particularly fond of this verse because it recalls the plight of the Advanced: "Try to be pure at heart, they arrest you for robbery / Mistake your shyness for aloofness, your shyness for snobbery."

I believe that part of why Dylan's music from the 1980s has a bad reputation is that people just seem to be generally embarrassed about the aesthetics of that decade. The part that we don't like to admit is that if the TV, music, and movies of that decade are pathetic, then those of us who loved *Double Trouble*, considered getting the Flock of Seagulls haircut (if we just had the courage!), and felt that John Hughes totally got us must be several steps below pathetic. The solution is to turn our shame outward. For instance, VH1 has made a fortune by trotting out little-known comedians, TV personalities, magazine editors, and anyone else who is somewhat connected to the world of entertainment and works within a cab ride of the studio to mock people who were actual stars but have since fallen out of favor. Hating the '80s (or ironically loving them) actually began in the '80s, but many of the most influential music critics of the time were just being nostalgic for the '60s. The world had changed and the music industry along with it, which threatened the "purists" with extinction. This is why there was so much concern about how videos were going to kill music. To Kurt Loder's credit, he got with the program and joined MTV, but for the most part critics became, essentially, grumpy old men talking about how it was in their day.

Bob Dylan, on the other hand, adventured out into the new sounds of the decade to see what there was to find, just as he had when he was a young man going to New York to find Woody Guthrie. He wasn't so much changing with the times as acknowledging the changes that come with the passing of time without judgment, embracing what he found interesting. Obviously if one believes that the '80s were essentially worthless, Dylan's open-mindedness is going to come off as the willful destruction of his legacy or a decline in his artistic powers. But this is the same thing that got the folkies riled up when he picked up an electric guitar: rock 'n' roll is bad, Bob Dylan plays rock 'n' roll, Bob Dylan is bad. The Advanced way of looking at his '80s period is: Bob Dylan makes good music, Bob Dylan made music in the '80s, Bob Dylan made good music in the '80s. An oversimplification, to be sure, but the alternative seems to me an overcomplication. Whatever the case, the real question is whether the songwriting stands up, and I believe it does. There is great work on every Bob Dylan record of the 1980s, and that has been missed by a generation that has been brainwashed to believe that the '80s were a wasteland for Dylan.

About twenty years after he supposedly began sucking, Dylan got good again with *Time Out of Mind* and continues to be on a roll, having made three straight acclaimed albums. All the critics of the '80s have either softened with age or been replaced by a new generation that is able to judge the work with some objectivity because they didn't have much of a stake in preserving Dylan's legacy. This late-career resurgence is standard Advanced stuff, of course, but as usual Dylan has done it better than anyone.

Not only has Bob Dylan made great records the last fifteen years or so, he also wrote an autobiography, which is fascinating on a number of levels. First, after nearly a lifetime of keeping his mystery alive, Dylan all of a sudden decided to bare his soul. Second, he avoided the parts of his career that most people would want to read about, spending a great deal of time talking about a lesser-known record he made with Daniel Lanois in 1989. Third, it is intended to be part of a trilogy, which would be the literary equivalent of a double album. The book got favorable reviews, but some critics had a problem with the second point. Why, they asked, wouldn't he tell us more about the early years and the recording of *Blood on the Tracks* and the motorcycle accident and so on? I suspect part of the answer has to do with the first point, and perhaps there is more to come in the next two books (should they ever be written; it's

Advanced to announce ambitious projects and abandon them). But that stuff has been written about so many times, it really wouldn't have added much to get his take on it. Plus, he would have nothing to gain by revealing too much, as he would either prove his detractors correct or be called a self-aggrandizing liar. Or maybe he just didn't want to reveal his tricks. For whatever reason, he took the Mark McGwire route and answered the questions he thought were the most relevant to who he really is. It was, in a way, the sequel to *Self Portrait*.

The postsucking years have been Advanced for Dylan in other ways, as well. He embraced technology by hosting a satellite radio show, and he sold out spectacularly by appearing in a Victoria's Secret commercial; plus he made a Cadillac commercial. He has remained a big baseball fan, playing a tour of minor-league stadiums (stadia, for the Overt and dictionary hunters) and devoting an episode of the satellite radio show to the sport. He teamed up with Twyla Tharp to create a Broadway musical based on his music. And then there was *Masked and Anonymous,* a Super-Advanced movie that Roger Ebert called "a vanity production beyond all reason." This is interesting criticism coming from someone who has spent the last forty years telling people what movies they should like. Ebert also cowrote *Beyond the Valley of the Dolls* and *Beyond the Valley of the Ultra-Vixens,* so maybe when it comes to vanity, he knows of what he speaks. Finally, Dylan's 2009 Christmas collection, *Christmas in the Heart,* is the most Advanced charity album of all time.

Lou Reed and Bob Dylan are without doubt the most Advanced musicians ever, but is one more Advanced than the other? In preparation for this book, I listened to both artists' entire catalogs on a more or less endless loop for a few months, but I don't find myself any closer to a conclusion. Without Lou Reed, there would be no

Advanced Genius Theory, so I have a soft spot for him, but I find Dylan's music more satisfying. But that could mean that Reed is just more Advanced and I still have a way to go. Plus, Reed has always been a little behind Dylan, so perhaps his *Time Out of Mind* is imminent. Then again, his most recent project is the Metal Machine Trio, so unless the public suddenly develops a taste for experimental guitar, tenor sax, and the fingerboard continuum, it doesn't seem likely.

As I write this, I'm a Dylan man, but it's entirely possible that by the time you're reading this I'll have changed my mind. Or maybe my mind will have exploded.

Chapter Five

The Second Tier

B
ob Dylan and Lou Reed are the most Advanced musicians ever, but that does not necessarily mean they are the *greatest* musicians ever. All it means is that their artistic genius combined with their consistent adherence to principles of Advancement make them more Advanced than everyone else. So when we talk about Second-Tier Advanced musicians—artists like Elvis Presley, David Bowie, Chuck Berry—that should not be taken as a slight against these artists. They are all amazing, but either they didn't reach the heights of artistry that Dylan and Reed have achieved or they weren't as faithful to Advancement. There's no shame in that, and these artists have much to teach us about what it means to be Advanced.

Elvis Presley

It took a long time for Britt and me to realize that Elvis was Advanced, which I find astonishing today. The Theory could have been invented for him as easily as for Lou Reed or Bob Dylan, but I think he was such a big star—and maybe a bigger joke, at least for my generation—that it took us a while to get past it and see that he was the prototype of the Advanced musician. I say that because not only did Elvis like rock 'n' roll, he was the king, if not the outright inventor, of it. He was so Advanced that his early, misunderstood period happened during his childhood, when he was ridiculed for his love of flamboyant pink clothes and other fashion idiosyncrasies, not to mention his omnipresent guitar and constantly bouncing legs. He was multicultural before it had a name, with influences that ranged from gospel to hillbilly music to blues to opera to salsa and anything else that he could find. At his peak, he had not one but two sets of African-American backup singers. Teaming up with Colonel Tom Parker, Elvis sold out so completely and unabashedly that it may have been his greatest innovation. Someone was bound to put country, gospel, and blues together, but only a genius could have pulled off "An American Trilogy."

Elvis was a rebel who was unfailingly polite and loved his mother more than most therapists would recommend. He was the greatest rock 'n' roll singer of all time but really wanted to sing gospel. He was deeply religious, though a fantastic sinner. He embraced the martial arts (occasionally he would do lengthy karate exhibitions onstage during a concert, which some audience members might not have appreciated) and devoured books on Eastern religions. He invented Las Vegas as the most Advanced city in America (Austin is the most Overt). And when it was time for him to "come back," you may remember, he wore a black leather suit. Finally, no one had more Advanced hair than '70s Elvis.

The Overt take on Elvis is that he was great, briefly, but then the Colonel got his hands on him and wrecked everything. Even if you believe Elvis didn't make a good record past his time with Sun Records, the problem is that Elvis was fully on board with the Colonel's plan. He wanted to be the biggest star in the world, and he believed the Colonel could make it happen. Others believe that Elvis was ruined because he got locked into making terrible movies. There is some truth to this, especially toward the end of his contract, but there was nothing keeping him from making good records. But I think he was bored with making music during that period, so making even bad movies was more fun than trying to find songs that would inspire him and fill up his records at the same time.

What's important to understand is that Elvis was completely aware of what he was doing, and the movie period was necessary for him to get out of the spotlight for a while and discover some new way of expressing himself. It may not have been a conscious decision on his part, but making bad movies was for him what bed-ins were for John Lennon. Once you get to a certain level of fame, you essentially cease to exist, so you might as well let yourself be crucified, especially when you know you'll rise again, more powerful than ever. I'm not saying Elvis is a messianic figure or anything. (For the record, Jesus probably qualifies as Advanced; Mohammed, too. Buddha was great, but he feels Overt to me. It's hard to say, though, because of cultural bias.) Elvis was more like Obi-Wan Kenobe calmly allowing himself to be light-sabered by Darth Vader. If he is Obi-Wan, then we are Luke, yelling "No!" because we can't understand that by leaving the physical plane, Elvis/Obi Wan gets closer to the Force and will give us some of his power when we are ready to destroy the Death Star.

So when Elvis was ready to move the stone away from the mouth of the cave or, if you prefer, reappear for the great Ewok celebration, he put on a black leather suit and made the '68 comeback special, announcing with authority that he still ruled rock 'n' roll. Having succeeded in reminding everyone that he was King, Elvis moved the capital of his kingdom to Las Vegas and started dressing like Liberace, on his way to the Fat Elvis period. Gaining weight is not unusual for an Advanced Artist—Marlon Brando and Orson Welles are two examples of this—but it seems to me that his weight gain is more closely associated with the perceived decline of his artistic gifts than with any other Advanced Artist. It makes sense, then, to talk briefly about society's collective blind spot to overweight and otherwise unattractive people.

Britt has noted that if David Byrne weighed 300 pounds, no one would care a thing about him. The same could be said of Byrne if his face were covered in boils or he had a birthmark that caused a big bald patch on the upper quadrant of his head. But overweight people are seen as particularly loathsome because theoretically they "choose" to be fat. In other words, they have no self-control and deserve no respect. This view is fairly consistent across all types of people, even among those who consider themselves to be open-minded. For some reason, alcoholism, drug abuse, and other forms of self-destruction and self-indulgence tend to bolster an artist's reputation, but overeating and not getting enough exercise don't. It could be argued, then, that an artist's allowing himself to become fat is a completely valid form of rebellion, even more than swiveling one's hips on a television variety show. Especially if those hips are accompanied by one of the most beautiful faces anyone's ever seen. In the case of Elvis, he always struggled with his weight because he had such a big appetite, especially for fried foods, and because of medications he took that caused him to be puffy. So I don't think he was trying to be fat as a way to make an artistic statement. However, he must have known what people would think of him, yet he continued to perform regardless of the impact it might have had on his image. By now that might sound familiar to you.

Elvis never reached full Advancement due to drug abuse. Of course, his addiction was of a different kind from the Sid Vicious/Scott Weiland style, where the drugs were a way to be cool and a substitute for inspiration. Elvis just couldn't get to sleep or wake up. Regardless, his artistic decision making was impaired and thus cannot be trusted fully. Unfortunately, it's hard to sort through what was Advanced and what was drug-fueled insanity in his later years.

So all the great things he did in those late years will be obscured by the fat, the hair, the karate, the guns, the Nixon handshake, the fried-banana sandwich, and all the other baggage of that period. This is a tragedy, like millions of voices crying out in terror, then suddenly silenced. On the other hand, by striking him down, we've made him more powerful than you could possibly imagine.

David Bowie

Advanced British Artists are slightly different from the American version. They typically prefer blazers to leather jackets, and they tend to keep more of their fans (because Europeans have more Advanced tastes). Another example: David Bowie reversed the usual order of things by forming a band as an act of Advancement rather than going solo as most other Advanced musicians did. That band was not the Spiders from Mars but Tin Machine, one of the most Advanced projects in history.

Like most people, I was somewhat appalled when I heard Tin Machine for the first time. I was actually appalled before I even heard the music, which is a classic Overt mistake. I could not understand why David Bowie would need to start a rock band at that stage in his career. Then I saw them on *SNL*, and I was impressed—rocked even—but still I just couldn't get into the records. But a few years ago, I heard "Under the God" on one of my custom Pandora stations (not coincidentally named "Lou Reed"), and I finally understood why Tin Machine was not only awesome but completely necessary. Most Advanced musicians have multiple artistic personalities, but Bowie has had more than any other (Madonna is his only rival, though I'm not totally sure if she's Advanced). And it seems as if he comes up with the persona first and the music second. So not only did forming Tin Machine give Bowie a new persona to explore— front man of a real band—it made it easier for him to rock.

I've been preaching the Advanced Theory for fifteen years or so (which makes the Theory eligible for Advancement), but I can still be surprised by how correct it really is. There's nothing more basic to the Theory than the idea that those who are ahead of their time like David Bowie will be ahead of their time. So it's funny that I was surprised that Tin Machine was actually good because of course it was good. David Bowie was a member!

Aside from Tin Machine, there are countless examples of Bowie's Advancement. He recognized Lou Reed's greatness from the start. He plays the saxophone and made a slick sellout album (*Let's Dance*). He took selling out to a whole new level by selling shares of "David Bowie" in the stock market. He has used the term rock 'n' roll liberally, acted in movies, been gay, married Iman, done tons of cocaine, and gotten clean. He was an early adapter of music technology, especially synthesizers, but he also started his own ISP, showing that he is technologically Advanced in other ways besides music. He has been particularly Advanced in his choice of collaborators, including Trent Reznor, Bing Crosby, John Lennon, Nile Rodgers, and Peter Frampton. More recently he worked with Scarlett Johansson on an album of Tom Waits covers, which may be even more Advanced than the pants he wore in the video for "Dancing in the Streets" with Mick Jagger. And that is really saying something.

David Bowie is in many ways the perfect Advanced British musician. But I do have two issues with him: As noted earlier, everybody likes him no matter what he does, so his fans have never fully rejected him. *Let's Dance* was something of a disappointment, but it was no *Metal Machine Music*. The other issue is that he doesn't keep up with the journal on his Web site. The last entry is from October 5, 2006, when he announced that he was going to play a character on *SpongeBob SquarePants*. He wrote, "Oh Yeah!! We, the family, are thrilled." I get a lot of satisfaction thinking about Bowie, Iman, and the family watching cartoons together. Later in the journal entry he writes, "Nothing else need happen this year." Judging by his silence, nothing has happened in a few years, or at least nothing as exciting as getting the *SpongeBob* gig. I'm guessing Scarlett Johansson must feel a bit slighted.

James Brown

One of the great challenges all parents face is having "The Talk" with their child. Some children are ready for The Talk when they are as young as seven, while the late bloomers may not be ready until they are twelve, thirteen, or even older. But whenever the time comes—and it will—we parents are going to have to sit down and try to explain where James Brown came from.

In many ways his was the typical rags-to-riches story, with a liberal dose of *Behind the Music* thrown in. He was born in South Carolina, moved to Augusta, Georgia (where I happened to be on the day he died), grew up in extreme poverty, was raised in a brothel—where he was exposed to many types of music—served some time in prison for robbery, cleaned up his act, and then worked harder than anybody to become successful in the record business. Brown lists among his influences Little Richard, Westerns, comic books, and the wrestler Gorgeous George (who had to be the most influential man in the middle of the twentieth century). Late in life he had money troubles and an escalating drug problem that caused him to behave erratically, eventually landing him in prison in Columbia, South Carolina (where I happen to have been born). Yes, the body of his life was typical, but the soul was anything but.

Many facets of the man James Brown became can be explained by his upbringing. For instance, he was obsessive about money because he grew up without any. And because he was Advanced, he knew how to make it (if not necessarily keep it). While Overt Artists are typically unable or unwilling to deal with the business side of art because they think it is beneath them, the Advanced make sure they get paid for their work. One of my favorite examples comes from the concert he played in Boston the weekend after Martin Luther King, Jr., died. First of all, he didn't agree fully with Dr. King's peaceful message, but he did respect what MLK was trying to achieve. So it's a little ironic that it was Brown who "saved Boston" by putting on a concert in King's honor.

After the assassination, there was rioting in the major cities across the nation, so there was some question about whether the Boston concert should even take place. The mayor at first thought it shouldn't happen but then was persuaded that not only should the concert go on but it should be aired on public television. The mayor called a press conference announcing the broadcast, and the venue told those who had bought a ticket that they could get their money back if they preferred to stay at home and watch on TV—the idea being that if people had an incentive to stay home, they wouldn't be out in the streets burning down the city. Unfortunately, no one had asked Brown if it was okay, and when he found out, he was furious. He told the mayor that he wouldn't do it unless they promised him that the city would pay him the money he would lose from all the refunded tickets. The mayor had no choice but to agree to Brown's demand, so the concert went on and the city was saved. You could say it was crass of him to insist on getting paid and that he should have just donated his services in honor of the memory of Dr. King. But he had a lot of musicians to pay, and their salaries would have come out of his own pocket. And there is something poetic about an African-American man insisting on his value being recognized by the white mayor of a major American city. It might not have been the way Dr. King would have gotten there, but James Brown made it to the mountaintop the only way he knew how: by making money for making music.

The Boston concert is just one of the many fascinating ways his career was entangled with political figures. As he relates in his autobiography *I Feel Good* (an incredibly Advanced title that I will talk about a little later), his friend Hubert Humphrey once considered him as a potential running mate. While that makes some sense, considering Humphrey's standing in the liberal community, Brown's friendships with the segregationists George Wallace and Lester Maddox are a little more surprising. Best of all, though, is that the man who wrote "Say It Loud (I'm Black and I'm Proud)" fully embraced Richard Nixon, the man who said, "I have the greatest affection for them [blacks], but I know they're not going to make it for five hundred years. They aren't. You know it, too. The Mexicans are a different cup of tea. They have a heritage. At the present time they steal, they're dishonest, but they do have some concept of family life. They don't live like a bunch of dogs, which the Negroes do live like." Maybe he was working from the inside, maybe he was being a good Christian, or maybe he just thought they were fun to hang out with. Maybe. But there are some things that are just too Advanced for explanation, and Brown's relationship with these three men is one of them.

His music doesn't need an explanation because it is so undeniably brilliant. After tiring of writing hits that were palatable to a wide audience, he invented funk music that widened that audience's palates. Along the way he ended up providing the samples for every rap song from 1979 to 1994, years before the genre even existed. Inventing two genres of music is a fine example of being ahead of one's time.

The Advanced are hard to work with and even harder to work for, and James Brown's treatment of his band was a good example of this dynamic. His band was made up of hundreds of musicians over the years and was as large as thirty-five in his later years, including three horn players, three drummers, three guitarists, two bass players, three background singers, and a twelve-piece string section.

Interestingly, Brown admits in *I Feel Good* that many of the musicians onstage were completely unnecessary. The giant band was more for visual effect than to create a certain sound. But Brown wouldn't reveal which ones were superfluous because that would have punctured the mystique.

Necessary or not, all of his musicians (many of whom still refer to him as Mr. Brown) were held to an incredibly high standard, even in concert, where mistakes are rarely noticed by the musicians, much less the audience. But when Mr. Brown heard a missed beat or a stray note—and he heard every one—he would flash a smile at the offending musician that said, "I got you." That musician would also be fined. And if you didn't like it, you would be fired, because if you wanted to play with Hardest-Working Man in Show Business you had to be among the Second Through Thirty-Sixth Hardest Working People in Show Business.

James Brown believed just as much in the show part of the equation as he did in the hard work. When you saw him live, you saw a real show, designed to give the audience what it wanted. The huge band was part of this. At first glance, this might seem inconsistent with the usual Advanced technique of making the audience uncomfortable. But Brown managed to give you what you wanted in an Advanced way. For instance, he played the hits but might leave out the hits you most wanted to hear, such as "Living in America" (an underrated song) and "Papa's Got a Brand New Bag." In lieu of those you might hear a bit of "The Way You Move" by Outkast and a Spanish rap. There's nothing like going to see the Godfather of Soul and being treated to a Rico Suave hook.

As mentioned earlier, James Brown's second autobiography (it's Advanced to write two autobiographies) is titled *I Feel Good*. Lesser artists might try to avoid being associated so closely with a single song, especially when they have written so many other songs that might not have been as popular but were more respected by critics. But like Lou Reed with "Walk on the Wild Side," he cultivated the idea that his biggest hit was also his favorite song because there was no way and no reason to fight it. I think also that he genuinely loved the message behind the song and that by saying "I feel good" as often as people wanted him to, it really did make him feel good. And feeling good is Advanced. Unfortunately, he didn't feel good enough to avoid the pitfalls of drug abuse.

Any discussion of James Brown, and especially his Advancement, has to include something about his use of drugs. The foundation of the Theory is that the Advanced are completely aware of what they are doing, and when you are on drugs, your judgment is impaired. In Brown's autobiography, he attributes many of his problems late in life to racial conspiracies and the government's use of "reverse x-rays or something" to spy on him through his television. If your judgment has lapsed enough to believe that, you probably don't have a good handle on whether your art has declined. So Brown's drug problem, while amusing to celebrity mug shot fans, is the only strike against his status as Advanced.

I'm compelled to add that I would not be in the least bit surprised to find out that David Duke and the CIA conspired against James Brown to ruin his career and that reverse X-rays were used widely to spy on celebrities who were judged to be too Advanced for the good of society.

Prince

I have no explanation for much of what Prince has done over the years, but I do know that I like it and that it is Advanced. Let's look at the proof: Obviously he is a prodigiously talented musician (he has taught himself how to play as many instruments as was necessary to realize his vision), songwriter, and producer, so he passes the greatness test. He has been active for thirty years, so he's passed the time test two times over. He has released a string of "disappointing" records. And he became a Jehovah's Witness, so he's got religion, too. (There was a nice article in *The New Yorker* about Prince's religion in which he revealed that he goes door to door to spread the faith, just like all good Jehovah's Witnesses. Having Prince show up with an armful of spiritual pamphlets would be second only to being revived by an EMT, only to realize that he is David Lee Roth.) The superficials are there as well: he's acted; he was among the first to release his music exclusively on the Internet; he's had the hair, the leather, and the sunglasses; and he has done countless irritating things to his fans, members of his band, and especially his record company.

All the prerequisites are taken care of, but few artists have fulfilled the obligations of Advancement with as much style as Prince. His early music was more or less traditional funk, but with *1999*, it became clear that Prince was going to be something more than just another George Clinton or James Brown knock-off. What he *was* going to be was a mystery, even after he became it (at least before Advancement came to be known), though I suspect that the key to understanding Prince is hidden in his movie *Purple Rain*.

As we have seen, Advanced musicians are drawn to acting, if for nothing else than as a means of expressing themselves imperfectly. But Prince's performance in *Purple Rain*, which is part *Rebel Without a Cause*, part *Jo Jo Dancer, Your Life Is Calling*, is perfection, though I can't recall a word of dialogue from the movie. What I do remember is his tearing through the most blistering guitar solos I had ever heard as a twelve-year-old and a certain combination of hair, sunglasses, and motorcycle jacket. I've never seen *Under the Cherry Moon*, mostly because I don't think I've progressed far enough to enjoy it, but I have seen *Sign o' the Times*, which somehow outdoes the live performances from *Purple Rain*. At that point he was on top of the world, so of course he changed his name to an unpronounceable symbol and fought with his record company for what seemed like forever.

Actually, first there was "Batdance," a classic of Advancement if there ever was one. (There's some connection between Advancement and Batman, but I haven't been able to connect all the dots yet. Perhaps I'll have to write a sequel to this book to sort it all out.) So what on earth was Prince so upset about that he should destroy his own name? When it was happening, I couldn't exactly figure that out, but it was so bad that he had to let his beard do his talking. And in one of the all-time great Advanced Irritant moves, he threatened to rerecord every note of *1999* and release it to coincide with the coming of the new millennium. That he *didn't* do it was even more Advanced than if he had, somehow.

What I understand now is that he was challenging himself as we've seen so many Advanced Artists do, but on top of that he was blowing up the record industry. I can't think of a more noble cause, and he was prepared to go down for it. But because he's smarter than everyone else, he didn't suffer a bit. Instead he pioneered the release of music through the Internet, which was so ahead of its time that most bands still haven't been able to figure out how to do it successfully.

During his slave period he was invisible but at the same time unavoidable because of his enormous output of music. Even with his record company woes he wasn't going to hole himself up like Axl Rose, tinkering away on some potential masterpiece. Instead he followed the Guided by Voices model, putting out what seemed like a new record each month. Those albums seemed like throwaways at the time, but now I realize that Prince's music from that era is similar to Dylan's *Self Portrait*. Here was an artist in transition, and we were privileged enough to be invited in to observe the process.

Once he got out of his contract (who knew that slave owners honored contracts?), he became Prince again, in both the literal and figurative senses. It was time for a "comeback." There was a buzz around Prince that had been absent a long time, besides the ubiquitous "artist formerly known as" jokes that circulated for about five years. So he rode that wave of renewed popularity and critical acceptance right into a Super Bowl halftime-show gig. This is pure Advancement. What's more, he covered a Foo Fighters song during the show. Think about that for a moment. The guy has written thousands of songs and dozens of hits, and in his fifteen-minute performance in front of however many billions of people, he plays a song by the Mike and the Mechanics of grunge. I thought he might give an explanation during his postgame press conference, the first instance of the musical act giving a postgame press conference I've ever heard of, but his "answer" to the first question was to launch into a song with his band. The song was a Prince original.

I have to give just a few more examples of his Advancement because they are truly remarkable. As you know, one of the ways the Advanced upset their fans is by changing styles. But Prince upset his fans by threatening to sue them for using his likeness. He made this threat through a song he released on a Web site. In the song, he tells his most dedicated fans that he loves them, "but don't you ever mess with me no more." One way of messing with Prince, apparently, is to post a picture of your Prince-inspired tattoo. And finally, for the twentieth anniversary of *Purple Rain,* he played a show featuring Morris Day, Wendy Melvoin, and Sheila E. Kind of a typical crowd-pleasing thing to do, but he started out the show on Rollerblades, disguised in a blond wig, hat, and beard.

I hope that one day I'll be Advanced enough to understand what Prince was up to that day.

Neil Young

In my experience, people either worship Neil Young or hate him, but both camps agree that his synth-heavy record *Trans* is awful.

And it is nearly universal that his fans want him to play songs they've heard before when they go to see him in concert. However, my cousin went to see him a few years back, and she reported that he played almost nothing but the music from his upcoming film *Greendale*, which hadn't been released yet. She was all primed to hear "Heart of Gold" but got "Grandpa's Interview" instead. When she found out that I was writing this book, she asked me if maybe Young's behavior could be considered Advanced. Yes, Amy, it could.

Young has managed to make just about everyone mad at him, from band members to audiences to record companies to an entire southern state and so on. He was in a band with Rick James. He hangs out with Eddie Vedder. And he is the only musician I know of who has been sued for not sounding enough like himself on a record. (Meanwhile, John Fogerty was sued for sounding too much like himself. Record companies are awesome.) He directed a movie called *Human Highway*, described on IMDB.com this way: "The new owner of a roadside diner stuck in a town built around an always leaking nuclear power plant plans to torch the place to collect insurance. However, an assortment of bizarre characters and weird events (such as spaceships flying around) gets in his way." Sounds pretty Advanced, and that's without mentioning that Dennis Hopper and Devo are in it. Young's in it, too, with buck teeth and glasses, and sings a song from *West Side Story*. All of this is very Advanced behavior for a man who made his name as a fairly earnest singer-songwriter.

Slate.com described Young's career very nicely: "He has been a model of iconoclasm, nearly letting his career implode many, many times—most notably in the early 1980s, when he leaped from punk-approved arena rock to isolationist country to synth-pop to rockabilly, all while supporting Reagan." Now, if that's not the perfect description of Advancement I don't know what is. So if you're planning to see Neil Young in concert, expect to see a very Advanced Artist, but you shouldn't expect to hear any songs you recognize. But don't worry, you'll love the songs you do hear, though it might take another fifteen years for you to realize it.

Chuck Berry

Chuck Berry is surely one of the strangest and most brilliant musicians of all time. His greatest achievement with regard to Advancement is "Johnny B. Goode," not only because of the guitar playing that everyone has ripped off at one time or another but because it was the birth of "Johnny" as the quintessential rock 'n' roll name. Berry turned "Johnny" into the black leather jacket and sunglasses of the world of names, and many Advanced Artists have recognized this (David Bowie's "I'm Afraid of Americans," for example). The song is also regarded as quintessential Chuck Berry, though he has written countless songs that sound nothing like it. But since he is Advanced, he has done little to discourage the idea that all his songs sound like "Johnny B. Goode." In fact, for years his touring routine has been to fly by himself rather than with a band, check his guitar, play with whatever local band the promoter can find without much (or any) rehearsal; change key on them without warning; play a bunch of songs that sound almost exactly alike; and finally get back on the plane by himself to go home. It is my belief that this is how he keeps his art interesting because even though no one wants to hear new Chuck Berry songs, he still wants to play live. By playing with a strange band that is unrehearsed, he gets the thrill of doing something new, even though he's doing the same old thing. And sometimes magic happens when the local band turns out to be great. Like for instance when his backup band just happened to be Bruce Springsteen and the E Street Band before they made it. Had

Berry been more conventional, that kind of thing would never have happened. Of course, the experience of playing with him can be extremely frustrating for a band, even if it's great. The most Advanced example was when Keith Richards got an all-star band together to back him for the documentary/concert movie *Hail! Hail! Rock 'n' Roll*. Richards made Berry rehearse a set over and over until everything was just right, thinking that he was finally getting the backup band he deserved. But when the actual concert happened, Berry did the same key-changing trick he always does, which rendered all the preparation more or less worthless, much to Keith Richards's hilarious dismay. So what does this say about Keith Richards?

The Rolling Stones

If I haven't heard the Rolling Stones in a while, I can convince myself that they aren't that good. Then I hear, say, "Brown Sugar" on the radio, and I have to concede that it is truly one of the great bands of all time and definitely qualifies for Advanced status. Keith Richards is obviously an Overt lifer (which is why he thought he knew what Chuck Berry wanted), though unrepentantly materialistic. Brian Jones died too young to grow into Advancement. Bill Wyman is also Overt for liking young, pretty girls. And Charlie Watts is too hard to judge because I have no clue what motivates him, though I think he is probably the only one of them that you could tolerate for more than an hour at a time. Mick Jagger, though, is clearly Advanced, and were it not for his guiding hand, it's easy to imagine the Stones being just another band that was good for a while, like the Animals or Ebn-Ozn.

The case for his being a genius is airtight, so there's no need to go over that. I think he began his move toward Advancement when the Stones started playing disco music. To clarify, I don't really hear the disco in their disco songs, plus the songs were huge hits and very good, but still rock purists were pretty unhappy with the development. He embraced internationalism in the form of Bianca Jagger, he was in *Freejack,* he went solo, reunited with his band, sang with Bette Midler, appeared in a sitcom, sold out a million times over (starting in the '60s with a Rice Krispies commercial), and played the Super Bowl. And then there's the matter of his look, which may be the most Advanced thing about him.

At various points he had the correct hair length, leather color, and sunglasses tint, but he developed a style of dress that no non-Advanced person could ever have dreamed up. I'm talking about the tights with knee pads, the jerseys, the striped leotards, and the puffy jackets that he has worn on stage the last thirty years or so. What is so baffling is that he was such a stylish dresser at the start of his career; no one has ever rocked sweaters and oxford shirts like he did (Eddie Haskell came close). But once the dress code was relaxed for rock musicians in the late 1960s, his Advancement blossomed. He lost the bad-boy-in-nice-clothes look, choosing instead a wardrobe that was a mixture of Gandalf and Philadelphia Eagles cheerleader. Even more amazing is that he dresses normally, even well, offstage. So what's going on?

One thing about Advanced front men is that they cannot be embarrassed. They will sing in falsetto, sing with a pronounced southern accent even though they are from England, dance like a chicken, and do Ink Spots–inspired voice-overs about fine Arab chargers. It is this fearlessness, though, that makes them able to give full voice to their genius. In the case of Jagger's clothes and general onstage persona, it does seem ridiculous, but he is an incredibly effective performer. He comes from an era when entertainers took their jobs seriously, which included wearing clothes that separated them from the audience. Jagger certainly meets this objective. As I said before, he is the reason the Stones are still around, and a big part of that is because he is still so interesting to watch. Make fun of his clothes, his pointing, and his lip contortions all you want, but the guy gets the crowd worked up, even those who are sitting in the top row of a football stadium a half mile from the stage. (I think he got into the garish costumes when they were playing in stadiums before the advent of Jumbotrons. It was just a way to be seen.)

Many Overt people feel he shouldn't be on the stage anymore, regardless of his clothes. They say that Jagger and the Stones tour only for the money and their recent records are just irrelevant throwaways. This is ridiculous, as they certainly have more money than they could possibly need, and it would keep pouring in whether they were touring or not. They tour because they love playing live and all the musicians they worshiped played until they couldn't play anymore. If they didn't like it, they wouldn't do it. As for the records, it is extremely difficult and time-consuming to make records, and they really don't make that much money for an artist. Sure, the records since *Steel Wheels* are hard to get into right away because they don't sound like the old Stones, just as it is difficult to enjoy any new music put out by a musician whose "prime" has passed. But if you haven't listened to *Voodoo Lounge* as many times and with as much care (or drugs) as you did *Exile on Main Street*, how do you really know it's not as good? You may dismiss this idea, but you probably also dismissed *Voodoo Lounge* before you even heard it. There aren't that many musicians as Advanced as Mick Jagger, so you could only benefit from giving him the benefit of the doubt. Maybe you've been hoping that there would be another great Stones record someday, so wouldn't it be great if it's already on your iPod?

If Mick is the most Advanced Rolling Stone and the Rolling

Stones are the only band that compares to the Beatles in terms of success and influence (sometimes I think the Kinks are better and more Advanced than both), who was the most Advanced Beatle? To answer that, we'll need a whole chapter.

Chapter Six

Who Was the Most Advanced Beatle?

I want to preface this section by acknowledging that average people would say that it's a waste of time arguing about who was the best (or most Advanced) Beatle. This is not because they aren't capable of understanding the argument but because they sensibly believe that Lennon and McCartney were both terrific, so there is no need to proclaim that one is better than the other. Just put their best stuff on your iPod, hit "shuffle," and enjoy. But those of us who think and write about music have to keep ourselves occupied, and it's a lot of fun to argue passionately about something that has no right or wrong answer. It's the equivalent of arguing about whether Willie Mays or Babe Ruth was the better baseball player, when everyone knows that Hank Aaron was better than both of them. So while I'll put a stake down, I realize that the ground I'm claiming is quicksand.

Maybe the only thing one can say about the Beatles that hasn't been said a thousand times is that they are underrated. Luckily, that is exactly my position. While the Rolling Stones are generally credited with being the bad boys of rock 'n' roll and the Beatles are seen as the cute, harmless ones, this is all wrong. Sure, Mick Jagger wrote a song about Satan and a guy got killed at the Stones concert at Altamont, but Paul McCartney wrote a song about an amusement park ride ("Helter Skelter") that got a lot of people killed, so I say the Beatles were just a bit badder than the Stones. How many more people have to die before the Beatles get the credit they deserve?

The most underrated member of this underrated group was not George or even Ringo but Paul, who had the great misfortune of not being killed before people started hating him. John got the reputation of being the most "way out" Beatle because he looked more ridiculous than Paul and married a Japanese artist. Paul was just too cute for people to realize that he was farther out there than the rest of the band. He was the one who brought tape loops to the Beatles, he was the one who was into avant-garde art, and he was the one who was interested in Cage and Stockhausen. But he was also the one who wrote pop songs that are so easy to like, the only choice any self-respecting Overt person has is to hate them.

I'm not saying that John wasn't Advanced, because he definitely was. And George Harrison was borderline Advanced; I'm inclined to give it to him for the video for "Got My Mind Set on You" and the song "When We Was Fab." As for Ringo Starr, he was a fantastic drummer, better than he is given credit for. He has also done many of the things that the Advanced do, such as making movies and playing with Tom Petty. Still, he doesn't quite rise to the level of real Advancement, though don't you dare change the channel if "It Don't Come Easy" comes on the radio. No, it was Paul who paid his dues, so he gets the title of Most Underrated Beatle. I know that the title of Favorite Beatle is probably always going to belong to John, but at least we'll give Paul the credit he deserves.

Speaking of favorite Beatles, they say that your choice of favorite Beatle supposedly says a lot about you. It has even been said that the Beatles were a microcosm of humanity: everyone is either a John—artsy, sensitive, a little angry; a Paul—artsy, sensitive, a little sappy; a George—artsy, sensitive, a little holy; or a Ringo—bearded, big-nosed, and a little lucky. Though that is a fun thought, I don't really believe it. In fact, I wouldn't even say John was a John. He was more of a Paul with a smidgen of George. And of course if everyone were one-fourth of the world's greatest rock band, then how could you explain why there are so few good songs on the radio? You're on firmer ground to say that a bigger band, maybe the Commodores, or maybe the cast of *Gilligan's Island,* represented the whole of humanity. (I'm a Lionel and a Professor.)

I bring all this up not to deprive you of the joy of feeling a kinship with your favorite Beatle but to introduce a related concept: the Beatles were a microcosm of Advancement. Within one group you find rejection, acceptance, selling out, genius, luck, religious awakening, rock-'n'-roll worship, love of technology, world-beat sounds, long hair in the back, black leather, musicals, drugs, Eastern influences, going solo, irritants, duets, and on and on. But before we discuss their Advancement, I have to address whether they qualify in the first place. You may think it's a given, but one very important person would disagree with you: Britt Bergman, cofounder of the Theory.

Britt and I disagree about a lot of things within the world of Advancement. I think this makes the Theory stronger. Out of the debate comes more certainty about what we agree on, which is the core of our faith in Advancement. So while I'll always say that Bob Seger's slow songs are better than his rockers, I can at least understand why Britt would disagree. So it goes with our Beatles argument: Britt says they are the New Kids on the Block of the '60s (NKOTBOTS), while I believe they are the most underrated greatest rock band in history. I used to dismiss his point of view as pure contrarianism until I heard someone else say essentially the same thing. I realize now that I was being Overt in just accepting without question the Beatles' place in rock history because I was basically brought up to believe it.

As I have looked into the question of whether the Beatles really were the NKOTBOTS, I found some corroboration from an unexpected source: the Beatles themselves. Both John Lennon and Paul McCartney have said that their early songs were pure pop confections, written to communicate with teenage fans by employing the word "you" as often as possible. By saying "you" frequently, they allowed the listener to become the subject (or object) of the song, which bound the listener to the song. This is exactly the kind of thing NKOTB and other boy bands did to hook screaming teenagers. That the Beatles did it first is really only a modest achievement.

The more you think about it, the more the Beatles have in common with NKOTB and other boy bands. Like most of the boy bands since Menudo, the Beatles were discovered and managed by a Svengali type, Brian Epstein, who chose their clothes, their stage moves, and even what they said to the press. For instance, they weren't allowed to talk about Vietnam, and there was certainly no talk of John's being married. And like NKOTB, they assiduously cultivated personas for the teenybopper magazines—the cute one, the sensitive one, the quiet one, the funny one. There are more similarities, and if you focus on them enough, you can actually convince yourself that the Beatles were just another boy band. But there is one major difference between the Beatles and NKOTB, Menudo, or Color Me Badd: they wrote their own songs, and those songs were among the best written in the second half of the twentieth century. So even if Color Me Badd had written "I Wanna Sex You Up," it wouldn't measure up to what the Beatles did in their boy-band period. With all due respect to the NKOTBOTS theory, the Beatles qualify as Advanced.

Now that we know that Paul is the most underrated Beatle and that the individual members of the band at least qualify for Advancement, let's get back to the question of who is the most

Advanced Beatle. George and Ringo can't be the most Advanced because as we've seen, George was barely Advanced, if at all, and Ringo is not Fully Advanced. The question is, then, was it John or Paul?

John Lennon certainly came by his Overt rebellion honestly: his mother and father basically abandoned him when he was about four, leaving him with an aunt (or, as they say in England, "auntie," but I'm not English and only Overt Americans use English terms like "auntie" or "the loo" or use British spellings like "grey" instead of "gray," so I'll be sticking with "aunt," which I pronounce "ant" instead of "awnt" because I'm not only American but a southerner). This aunt reports that Lennon was an inventive boy and a born leader who sang himself to sleep every night. Most aunts think that about their nephews, I guess, but this particular aunt saw that she had a truly special boy on her hands. Lennon loved his aunt but says that he lost his mother twice because the two of them reconnected in his adolescence, only for her to be killed by an off-duty policeman who was driving drunk. In other words, the source of his rebellion was no trifle; he came by his aversion to authority the hard way. He was an angry kid, then, whose life was saved by none other than rock 'n' roll. I find it particularly interesting that he talked about how inspiring it was to watch girls go crazy over Elvis movies, the same movies that are the source of much Overt derision. Lennon would have probably been in a band even without *King Creole,* but no one could absolutely guarantee it.

We can skip all the familiar stuff about how he was in the Quarrymen and asked Paul to join his band and how Paul brought George into the mix and how John was envious that Paul knew chords that he didn't and how they eventually changed the name to the Beatles. The period in Germany, though, is important enough to discuss a little, as it was when they stopped being just another band and became "The Beatles." For our purposes, this is the period when they embraced Overt weirdness, dressing in leather, hanging out with avant-garde painters, and getting their famous haircuts, which had previously been reserved for female German art students and their androgynous boyfriends. This is also the period where Stu Sutcliffe made one of the all-time Overt decisions: he left the band because he wanted to be an artist, not a rock 'n' roller. Little did he know that had he just stuck with the music—and possibly avoided the intracranial hemorrhage—he could have made all the art he wanted, just like Tony Bennett and John Cougar Mellencamp.

Understanding this period in Germany is important for those who think that Paul McCartney was some kind of wuss. The clubs they played were extremely rough, frequented as they were by Hamburg gangsters, and Paul was right in the mix, drinking himself into a stupor, taking speed to keep up the energy onstage, and commingling with hookers and strippers. He lived the hardcore Overt lifestyle of sex, drugs, and rock 'n' roll, the kind of life that killed Jimi Hendrix, Janis Joplin, and Jim Morrison, but while they couldn't hack it, he emerged essentially unscathed. John Lennon did the same, but no one ever questions his street cred.

They got to leave that lifestyle behind thanks to Advanced manager Brian Epstein and Advanced record producer George Martin, both of whom not only saw the band's potential but helped them realize it. Despite moving to nicer quarters, though, they still rocked pretty hard for their day. In fact it could be argued that "Twist and Shout," which featured vocals by John Lennon, whose vocal cords were shredded because the band had to record an album's worth of material in one day, was the first punk song, not "All Day and All Night" by the Kinks. But no one ever says that because their influence on punk is as underrated as their ability to make serious rock 'n' roll. I blame "Yesterday" for this and other slights.

Paul McCartney had Overt qualms about "Yesterday," worrying that it was a bit fey for a fire-breathing rock band like the Beatles. Luckily, George Martin was a bit more Advanced at that time and talked him into recording it. To put it simply, that song is freaky good, and though you're entitled to your opinion, if you don't agree you're totally crazy. Everything about it is perfect; so perfect, in fact, that some people have to hate it because it reminds them how imperfect they are themselves.

The song was a huge hit, but it was the beginning of the end for Paul McCartney the rock 'n' roller, despite the fact that he wrote some of the greatest rock songs of all time long after he did "Yesterday." Sure, he tended to be a bit on the sweet side, but if I can borrow a line, What's wrong with that? I'd like to know. Sure, I skip past "Let It Be" when I'm listening to *Let It Be,* not because it's bad but because it is good. So good you can listen to it only so many times, like a dessert that is so rich you can have only a little portion and no more than once a year. Or maybe it's more like the joke in the Monty Python sketch that was so funny that it killed anyone who heard it and injured those who heard only part of it. In any case, just because "Let It Be" kills you, that doesn't mean it isn't a great song.

Meanwhile, John Lennon is somehow seen as the big rocker, even though he wrote just as many sweet songs as McCartney. The issue is that while McCartney was equally effective writing pop songs, hard rockers, and ballads, Lennon's lighter songs weren't as great as his rockers or weird ones. Many were great, but there was no "Yesterday," "Penny Lane," or "Hey Jude," leaving us to remember "Revolution" and "Strawberry Fields" instead.

It's difficult to compare Lennon and McCartney during their time in the Beatles because they were collaborating, and even when they weren't actively writing together, the end product of both writers' songs was greatly influenced by the rest of the group. The way a band dynamic works, even if you write a song by yourself, it can be completely changed because the drummer decides to play a part on the toms instead of a more traditional kick-snare part or because the bass player emphasizes the F on a D minor instead of the D. Both writers talk about how great it was to play with Ringo because in addition to being a good drummer he was just a pleasure to be around. You don't get a songwriting credit for lightening the mood before take sixty-three of the second chorus, but anyone who has been in a studio will tell you how valuable that contribution is. Since it is so difficult to figure out how each Beatle influenced the others—and an intact band can't Advance anyway—we have to look at the solo work to make our judgment. It is during the post-Beatle period that Paul proves that he is the most Advanced Beatle.

John Lennon's solo career had greatness, of course, but it wasn't as consistently Advanced as Paul McCartney's because despite recording an album called *Rock 'n' Roll,* his Overt period was much longer. In fact, though he had some moments, his first truly Advanced album was his final album, *Double Fantasy.* The album was a sort of back-and-forth between Yoko Ono and Lennon, and it was his return from a five-year break from recording. My favorite bit about the record is that the reason he decided to make music again was that he was inspired by New Wave music, especially the B-52s, who he thought sounded a lot like Ono (and they were, in fact, inspired by her). Of course, the record he ended up making sounded nothing like New Wave, as he opted for a slick production featuring lots of fancy studio musicians. All of these elements—the irritant move of letting Yoko write half the songs; simultaneously embracing and ignoring new forms of music; using studio musicians; writing songs about his happiness in being forty, a husband, and a dad—resulted in an Advanced album that disappointed many critics (though their reviews were pulled after Lennon was killed).

Between his first solo album and *Double Fantasy,* though, Lennon was pretty much a mess as he tried to understand what his role was in a post-Beatles world. He was kind of like the United States after the fall of the USSR, with Paul as Mikhail Gorbachev because he moved pretty seamlessly from being a Beatle to being just Paul. McCartney's first solo album, which would have been described as "lo-fi" if that term had existed yet, was a family affair, recorded at home and featuring his wife and kids. Like many Advanced musicians, he formed a new band, Wings, knowing that the new band would be compared unfavorably with the band that had made him famous. On top of that, he included his wife in the group, which was highly criticized by morons who apparently don't realize that people who love each other enjoy being together. Even with all that, Wings went on to record huge hits through the '70s. It was in the '80s, however, that McCartney cemented his Advanced status, with a big assist from Stevie Wonder and Michael Jackson.

The '70s were very different for John Lennon, who went back and forth between Overtness and Advancement. He recorded the soul-bearing, primal-screaming *Plastic Ono Band* but also did a week of *The Mike Douglas Show*. He made music with David Bowie ("Fame") but drank Brandy Alexanders with Elton John and Harry Nilsson. Sometimes he blended Overtness and Advancement, for example using traditional advertising techniques to promote peace, including putting up billboards (if only they had read "War Is Overt," the Vietnam War might have ended a little sooner). He also went back and forth from being completely focused on his wife to carousing about in California with an "assistant" (plus those Brandy Alexanders). But finally he settled down, had a baby, took time off from music, and devoted himself to his family. After all that, he was finally ready to be a Fully Advanced musician, writing music about his child and his woman. In other words, he finally reached the place that McCartney had ten years before.

As with all Advanced Artists who die before they reach full Advancement, we can only speculate about what John Lennon might have done had that pathetic lunatic not shot him. Maybe he would have put out a true New Wave record with the Cars as the backup band, produced a Shakira album, toured with Chuck Berry, campaigned for Ronald Reagan, or appeared with Paul in *Cannonball Run*. Even without that last possibility, there would have been a reunion, at least for Live Aid, Amnesty International, or a corporate gig on the Microsoft campus. It's hard to say if it would be like the Page/Plant shows that left out John Paul Jones, but I imagine the whole band would have been there, and the stage show would have featured several African-American women backup singers, an extra percussionist, Paul Shaffer on keyboards, Kanye West's string section, Kanye West, and Steve Miller on lead guitar, while the set list would include nothing but new tunes and material from their days in Hamburg. I could go on, but it's just too painful to think about.

Chapter Seven

The Curious Cases of Sting and Bono

S ting and Bono have a lot in common—both are single-named political activists who at one time fronted the biggest (and best) band in the world, both have played the Super Bowl, both have stayed with the same woman for many years, both have grown beards—but the ways in which they differ are more important. With regard to their careers, Sting has made one disastrous artistic decision after another, embracing lite jazz and adult contemporary, insulting his former bandmates, and recording an album of lute music from the seventeenth century. Bono has managed to stay cool for thirty years, changing his image just when people were about to be sick of him, sticking with his band when he could have gone solo long ago, and making music that still has street cred. Having been abandoned by radio, Sting resorted to selling his music to car companies to increase awareness of his albums. The release of a new U2 album is an international event. Sting not only fights for the rain forest, he employs residents of the rain forest in his band. Bono plays with white guys and Americans, plus the occasional blues or opera legend. In other words, Sting is Fully Advanced, but Bono is not.

Sting

Several years ago, I went to Germany for a while, and during my stay in Berlin I took some dance classes (I was a dancer for about ten years). I signed up for a "modern" class, not realizing that in Berlin "modern" meant "jazz," as in "jazz hands." I didn't realize this until after the warm-ups, which meant I was stuck taking a jazz class, in German, dancing to some of the most aggressively bland music I had ever heard. However, I was too preoccupied with executing my jazz moves to pay much attention to the music. But when I was waiting my turn to do the combination, I realized to my horror that we were listening to Sting. The guy who wrote the songs for my first-ever favorite band (followed by U2, then R.E.M., then the Pixies, then I outgrew having a favorite band) was now making straight-up smooth jazz. I was so distraught, I almost considered not taking advantage of the coed shower system they have in German dance schools. Later, as I wandered the streets of Berlin, I was fixated not on the images of sudsy naked German dancers recorded in my peripheral vision and stored in my brain for later use but on a terrible question: "Is Sting Advanced or just awful?"

Back home in New York I reviewed my relationship with Sting and his music. There was the Police-worshiping era, the somewhat uneasy enjoyment of *Dream of the Blue Turtles,* the period of doubt around the time of "Russians," the disappointment at hearing the first single from *Ten Summoner's Tales,* and finally that dark day in Berlin. I realized that he hadn't made a song that I truly liked since the late '80s, and even the ones I did like I wouldn't ever buy.

I went back to the Police's early days to see if maybe I had been wrong about them all along and they were actually bad. I needed this to be the case because the only way that Sting could not be Advanced is if he hadn't been that great in the first place. But if he really was as great as I had always believed and was still somehow not Advanced, the whole Advanced Genius Theory would fall apart.

Just as Einstein's math predicted black holes, Advanced math predicted that Sting is Advanced. But as with black holes, Sting's Advancement would always be doubted by some until it could be observed. The problem was that I was the one who doubted it most, and I was afraid that Sting would turn out to be the black hole of Advancement in another way, by sucking all the light and energy out of the Theory. The other problem I faced was that if I were to prove that he is Advanced, I would have to listen to every one of his solo records. I surely wasn't up to that, so I went in the other direction: I set out to prove that the Police sucked.

I started in reverse, beginning with *Synchronicity*, my least favorite album. I figured if I were to listen to that, I could begin some negative momentum that would carry me all the way through to *Regatta de Blanc*. Unfortunately, *Synchronicity* had aged better than I had expected. On some level I liked all the songs, and I was particularly appreciative of the way the group's sound had evolved using technology. Damn. Plus, how could *that* record be the biggest album in the world? Think about the average music listener's record collection and try to place where *Synchronicity* fit into it. This was a very weird record that was not just a number one album but an era-defining achievement. Damn again. There was no reason to go on past *Synchronicity* because I was a fan again. Still, I listened to all the records and loved every second of each one. Loved and hated, because the survival of the Theory hung in the balance. Plus, even with my renewed enthusiasm for the Police, I really, really did not want to listen to Sting's solo material.

After thinking a little, I came up with another explanation: the Police really were great, but *despite* Sting. Stewart Copeland started the band, and it could be that he was the primary force behind its greatness. Even though Sting wrote most of the songs, it was still possible that they weren't very good until the band got hold of them, sort of like a great actor making poorly written dialogue seem believable. If it wasn't Copeland's input that made the Police superior, maybe it was Andy Summers's interpretation of Sting's songs that elevated them to greatness. This was promising, because though it would be hard to prove completely, reasonable doubt was sufficient. Anything to escape listening to those solo records.

This time I listened to all my favorite songs first, but focusing on the other guys. I started to believe I was onto something. I knew the band fought all the time and that a big reason was that Stewart Copeland played too fast. But if "Regatta de Blanc" had been slower, it might have been terrible. Plus, the bass playing isn't really that interesting, certainly not as interesting as the guitar work. A picture was developing in my mind: Sting brought in a slow, boring song, and the band turned it into the amazing song we all know. Though I knew it was an inelegant placeholder, I could live with it, even though it made me uncomfortable. Keeping with the Einstein thread, I guess you could say it was the Theory's cosmological constant.

A couple of years later I happened to watch Stewart Copeland's movie about his time with the Police, which I had hoped would strengthen my case against Sting. It's called *Everyone Stares* and is just a bunch of home movies Copeland shot while on tour and in the recording studio. The scenes are accompanied by his narration, providing some context for what we are seeing. There is one particularly amazing scene where he is playing drums at a concert, filming himself, and talking into the camera midsong, while the rest of the band plays to the crowd. I also loved his Advanced stance regarding his drum kit. Overt drummers insist on having as simple a kit as possible, but Copeland's made nearly a full circle around him, featuring just about every form of percussion he could find.

His explanation was something like "Why not? I don't have to set them up!"

Things were rolling along nicely until I saw a clip of Sting teaching Andy Summers how to play a transition in "De Do Do Do, De Da Da Da" (the building part right before the final chorus, which happens to be my favorite part of the song). The scene was so unsettling because not only was Sting teaching the part, he was explaining how it all fit together. In other words, the final version was in his head, and Summers was essentially a hired hand. However, Copeland says that they were still a collaborative unit at that point, so maybe this was just an isolated incident where Sting lucked into a great idea. I imagined that most Sting songs sounded like "Don't Stand So Close to Me '86" (from their singles collection) before the rest of the band made their contribution.

That sufficed for a few minutes, until the movie entered the *Ghost in the Machine* era. To me, that was always the Police's masterpiece, with all the edginess of the early stuff and all the sophistication that characterized *Synchronicity* (and Sting's solo work). I was devastated to hear Copeland report that it was on this album that their music stopped being collaborative. Apparently Sting walked into the studio with the whole album more or less complete. He had always done demos of songs (I've since heard the demos, and they are depressingly similar to the final product as far back as "Message in a Bottle"), but on *Ghost in the Machine* he had the whole thing mapped out. It was now impossible to argue that either the Police weren't so great or they were great despite Sting. I could either admit defeat and forget all about Advancement or listen to the solo albums. I had to choose the latter, but first I had to get inspired, so I turned to an old standby: Lou Reed.

It took me a long time to learn how to like *Mistrial* on an Advanced level, and that was an album I kind of liked already or at least had been predisposed to liking. So I thought I would apply the lessons I learned with that experience to Sting's solo career.

One of the reasons I don't care for Sting's solo music is that it feels too much like adult contemporary, which people like me aren't supposed to like. That was easy to get over, as Advancement has taught me that you have to judge musicians' work by how well they execute their goal within a chosen genre rather than their choice of genre. To make an informed judgment about how Sting compared with other artists in the genre, I started to pay attention to adult contemporary music to understand what it was all about. It is boring, definitely, but at the same time, it's kind of relaxing. Frankly, the older I've gotten, the more I appreciate "boring" things. I don't need to be highly engaged with my music as I did in high school because I've got enough to think about without having to bang, or think with, my head. Plus once you've decided that adult contemporary is your kind of thing, you start to hear little interesting bits, like an unusual riff or drum part (check out the drums on Sade's "Sweetest Taboo"). Overt music is designed to wow you with its brilliance from the first listen, while adult contemporary musicians aren't trying to impress anybody, which can make their music ultimately more interesting. Think of it like this: You buy a new album by a band you really like. You listen to it all the way through and are blown away by the song that eventually is a hit, while pay little attention to a deep cut. But eventually you get sick of the hit (not just because it's on the radio) and grow to love the deep cut. Sting's adult contemporary music is perhaps the deepest cut of all.

Having prepared myself, I was ready to listen to Sting's 2003 album *Sacred Love,* featuring Mary J. Blige, the flamenco guitarist Vicente Amigo, Anoushka Shankar on sitar (duh), and somebody on the duduk, a traditional Armenian woodwind instrument. If ever there was a more Advanced lineup than that, I've never seen it. Since I'm not allowed to listen to Sting in the house, I popped the CD into my car stereo and took a ride.

The progression one follows when embracing something Advanced is a lot like the stages of mourning, in that you pass through different levels—despair, guilt, irony—until finally reaching acceptance. I figured for the Liking Sting Project it would take me weeks (months?) to get past even the first stage, considering the years of enmity I had built up. But something amazing happened: I liked the first song instantly, but not in the Advanced way. I liked it the regular way, the way people who don't know about Advancement like a band they might go to see in concert sometime if someone at work had two tickets they couldn't use and were selling them at face value. I was shocked, but some skepticism remained. It was still possible I wasn't really enjoying the music; instead I might have been subconsciously making fun of Sting or myself by liking it. Or perhaps because I was preparing for this book at the time, I had a professional incentive to like it.

I kept listening and liking, with just a few awkward moments here and there, like when your new girlfriend uses an expression like "I could care less" that had always embarrassed you when other people said it. But I was sure those bumps would be smoothed out upon repeat listening, and that has turned out to be the case. *Sacred Love* has made it onto the regular shuffle rotation (still headphones only in the house). Some songs still require my being in an Advanced state of mind to enjoy them, but that's really no different from not being in the mood to listen to Sonic Youth in the car with my mom on the way to my first-grade teacher's funeral. The music is still good, I'm just not in a mental state to enjoy it.

The progress I made with *Sacred Love* was encouraging, but I know I have a long way to go to fully embrace Sting. I haven't completely unlocked the mystery of his Advancement and maybe I never will, as I don't think I have the courage to like all of his solo material (1996's *Mercury Falling* scares me to death). Unlike Marie Curie, I'm not willing to poison myself irreversibly for the sake of discovery, no matter how important that discovery may be to mankind. Still, I'm as confident as possible that Sting is Advanced and will not rip a hole in the fabric of the Advanced universe. Perhaps he has achieved some kind of Super Advancement that will be understood by people not yet born. Maybe his appearance with No Doubt at the Super Bowl will one day be seen as classic Advancement and his lute suite will be on *Rolling Stone*'s list of top 500 albums of all time in 2050.

Bono

Bono has done many things that suggest that he wants to be Advanced: he and the rest of U2 always wanted to be the biggest band in the world (Overt bands usually turn up their noses at success); he had a mullet; he is religious; he loves Lou Reed, David Bowie, and Iggy Pop; his band invented its own distinctive sound; he collaborated with Brian Eno (the most Advanced producer); and he has been making great music for more than fifteen years. Plus U2 made the greatest debut album of all time and kept topping itself until it became the biggest, most respected band in the world, without ever compromising its principles. That's why Bono is such a huge disappointment to me.

Adding insult, there was actually a period, beginning with *Rattle and Hum,* when I thought he was ready to commit to Advancement. *Rattle and Hum* was essentially a road movie, as well as a meditation on what it meant to be U2, like *Some Kind of Monster* with less therapy and better music. But with its celebration of Elvis Presley, Bob Dylan, the blues, rock stopping the traffic, and America, it was also a portrait of four artists on the verge of Advancement.

The movie marked virtually the first time U2 had gotten negative criticism, other than some complaints about Bono's taking himself too seriously. Even their biggest fans were down on *Rattle and Hum,* feeling that the music wasn't up to U2's standards and that the whole exercise was narcissistic and self-indulgent. In other words, the time was right for Bono to Advance; the only question was whether he was ready. It appeared that he was indeed ready when the World's Most Serious Band named its next record *Achtung Baby* ("baby" is an Advanced word, you may remember), but this turned out to be just another case of Fool's Advancement, like the movie version of *Tommy* or *The Return of Bruno*.

In an eerie case of synchronicity, the album was released at about the same time the Advanced Genius Theory was being developed. Eerie because everything that Britt and I were thinking was being played out before our eyes. For instance, Bono started wearing black leather and sunglasses all the time. And when I saw U2 during the *Zoo TV* tour (Advanced name for a tour), there were signs of imminent Advancement before U2 even took the stage. First of all, BAD II and Public Enemy were the supporting acts, which is quite an Advanced opening combo. (BAD II seems Advanced, but I'm not totally sold on the Clash's music; nevertheless it is a pretty Advanced choice for an opening act.) After BAD II and Public Enemy, music came on over the PA, with the last song played before U2 started being "Rock 'n' Roll" by Led Zeppelin. Then the first song played after they finished was "Can't Help Falling in Love" by Elvis. Best of all, Bono did a Natalie Cole–style "duet" with Lou Reed on "Satellite of Love" (Lou Reed prerecorded his vocal part and lip-synced on a giant screen, while the band played live). At that moment, it felt as if Bono and Lou Reed were trying to communicate directly to me.

Another promising development came in the form of Mac-Phisto, a sort of devil-went-down-to-Vegas character Bono created during the *Zooropa* tour. It was very difficult to criticize Bono for being too serious when he was wearing powdered makeup and devil horns while singing in a falsetto. The following tour (*PopMart*) saw the band get even less serious, featuring as it did Village People costumes, a giant lemon-shaped disco ball, and a karaoke-style version of "Daydream Believer." That tour was almost enough to make you forget *The Unforgettable Fire*. Interestingly, Bono toned down his look a bit for *PopMart,* but the Edge often wore a body suit and cowboy hat. When I was at that concert I had half a thought that the Edge could become even more Advanced than Bono, but I certainly didn't question whether Bono would Advance eventually. Yet here it is more than a decade later, and I'm still waiting. But why?

Bono, like Mick Jagger, is impervious to embarrassment. But unlike Jagger, he seems to be susceptible to criticism. For instance, as Advanced as *Achtung Baby* seemed at the time, in retrospect it was just a reaction to the negative feedback the band got for *Rattle and Hum.* It was, to put it in familiar terms, the opposite of what was expected of Bono. He was supposed to be earnest, so he became frivolous. He was supposed to be God-fearing, so he dressed up like the devil. Not only was it the opposite, there was always a whiff of irony to go along with the sulfur. Then, when critics started to tire of this new version of Bono, he reverted to serious Bono (though not *too* serious), strapping the debt of third-world nations on his back while making music that everyone loves. To his credit, he kept the sunglasses from the *Achtung Baby* days, even when talking to George W. Bush, the pope, and other world leaders/powerful nerds.

In the end, Bono is like a doctoral student who has done all the course work but can't finish his dissertation. And at times I feel like the parent who paid for all those classes. Still, even though he's been around for such a long time, he's not so old that he can't yet Advance. With each passing year, though, the prospect seems less likely. After five years away from the studio, there was a new U2 album in 2009, which got five stars from *Rolling Stone.* So it doesn't seem as though we'll see an end to U2 anytime soon, and until Bono goes solo and does a techno-salsa version of *Boy,* he can't be Advanced, no matter how many Super Bowls U2 plays.

Chapter Eight

On the Bubble

An Echo & the Bunnymen fan once wrote a passionate letter to me explaining why the band deserves a spot in the Advanced pantheon. I don't agree, but maybe that's because I never really listened to them that much, so I can't judge properly. (A band can't qualify anyway, but that's beside this particular point.) Even though I coinvented, or codiscovered, Advancement, there is still a lot of subjectivity about who is Advanced. For example, it's possible that artists I don't appreciate actually are great enough to qualify for Advancement, but for whatever reason I missed the boat. It's almost certainly my fault that I can't stand the Clash and don't understand why people are into the Replacements, because almost everyone my age feels differently. I just happened not to listen to them much until I was too old and jaded. There are also artists who "feel" Advanced even though I never loved their music the way I did the Velvet Underground's or James Brown's. These artists are on the bubble of Advancement, and, as Carlo Marangoni or Lawrence Welk could tell you, bubbles are endlessly fascinating.

Eric Clapton

I want to like Eric Clapton, I really do. He seems to be the ideal candidate for Advancement—aging rock 'n' roller, sold out by doing beer commercial, participated in a Cream reunion—but I think he's just authentically terrible. I know that some people, people I respect, revere him, but I find his style of guitar playing incredibly boring. And his songwriting is truly dreadful. The obvious examples are "Tears from Heaven" and "Wonderful Tonight," neither of which I can sit through from beginning to end. Don't even get me started with his idiotic nickname, Slow Hand. I think the biggest reason I can't get on board with him is that he is so devoted to the blues, which I also really can't stand. (Again, my fault.) I say he's devoted because he says it, not because there is much evidence that it's true, at least post-*Unplugged*. That aside, the kind of blues he worships is particularly irritating to me. If there is anything more predictable, it's straightforward electric Buddy Guy–style blues, especially played by a chinless, wife-stealing British white guy. At the very least he could have emulated Robert Johnson, whose style was genuinely strange. Of course, Johnson is the most Overt of all possible blues influences.

As usual, I'm perfectly willing to accept the fact that I'm probably the idiot here. Clapton was in the Yardbirds, a decent band, but he quit it for his Overt love of the blues. Pretty tedious, but at least there was a principle involved that he could later betray. Cream was in fact a pretty good betrayal of those principles, and it rocked pretty hard at that. If there *were* an argument to be made inside my head for the Advancement of Eric Clapton, it would have to be his involvement with Cream. It was one project that he didn't ruin by his presence, kind of like how people loved *The Matrix* because Keanu Reeves wasn't all that terrible in it. Clapton, then, was the Reeves to Ginger Baker and Jack Bruce's Laurence Fishburne and Carrie-Anne Moss. Just as Reeves was needed in *The Matrix* to play a character in permanent "whoa!" mode, Clapton was necessary to keep Cream grounded. Without his wah-wah solos, "Tales of Brave Ulysses" could have wound up sounding ridiculous, and that's a possibility I'd prefer not to contemplate.

Everything after Cream has been awful as far as I can tell. There wasn't even a *Dream of the Blue Turtles* for me to look to as proof that he could achieve something as a solo artist. Even so, I'm leaving the door open for someone to prove me wrong about him. It's possible that, like Sting, he is just beyond my comprehension. He could have lapped boring into being interesting. I do find it somewhat compelling that he has gone preppy in the last few years, wearing khakis and short-sleeved cotton shirts onstage instead of the suits he wore there for a while. He's chosen a look that reminds me of what a retired man who has given up suits would wear to a nice restaurant. It's strange, yes, but not Advanced. If he shows up in leathers for the next Cream reunion, then I'll be ready to change my mind.

Elvis Costello

Elvis Costello is almost surely Advanced, though I have some reservations about him: I absolutely love a few songs on each of his albums, but I just never find myself sitting down and listening to any of those albums from beginning to end. I'm much more of a greatest-hits sort of Costello fan. There's no shame in that—for him or me—but it's just difficult for me to pronounce someone Advanced because I love twenty of his songs but merely like all the rest of them. Still, he has a lot to recommend him.

Costello started out more or less part of the punk scene, though he never really thought of himself as a punk. This is probably because instead of lip-syncing to Alice Cooper for Malcolm McLaren like Johnny Rotten, Costello was going to work every day as a computer programmer. That he was doing this in the '70s just goes to show you how ahead of his time he really was, and not just in the musical sphere. Besides being a punk rock computer programmer, he played in country bands on the side. All of this is good stuff, but his greatest accomplishment is that he took Elvis as his stage name—and got away with it. I can't think of anything more audacious, or Advanced, than taking the King of Rock 'n' Roll's name. He could've taken an easier road and called himself Jerry Lee Costello or Ringo Costello (though Lou was obviously out), but he called himself Elvis and threw in Buddy Holly's glasses for good measure.

It wouldn't have mattered what he called himself had he not also been such a good songwriter. *My Aim Is True* is indisputably great, or at least three-fourths of it is. Though that album was also indisputably Overt, there were still hints of Advancement to be found. Most notably, Costello was right in the middle of the golden era of British punk, and, for a backup band, he chose a group of musicians that ended up being the News, as in Huey Lewis (*Sports* is an all-time Advanced album title). And though it might have been uncool of him to choose such an unpunk group, they helped him make one of the all-time great debut albums. The reality is that the News was a thousand times better than a band like the Clash, and Costello knew it.

What's great and challenging about him is that he has never limited himself to a certain type of music. He used a piano riff from Abba's "Dancing Queen" and put it into "Oliver's Army," made a country record with a big-time Nashville producer, and cowrote songs with Paul McCartney. But things really started to get Advanced when Costello recorded with the Brodsky Quartet, creating a genuine "song cycle." He turned it up a notch when he collaborated with Burt Bacharach and then appeared with him in *Austin Powers: The Spy Who Shagged Me.* He was also in a movie with Joe Strummer and Courtney Love, and, even more Advanced, he did a cameo in the Spice Girls movie *Spice World*. By the time of that cameo, it wasn't that surprising that he would show up in a movie like that (it was more surprising to me that I was watching the movie in the theater), but who would have ever guessed that a guy with the guts to switch songs in the middle of a performance on live television (the famous "there's no reason to do this song here" incident on *SNL*) would tacitly endorse the existence of the Spice Girls?

Though now he rarely displays the cheek that made him the only person to cross Lorne Michaels and live to tell about it, he hasn't given it up completely. On one tour, according to All Music, he closed with "Couldn't Call It Unexpected No. 4," but did it without a microphone, "forcing the audience to sit in complete silence . . . with nothing but his dulcet baritone filling the auditorium." Telling your audience to do anything is Advanced, but it's especially Advanced if they do it themselves.

Of all that he has done, perhaps the most Advanced of his moves was also the simplest: after years of developing the Elvis Costello look (basically the Buddy Holly look with more colorful jackets), he decided to grow a long beard. It won't surprise you to hear that he also got rid of his trademark glasses in favor of black sunglasses. This was an interesting twist on the traditional Advanced look, substituting long hair in the back for long hair in the front (also known as the ZZ Top model of Advanced hair). He didn't take up black leather, but his Britishness excuses that omission. After a year or so, the beard disappeared just as suddenly as it appeared (probably more so, as it takes a lot longer to grow a beard than shave it off), and he looked exactly like he used to again.

In looking over his case, I realize that Elvis Costello meets nearly every requirement for Advancement, including inventing a new way to be Advanced. So I'm forced to conclude that the only argument against his being included among the Advanced (my personal lukewarm reaction to 60 percent of his music) is my problem. So Elvis Costello is almost certainly Advanced, but not to me.

Madonna

You may have noticed that I haven't written much about Advanced women, but I don't mean this as a slight against female artists. I admit that looking over my collection of music and books that I favor male artists, and I'm definitely the poorer for it. But I think it is possible that Advancement might just be more of a male thing, like watching *Just One of the Guys* for ninety minutes to see a five-second shot of bare breasts. (Totally worth it.) This is not to say that women artists can't be geniuses, just that most female geniuses don't usually aspire to Advancement. However, there are some exceptions, and Madonna may be one of them.

Examples of her possible Advancement are the blasphemous Pepsi commercial (selling out *plus* religion), *Truth or Dare* (Advanced Artists like movies about tours or themselves in general), and her cover of "American Pie." She has acted; worn black leather and sunglasses (*Desperately Seeking Susan*); developed an accent that can only be described as international; and embraced younger, rival artists like Britney Spears. Finally, she has transformed herself many times, which is a hallmark of the Advanced Artist (Lou Reed, David Bowie, Bob Dylan). Not only has she reinvented herself every five years or so, but every new incarnation is enthusiastically embraced by her fans. This ability to anticipate what people will like is maybe her most Advanced characteristic (even though pleasing one's fans is not Advanced). In fact, she's *so* right *so* often, I'm convinced she can see into the future. So if you ever want to make a lot of money, ask Madonna which team is going to win the World Series next year, and bet everything you have on her pick. There is no surer bet.

I saw her at Madison Square Garden a few years back, and I

came away impressed. Her band consisted of a spectacular drummer, a guy playing serviceable bass/keyboards, a couple of African-American backup singers, and a Mohawked lead guitarist. Having a guy with a Mohawk in your band might be Advanced if you are Madonna, though it would not be Advanced if you are in Green Day or No Doubt. The show got off to a slow start with an okay version of "Vogue." Speaking of "Vogue," she has been criticized for merely lifting elements of gay-club culture, with that song being a favorite example. All I can say to that is that there aren't many artists who can take what is found in underground gay clubs and make it acceptable to the mainstream. If Madonna can in fact see into the future, her crystal ball is apparently totally gay.

Things got better and more Advanced during "American Life," when a bunch of dancers came out dressed as nuns, Hasidic Jews, Muslims, and just about every kind of person with international flavor you could think of. The song rocked, sounding a bit like Ministry, and she seemed finally to be getting into it. Then she picked up a guitar to play "Burning Up." She was clearly still a novice (you can tell because she constantly looked down at the fret board and held the pick in a certain way, as if she would be lost were the pick to shift in her fingers), but she made up for that with her enthusiasm. People might make fun of her lack of ability, but I think it's rather brave to be a beginner and play in front of all those people. Plus, if you've been making music as long as she has, you have to make it fresh any way you can. So I love that she played the guitar.

If she is in fact Advanced, the most Advanced moment of the night was her cover of "Imagine." Most reviews (for the MSG show and others from that tour) mentioned this as the low point of the evening. I would have expected to feel the same way, but the song was actually pretty moving. This was a moment that I think most critics couldn't enjoy because "Imagine" has become a cliché. But at one point, I'll bet even the most seasoned of critics loved the original version of that song, even though that moment may be long forgotten. Now if, say, Britney Spears covered "Imagine," it might be awful (even if you love her as I do). But Madonna is one of the few people whose impact on popular culture rivals John Lennon's, so I say she has the right to cover it if she wants to. And it really was a nice moment in the show.

Madonna has many things going for her, but there are some major strikes against her. I can't say that her music has ever been innovative, and she was never really misunderstood. Plus, even through all her changes, she has never disappointed her core audience from the very beginning. So though she can see into the future, she uses her powers to see what her fans will like in a couple of years rather than fifteen or twenty years down the road. This may be the prudent course, but it is no way to be Advanced, regardless of gender.

Patti Smith

I had a pretty Overt stance on another potentially Advanced woman, Patti Smith, for a long time. For example, I once wrote a post about her on the blog with the headline "I'm So Overt, I'm So Goddamn Overt." Without really doing the research, I dismissed the possibility of her being Advanced. The irony is that it was her most Advanced act—leaving music to focus on her family—that led me to believe she was Overt. I became aware of alternative music during her hiatus, and when she did come back, I just figured she was a sort of punk rock Grace Slick. But while working on this book, I've been forced to rethink my position.

First of all, the music that made her reputation was really just straight-ahead rock 'n' roll with poetry on top. I can forgive anything, even poetry, if it rocks. Second, her biggest mainstream hit was a song she wrote with Bruce Springsteen. I can't imagine a

New York downtown weirdo like, say, Lydia Lunch, even admitting that she likes the Boss, much less writing a song with him. Third, she did a straight-ahead cover of "You Light Up My Life" on a television show for kids (ah, YouTube). On that show, the host asked her if she was the next Mick Jagger. At the time a more apt comparison might have been the other great rocker/poet, Jim Morrison. It turns out, though, that the artist she is most like is John Lennon, who also took a long break from the music business to concentrate on his family. At a time when a woman, especially a woman like Smith, was expected to be just as dedicated to her career as a man, she gave it up to raise a family. This decision caused a lot of anger in Overt people everywhere, who felt she was somehow betraying her principles when in fact she was just betraying their principles. All I knew was that she had been cool and then disappeared, only to come back Overt.

In hindsight all of her moves after coming back seem pretty solid and not boring at all: she moved back to New York to begin her Second Stage Advancement with new music, a tour with Bob Dylan, a cover of "When Doves Cry," and getting inducted into the Rock and Roll Hall of Fame, performing "Gimme Shelter" for the occasion. Maybe she was the next Mick Jagger after all.

Joe Walsh

As a kid, I was fascinated by the weird noise in the middle of Joe Walsh's single "Life's Been Good." To this day, I still don't really know how it was made, but I like to think that it is what Walsh hears inside his brain, sort of like the way kids in Charlie Brown specials hear adults. Much later I discovered the James Gang, the best American rock trio of all time, which made his participation in the Eagles confusing. He was so great in his own band and as a solo artist that it made little sense that he would join a band where he would be relegated to writing a couple of songs, playing an occasional solo, and being a backup singer. At one time I thought that maybe that arrangement was pretty good for him: he got to be in one of the biggest bands in the world without having to be the front man, which would leave plenty of time for his true loves, drinking and doing drugs. Since the Theory came to me, however, I've realized that the problem was that I was trying to make sense out of someone who makes no sense. You could go out of your mind trying to figure out why one of the greatest rock guitarists ever would make an album called *Got Any Gum?* There's just not a satisfactory answer to it. Sadly, though I'd like to say that his behavior is attributable to Advancement, I really can't. True, he did go solo, join another band, abuse drugs, and clean up, which is commendable. But he doesn't quite make the cut and belongs in either the Refined Overt class or perhaps the Authentically Weird class.

Johnny Rotten and the Sex Pistols

Most people are familiar with the story of how Johnny Rotten got the gig with the Sex Pistols, but few have understood how much is revealed by it. If you haven't heard the story, it goes like this: Malcolm McLaren was putting a band together and needed a singer. He had seen John Lydon—who was famous around town for adding "I hate" to a Pink Floyd shirt—hanging out at his boutique, and he thought he would be a pretty good front man for the band. He and the band had Lydon "audition" by singing along with a jukebox playing "18" by Alice Cooper, while channeling Richard III. Naturally he got the job.

The story is revealing because it shows that from the beginning, the band was pretty much no different from the Monkees or the Spice Girls, bands that were put together for the way they looked and behaved (or misbehaved). Also, it shows how influential

Alice Cooper was before he became a golfing sports-bar owner. The Johnny Rotten character, after all, was really just Alice Cooper with a faster band. He even wrote a song called "Seventeen" in an attempt to one-up Cooper. The part I love the best is that Chris Thomas, the engineer on *Never Mind the Bollocks,* also worked on *Dark Side of the Moon* by a band called Pink Floyd. So Johnny Rotten was really just Scary Spice + Alice Cooper + Roger Waters, which is why he is three times as awesome as just about anyone else from the punk era.

Obviously his Overt period was about as Overt as it gets, but is he Advanced now? His name certainly is. As you know, there is no more Advanced name than Johnny. His post–Sex Pistols band, Public Image Limited, which featured Steve Vai (you may remember him from his guitarversation with David Lee Roth in "Yankee Rose"), was in essence a solo project. He doesn't give honest interviews, or else he is so honest in interviews that he sounds dishonest. He had a talk show on VH1. He is certainly irritating in an amusing way. And he was a part of a Sex Pistols reunion tour, admitting that he was doing it mostly for the money. He has definitely worn leather and sunglasses, and I feel he had a rattail for a while. It doesn't matter if he did or didn't, though, because he doesn't qualify. He made two great albums and a few good songs over the years, but so did Colin Hay of Men at Work (yes, two great albums; you really need to listen to *Cargo* again). Plus, there is just too much sarcasm and irony in his act. I give him credit for doing a show on VH1, but he still couldn't help saying disparaging things about himself and the network to show us that he knew that some people might think that he had truly sold out. He pretends he doesn't care what people think, but with as hard as he works to make us believe that, I just don't quite buy it.

In my opinion, if there was an Advanced Pistol, it was Glen Matlock. He was the one who wrote most of the hits, writing them for acoustic guitar and trying to sound like the Beatles and other pop bands that he liked. But because Johnny Rotten and rest of the band were so Overt, they had to transform Matlock's pop songs into something much heavier, reminding us once again that most original-sounding bands are usually just trying to sound like someone else but aren't capable of pulling it off. Matlock left the band, replaced by Sid Vicious, who could barely play (or so it is said) but looked cooler and had a much dumber name. Despite being mistreated by the band so publicly, the pragmatic Matlock agreed to be a part of the reunion tour. Unlike Johnny Rotten, Matlock was in it for the great rock 'n' roll, not the swindle.

Morrissey/Johnny Marr

There is not a better band than the Smiths. Every song they wrote was good, usually great, and every member is among the best musicians of the alternative era. Morrissey and Johnny Marr were among the best in the history of popular, not just alternative, music. No one has ever written more unique and interesting lyrics or sung those lyrics with more skill and wit than Morrissey. No one has written more tasteful and tuneful guitar parts with more subtlety and dexterity than Johnny Marr. I really, really like the Smiths.

Surprisingly, though, neither of them is Advanced. Morrissey went solo (though he blames Johnny Marr for the breakup), but he never really changed his sound other than flirting with a quasi-rockabilly band for a while. He also says things like "When was the last time you were surprised by the lyrics of a pop song?" (that's not a direct quote, but it's close), to which one could respond, "When was the last time you were surprised by anything in a Morrissey song?" He might be an Advanced Irritant, but that's as far as I'm willing to go. And really he's just irritating the same people he's always irritated, so even Advanced Irritant status is questionable. Johnny Marr has jumped around from playing with the Talking

Heads to doing electronic projects to joining Modest Mouse. Of the two, he's probably shown more signs of Advancement, especially that joining Modest Mouse move. Nevertheless, he's never really been a solo artist, so I can't grant him Advanced status.

The good news, though, is that they both have the greatness and the longevity to become Advanced. If Morrissey writes a few love songs, does a duet with Posh Spice (the video would feature him playing soccer with David Beckham), and stars in *The Love Guru II* while Marr does a bluegrass record and maybe renounces the guitar before re-forming "the Smiths" with Morrissey but with Flea and Beck's drummer rounding out the lineup (Morrissey and Marr would insist that they are better than ever), then I could say that they are both Advanced. But until then, they are just way, way better than just about anyone else.

Roy Orbison

No one is more revered by great musicians of a certain age than Roy Orbison. Luckily, before he died he got to play with many of them—Elvis Costello, Tom Waits, Bruce Springsteen—for a show that will definitely be a part of your next PBS pledge drive. Orbison's great claim to Advancement, as opposed to plain greatness, is his look: all black clothes, dark sunglasses, and ragged black hair that looked like a crooked wig (which it may have been). He was also in the Traveling Wilburys, which is another notch in the win column. What intrigues me is that he wrote maybe ten of the greatest songs in the history of rock 'n' roll, but growing up I thought the only song he ever did was "Oh, Pretty Woman," a perception he helped along by playing only that song on TV appearances. This is very similar to Lou Reed's playing nothing but "Walk on the Wild Side" for about fifteen years. I can only imagine how frustrated Tom Waits must have been watching Orbison play that song to Johnny Carson for the ninetieth time, especially since a lot of kids were probably wondering why some weird old guy was covering a Van Halen song. I don't think, though, that Roy Orbison is truly Advanced, even though he was such an inspiration to so many Advanced musicians. Ultimately I think he was just an angst-ridden, slightly mysterious nerd who wore black because it was a way for him to seem cool. I guess you could say he was the Trent Reznor of his time, only without all the weight lifting.

Billy Joel

Chuck Klosterman has defended Billy Joel eloquently in the past, so I won't dig too deeply into the career of the man known by some as the Long Island Loser. But I would like to talk about "We Didn't Start the Fire." I should preface by saying that no believer in Advancement can fail to appreciate Joel's earlier work, especially, for obvious reasons, "It's Still Rock and Roll to Me." But when I heard "WDSTF" the first time, I had to say "WTF." But when I broke it all down, everything became clear. The song is a sort of update of Dylan's "Subterranean Homesick Blues," and the video featured Joel, an aging rocker, in black clothes and dark sunglasses. (He also insisted on wearing dark sunglasses during all the interviews he did promoting that album.) It is pretty obvious what was going on: he wanted to be seen as Advanced, but as with most of the things he has done, it wasn't quite enough. He's had some great songs, but he was never really innovative, and though building a piano-shaped mansion is a nice touch, being bilked by several business partners is just not the Advanced way. But he *was* trying, and there is something to be said for recognizing at least the superficial aspects of Advancement and aspiring to that brand of greatness, even though it was in vain. I suppose in that way he's a bit like Antonio Salieri in *Amadeus*. Still, I have to admit that I have fond memories of *The*

Nylon Curtain and I'm always excited to hear "Only the Good Die Young," despite its Overt message.

Phil Collins

I missed out on the Peter Gabriel–era Genesis because I was too young and probably wouldn't have been very susceptible anyway. I'm just not into that sound (or masks). So I didn't discover Phil Collins until "Abacab" and "Paper Late," both of which were pretty interesting songs to hear on Top 40 radio. Then he went solo, recorded "Sussudio" and somehow became one of the biggest stars in the world. Since I didn't know much about his time behind the drums, I pretty much dismissed him as a cheesy singer, even though I enjoyed some of his singles, especially "Take Me Home." But now that I look at his career again, there is some reason to believe that he is Advanced: he was in an extremely Overt art band, is a universally respected drummer (he was the best musician on the stage when he played with Led Zeppelin at Live Aid), went solo, wore sunglasses, had long hair in the back, reunited with the original Genesis, and acted in movies. And when Britt introduced me to the speech about Genesis in *American Psycho*, I was leaning toward a positive verdict for Collins, but I've since thought better of it. He's a better musician than most people think and he's a decent songwriter, but even if he was the driving force of innovation in Genesis (though I believe it was Gabriel), his solo stuff has been almost completely middle of the road, so I'm forced to conclude that he is not Advanced.

The Rat Pack

Some artists, such as Frank Sinatra, Sammy Davis, Jr., and Frank Sinatra, were so far before my time that it's difficult to understand how ahead of their own time they were. It's a bigger problem with musicians who predated rock 'n' roll because a love of rock 'n' roll is one of the cornerstones of musical Advancement. It might be said that Sinatra embraced rock 'n' roll by adding some rock songs to his act, but with him, Martin, and Davis, Jr., we don't need to quibble: those three guys were definitely Advanced, albeit some earlier version that I'll call Early-Form Advancement.

All three acted, sold out, performed as solo acts, embraced Vegas, kept performing after most people thought they should stop (especially Sinatra), were dismissed as irrelevant only to make comebacks, abused alcohol, hosted variety shows, celebrated multiculturalism (Davis was a one-man band of multiculturalism), and reunited for a tour. Sinatra was the Lou Reed of the group; Sammy Davis was the Dolly Parton; and Dean Martin was the Ringo Starr. (Now, if only those three would get together we'd have a show on our hands.) By that I mean that Sinatra was gloomy and difficult to work with; Davis was beloved but had such an outsized personality that it overwhelmed people's ability to appreciate how talented he was; and Martin seemed as though he might have just been along for the ride when in fact he was as talented as and possibly more Advanced than the more celebrated members of his peer group.

I could go on and on about these guys, but I think that all you need to know is that for about ten years they were the coolest guys in the world and were surrounded by the most beautiful women in the world (plus Norman Fell). They were powerful, famous, talented, and good-looking, and their final movie together was *Cannonball Run II*.

Michael Jackson

The King of Pop was obviously a musical genius. I liked every single he ever released (particularly "Earth Song"), including those from his Jackson 5 days. He leveraged rap and rock 'n' roll, and he was religious. He embraced the Advanced Trinity, even adding his own touch with sequins and epaulets. He was innovative, acted in movies, and was *seriously* committed to changing his look. He reunited with the Jackson 5, sold out to Pepsi, married Elvis Presley's daughter, and played the Super Bowl. Plus he was one of the weirdest people on the planet.

Obviously Jackson was a complicated figure, and the more I think about him, the more questions arise. Just about everyone who worked with him says that he was not the weirdo people make him out to be. They say he was just a normal guy, though definitely a genius. So was his supposed weirdness merely his way of staying relevant in the constantly changing pop landscape? If that were true, would pretending to be that crazy be Advanced or Overt? What if he was crazy but only selectively? Can you be a crazy person in your real life but not in your art? Would that be Advanced? I confess that I just don't know. If the allegations surrounding his behavior with children are true, he is disqualified. Not because of the immorality of his actions but because his behavior was indicative of mental illness that would disqualify him from consideration. If he were truly innocent of all the worst charges against him, however, I would have to say that he was the most Advanced pop musician ever.

John Fogerty

In *Vicky Cristina Barcelona,* Javier Bardem plays an artist whose father is a poet who refuses to publish his work as a way to punish the world for not knowing how to love. No one could understand this logic better than John Fogerty, who punished the world by refusing to play CCR songs in concert for years because he was mad at Saul Zaentz, who owned the rights to those songs. Fogerty was an irritant, but he is not truly Advanced because he hasn't produced enough great material as a solo artist, and I don't think he was ever really ahead of his time. But he does deserve some recognition for singing as if he was from New Orleans when he was actually from California, being sued (by Zaentz) for plagiarizing himself, and writing "Centerfield," the best rock-'n'-roll song about sports. What's more, if you had gone to see Fogerty in concert in the 1980s, you wouldn't have heard "Lodi," "Have You Ever Seen the Rain?" or "Green River," but you would have been treated to "Centerfield," played on a guitar shaped like a baseball bat. Take that, Saul.

There are so many other potential candidates and interesting figures—Neil Diamond, David Lee Roth, Leonard Cohen, Alice Cooper, and Axl Rose, just to name a few—that I can't possibly include them all. Plus, by now you should have a pretty good grasp of what makes a musician Advanced, so you are more than capable of making your own list. It's time now to examine other areas, where Advancement is harder to identify and even harder to achieve.

Chapter Nine

The Stage and Mostly Screen

Unlike musicians, who can start a band and record with little or no financial backing, young directors and actors have no choice but to collaborate with writers, producers, editors, cinematographers, corporations, and so on. So while a director may do a spectacular job during filming or an actor may give a great performance, the end product itself might be terrible. This dynamic makes it difficult to judge the Advanced status of an actor or director. Further complicating matters is that while musicians are usually expected to stay within one style of music, great directors and actors are expected to explore various genres, so long as the quality of the work is high. Finally, actors have no real say in their wardrobes, so black leather, dark sunglasses, and long hair in the back aren't always an option. Directors, of course, have to wear cargo shorts and baseball caps.

So how do we spot Advanced directors and actors?

The fifteen-year rule applies, so we still have a large body of work to look at. This comes into play because while genre hopping is encouraged, it's generally uncomfortable for an audience to see a director or actor go away too quickly from what is expected based on their past work. For instance, Sir Ben Kingsley, who reportedly insists on everyone referring to him as "Sir Ben," decided to accept a role as Guru Tugginmypudha in Mike Myers's *The Love Guru*. Making a big deal of your knighthood and then appearing in a movie that features a sword fight with urine-soaked mops can come across as foolish. But he was Gandhi and Sexy Beast, so I have to conclude that there is something more interesting than mere foolishness going on there. Though I don't know what that something is, it feels to me like Advancement.

Another hallmark of Advancement, innovation in one's craft, is applicable. This is easy to spot in directing (for example, George Lucas's *THX*), but it is more difficult to see innovative acting. In addition to having to fit in with a director's vision, actors have to mesh their performance with that of other actors, who may not be as adventurous and talented as they are. So while the actor's technique may be truly innovative, it may not be effective within the context of the work as a whole. You see this a lot with Jim Carrey, who is often innovative, but his movies suffer from the *Roger Rabbit* effect, where it feels as if you're watching real actors interacting with a cartoon character.

James Dean, on the other hand, could be innovative in a way that was less jarring, at least to the audience. For instance, he understood that Raymond Massey, who played his father in *East of Eden*, was an old-fashioned actor who read his lines as they were written and would be uncomfortable with Dean's improvisational style. So Dean used this discomfort to his—and the story's—advantage in the scene where Massey plays a father rejecting a gift (money) from his son on the grounds that the money is dirty. This rejection is devastating to the son, so in the scene, Dean throws himself weeping on Massey. However, Massey didn't know he was going to be so physical and had no idea how to handle this outpouring of emotion. Consequently, Massey looks angry and confused, completely at a loss for how to deal with this crazy young actor. However, it is precisely this dynamic that brings power to the scene because the father in the story has no idea how to handle his crazy young son. The audience can sense Massey's genuine dismay, so instead of just being angry with the mean dad for rejecting his son's love, we also feel sorry for the dad, which elevates the scene from pathos to tragedy.

We still talk about James Dean because his talent was so rare (and his life was so short). Less common still are actors who have the talent and aspire to Advancement. Robert De Niro gets my vote, mainly because of his American Express commercials and *Rocky and Bullwinkle*, but he was pretty good in *Raging Bull*, too. Then there is Val Kilmer, who has played a genius, become a rock star twice (Nick Rivers and Jim Morrison), and appeared in *The Ten Commandments*, the musical. He was also in the highly Advanced *The Island of Dr. Moreau* with Marlon Brando. I wasn't completely sure of his Advancement until he started making up normal stories about himself when considering a run for governor of New Mexico.

Michael Caine is an incredibly talented and versatile actor, plus he has been in more bad movies than any other good actor I can think of. I've thought of some complicated reasons why he might have wanted to be in *Jaws IV* (including Advancement), but I think the simple answer is that he's just doing his job. As Alec Baldwin once said on *Inside the Actor's Studio*, a plumber doesn't come to your house and say, "I'm not going to work on that sink. It doesn't move me." A plumber just does the work and gets paid. That is not to minimize Caine as an artist. The more artists practice their craft, the better they become, even if the work is with a revenge-minded shark. And you have to give him credit for missing his chance to receive his Oscar for *Hannah and Her Sisters* in person because he was filming *Jaws IV*. Even so, Michael Caine doesn't meet the standard somehow, mostly because I can't say he's ever been ahead of his time.

Dustin Hoffman is a viable candidate: In addition to following up *The Graduate* with *Midnight Cowboy* ("Honey, let's go see that new movie with that nice boy from *The Graduate*. I think it's a Western."), he was in *Ishtar, Hook,* and *Meet the Fockers;* plus he dressed up like a woman (the Advanced like to be in drag or at least be androgynous). Jon Voight, his costar in *Midnight Cowboy,* played Howard Cosell (Advanced sportscaster, as you will soon learn), appeared in *Anaconda* with Ice Cube, and wears those actors' scarves at awards shows. Additionally, he doesn't get along with his daughter, possibly because she's so Overt. I believe that of the two, only Hoffman could be Advanced. Voight isn't because he didn't have a long enough period of excellence. But if you ever want to get really depressed, you should watch *Midnight Cowboy* by yourself on a Saturday night.

Before we get back to directors, it's important to consider actors like Tom Cruise who are not so much actors as "stars." Julia Roberts is another example of this type of actor. I don't know why being charismatic on-screen should be discounted, because it is as rare as other kinds of natural genius. Should we discount "stars" because they are born magnetic? Is it any different from other kinds of genius, which are also just something the lucky few are born with? In the past I've dismissed the idea that Cruise or Roberts or even Bruce Willis could possibly be Advanced, but is that just Overt of me? After all, Willis may be an action star without much range, but he did make *Return of Bruno,* was phenomenal on *Moonlighting* (plus he always wore sunglasses), is a right-wing Republican, made M. Night Shyamalan seem deep, and made Quentin Tarantino seem subtle. So shouldn't stars at least be part of the conversation? Probably, but I'm not Advanced enough to have that talk yet.

I've focused more on actors than directors up to now for a reason: there are more actors who qualify for Advancement than directors. To prepare for this book, I put together a long list of possible candidates, including all kinds of artists, as well as businessmen, athletes, and even a fictional character, Don Quixote. The list of actors was long, though most of them turned out not to be Advanced. The directors list was incredibly short, which surprised me a bit because movie directing would seem to fit the Advanced temperament perfectly. In fact, it's one of the few jobs where people *expect* you to be an uncompromising, megalomaniacal control freak. It may be that there is some subtlety in the craft that I'm missing, but it seems just as likely that the medium doesn't lend itself to Advancement. Movies just cost too much to take the kinds of risks required to Advance. If Bob Dylan makes a few records that don't sell, the record company can release a greatest-hits package and everything is okay. But if a movie director makes an expensive bomb, the movie's financiers can lose a fortune. Make two bombs in a row, and you're no longer a director. Just ask Orson Welles.

Chapter Ten

"A" Is for Advanced:
Orson Welles

As a sixteen-year-old Orson Welles got into Harvard, but he wasn't interested in going. So he avoided it by becoming a bullfighter, then making his way over to Ireland. There he offered his services as an actor to Hilton Edwards at the Gate Theatre "if any leading roles were available." In true Advanced style, he lied about his age and experience (he had never acted at the time), but he got a part anyway and was well received. So that was that for Harvard, and from there he went on to do the things that you know about: he had incredible success on the stage and then the radio, scaring half of America while he was at it. Then he went to Hollywood to take on the other half.

Even though it's a well-worn topic, we can't avoid *Citizen Kane*, as it was his greatest Overt achievement. (Maybe *the* greatest Overt achievement.) Welles, a twenty-five-year-old first-time director, managed to make a movie that is regarded almost universally as the best movie ever made, even by people who can't stay awake through the whole thing. Making such an acclaimed film was only part of the accomplishment, though. By choosing to take William Randolph Hearst as his subject, he ensured both that the movie wouldn't succeed financially (Hearst would take care of that) and also that studios would not want to work with him. This was a sort of kamikaze Overtness: by his crashing into Hearst, history will always remember Welles as the patron saint of unmet potential while Hearst will be seen as a bully and a fool. But it was especially Advanced of Welles to play Kane himself, because few people now remember what Hearst looked like, so it's Welles's face people picture when thinking of Hearst. It's as if Welles stole Hearst's face and replaced it with his own.

Welles's decision to play Kane was interesting in another way. Plenty of critics have written about the ironic similarities between Welles and Kane, but no one was more aware of them than Welles (which makes them not so ironic). I think he imbued the character with parts of himself, knowing that what they shared was their separateness from other people. Like Kane, Welles was a visionary who would do anything to achieve his goals, even if in doing so he destroyed others or even himself. (Again, a kamikaze.) Even as a young man, he could see that the destiny of his caliber of genius was to be denied his humanity by a misunderstanding world. But he was also self-aware enough to acknowledge his own role in others' misperceptions of him.

Welles had a penchant for playing characters that were like him or had some significance in his life. In addition to Charles Foster Kane, he played the fat, narcissistic Falstaff in *Chimes at Midnight,* was the seer Tiresias in *Oedipus the King,* and portrayed the studio mogul Lew Lord in *The Muppet Movie.* In this film, Lord greenlights a project pitched by a first-time director (Kermit) who has no experience, giving him full artistic control. This can be read two ways: One, he is playing a generous patron of the artist, the kind that would have allowed Welles to make all the movies he wanted without interference. So it was something of an exercise in wish fulfillment. The darker reading is that given Welles's real-life experience, we might assume that artistic freedom will end up dooming Kermit as it did Welles.

Actually it wasn't artistic freedom that killed *Citizen Kane* (and Welles by extension) but poor marketing. Welles knew that Hearst would try to keep the film out of theaters, so he hatched a plan to publicize the fact that the movie was being censored, spread rumors that the movie was much more salacious than it actually was, and then showed it independently across the United States from Boston to little towns in Minnesota to the Iowa cornfields and beyond. Welles was serious enough about this that he offered to buy the film and distribute it himself. But it never happened, so *Kane* was regarded at the time as an expensive vanity project by an egomaniacal star/director, and his reputation never recovered. In other words, *Citizen Kane* was the *Waterworld* of its day when it could have been the *Field of Dreams*.

But let's not lose sight of the fact that Welles was still Overt when he made *Kane*. As proof, one need only watch its hokey trailer, which includes scenes of chorus girls, various smiling well-known cast members, and the introduction of unknown actors (future stars, Welles promises) featured in the movie. Then Welles rattles off a bunch of contradictory descriptions of Charles Foster Kane, presumably to add an air of mystery. The humor was his way of protecting himself, because if people took him as seriously as he took himself, he would be vulnerable. And the ambiguity surrounding the main character is the height of Overtness.

As a counterpoint, the trailer for a movie he made post-Advancement, *F Is for Fake*, is twelve minutes long and features a voice-over speaking of connections between Picasso and Howard Hughes. Welles doesn't show any chorus girls, opting instead for shots of a tiger and plenty of nude pictures of his girlfriend, just to ensure its never being seen by anyone in a reputable theater. (He also appears in a black cape, which is his version of the black leather jacket.) There is a touch of Overtness even here, though, when he makes the claim that the *War of the Worlds* was, in fact, not a hoax but the result of collaboration between himself and actual aliens. At least I think that's Overtness.

The broadcast *War of the Worlds* was the main reason Welles was able to go to Hollywood to make movies, but he had been turning down contracts long before that. The more they offered, the more he asked for, and finally, after *War of the Worlds,* RKO gave him total artistic control, which no one had ever been given before by a major studio. Welles recognized that popular art is a commodity and that you have to be able to do business if you want to make art. A lesser artist might not have had the confidence to turn down the offers and would have ultimately had to compromise his vision. Welles didn't have to compromise at all. The result was *Citizen Kane,* a summary of everything that had come before and the blueprint for everything that would come after. Unfortunately for Welles, he would play only a small part in the future he foresaw (though he did get to narrate a film about another seer, Nostradamus).

The period after *Citizen Kane,* otherwise known as most of his life, is not well understood. The popular perception of him is as either some sort of rebel who wouldn't let himself get hemmed in by Hollywood or a one-and-done artist who wasn't up to the challenge of following up his debut. In fact, Hollywood rejected him more than the other way around. He was thought to be box office poison plus difficult to work with, and he could never overcome that reputation with the notoriously risk-averse Hollywood studios. Certainly he was uncompromising, but so are countless other less talented artists who work just fine within the system. He just wasn't wanted.

Now for the second part of the equation: his inability to follow up on *Kane.* Welles was not intimidated by his own achievement, as were Harper Lee, Truman Capote, and Ralph Ellison, whose blocks were purely mental. After all, to write a book you need only a typewriter and some paper. But a director has to get actors, build sets, scout locations, find/write scripts, and all the other million things that need to be done to get a movie made. Not only is it logistically difficult, it is extremely expensive. So since Welles was not welcome at the studios, he was forced to act as producer as well as writer and director. As it turned out, many of his backers ended up not working out, often pulling out at the last minute, causing him to pause filming—sometimes for years—or cancel altogether. He tried to raise the money himself by doing voice-overs and commercials, as well as taking acting roles that might have been "beneath" his talents (he was the voice of Robin Masters on *Magnum, P.I.,* for instance). The reality is that he wasn't afraid to finish projects, he just couldn't afford to.

The Case for Advancement

Orson Welles once said that it is only in your twenties and then your seventies and eighties that you do your greatest work. He added, "We must treasure old age and give genius the capacity to function in old age." True, this is a philosophy one would expect from an old man who did his best work before he was thirty (I don't believe that, but many do), but it also happens to be one of the pillars of the Advanced Genius Theory. This was just one way his philosophy was in line with Advancement. Like Elvis, Welles was, in both word and deed, Advanced before it had a name. Let's take a look:

1. He understood and rejected Overtness.
Unlike Overt Artists, who pretend not to care whether they are accepted by the mainstream, Welles wanted commercial success. He reported in *This Is Orson Welles* that he liked "popular artists,"

such as Dickens and Shakespeare, the most, and wished that he too could have been one. He believed that Hollywood deserved respect, and he added that he wasn't interested in making "art-house movies." He labeled the deliberate eccentricity of his early, celebrated work like *Kane* and *The Magnificent Ambersons* "virtuoso hamming." He didn't disown the achievements of his youth, but in his Advanced years he understood that the elements most celebrated (especially the technical achievements) were the most superficial.

2. He was an innovator and embraced technology.
Though he may have downplayed those superficial achievements, they were still achievements. Aside from the deep focus, low-angle shots, various special effects, sophisticated makeup, and so on found in *Citizen Kane*, he was also a pioneer of the handheld camera, he is credited by some to have invented narration on radio, and he was the first to take the gels out of stage lighting. Additionally, he embraced television, the enemy of serious filmmakers. Welles thought that "some of the most interesting filmmaking is in [TV] commercials," which he said could be "staggering." He believed that commercials made the public more accepting of "surprising things," such as fast cuts.

3. He wore black.
As discussed, he opted for a cape rather than leather.

4. He was a rock 'n' roller.
In 1984 he was featured in a song by Ray Charles and narrated "Dark Avenger" for the metal band Manowar (you'll find it on the 1982 album *Battle Hymns*).

5. He rejected drug use.

It's not necessarily Advanced to abstain from drug use, but Welles had a pretty Advanced reason for not liking marijuana. He said it was "very hard to get quantities of good enough quality to give anybody enough a bang to be worth all the carrying on that they do about it." (He also complained that it gave him bad breath.) He took the Advanced position on hallucinogens in an argument with the Overt Aldous Huxley, who believed that they could "help you." Arguing with Huxley about 'shrooms is at least extremely cool if not Advanced.

6. He was an irritant.

There are many examples of this, but my favorite is one told by Stacy Keach, who was Welles's costar in the Pia Zadora vehicle *Butterfly*. Apparently Welles decided that it was essential that he wear a prosthetic nose in his role, and, after insisting, he got his way. Keach found this odd because the fake nose looked exactly like Welles's actual nose.

7. He sold out.

This one is slightly more complicated because he sold out only as an actor and only to fund his movies. But his work in commercials made it much harder for people to take him seriously as a film-maker. For instance, I had no idea growing up that the "Sell no wine before its time" guy was a director, and I'm sure I'm not alone. Still, he did those commercials and others like them in an effort to fund movies that were never completed and would not have been seen even if they had been. One of those movies, as it happens, was *Don Quixote*.

8. He was quixotic and optimistic.

He was quixotic not only because he tried to film *Don Quixote* and other lost causes but for his attitude toward the past. Welles once said, "Even if the good old days never existed, the fact that we can *conceive* [italics his] of such a world is, in fact, an affirmation of the human spirit."

It's impressive to me that a man who had to fight most of his life for the right to do something he did better than almost everyone else should have had such a generous attitude toward the human spirit. For Welles, life must have been a lot like sitting in a theater watching a horror movie where the babysitter investigates the noise in the basement—no matter how loudly the audience tells her not to—when it is so obvious that she should just get out of the house and call the cops. Only instead of a teenager in her underwear, it was studio heads, financiers, and audiences, and instead of investigating a strange sound, they were preventing the greatest genius in cinema from making movies. But the frustration one feels at the character walking into certain doom is part of the fun of a horror movie, and similarly Orson Welles came to enjoy his role as the wasted genius, likely because the alternative was either to play the game by someone else's rules or to go insane from the frustration of seeing people with less talent making as many movies as they wanted. He chose the middle, Advanced way: he did guest spots on shows like *Magnum, P.I.*

Chapter Eleven

Overt Riders, Overt Bulls

Just as with everyone else my age, the late 1960s through the early 1970s is my favorite era of American filmmaking, which, not by coincidence, is around the time I was born. There is something satisfying about watching movies that look like pictures from your childhood, even if your dad doesn't look like Robert De Niro. But home-movie nostalgia aside, I do think that the directors of that time really were making excellent movies. And most of them have gone on to do interesting work to the present day. But while those "movie brats," as they came to be known, made some of the most respected (and commercially successful) films of the last forty years, only George Lucas embraced Advancement completely.

Francis Ford Coppola is a prime candidate for consideration, but he's not done enough Advanced work. On the plus side, he made a sequel (*The Godfather II*) that was better than the original, then made a sequel to *that*, casting his inexperienced daughter as the Jar Jar Binks of his trilogy. Also, he made Martin Sheen continue filming *Apocalypse Now* after Sheen had a heart attack and directed an episode of *SNL* when it was in one of its supposed "Saturday Night

Dead" periods. He directed Michael Jackson in the short film *Captain EO*, which also starred John Huston's daughter. I'm impressed that he cast Marlon Brando in *The Godfather* when it was thought that he was no longer worth the risk, then cast Brando as Kurtz when he definitely was not worth the risk. On the negative side, he didn't understand Brando's approach to the role, insisting that reading *Heart of Darkness* was somehow necessary to playing the character. I'm also not so sure that he has ever really been ahead of his time or particularly technologically inclined, though he did allow *The Godfather* to be made into a video game. The biggest strike against Coppola is that he has been highly regarded pretty much since he wrote the screenplay for *Patton* and is too comfortable with that to do anything that might lose him the respect of the film community. That wasn't always the case, especially during the *Apocalypse Now* era. But when he was confronted with the heart of Advancement in the form of Marlon Brando, he could not face the horror.

Peter Bogdanovich has his own take on Advanced glasses; I'm always impressed that he manages to wear the same frames in everything he appears in, from *Mr. Jealousy* to *The Sopranos*. He gets points for being Orson Welles's confidant, though I get the sense that he used the sentence "Yes, sir, Mister Welles" a lot. Like Coppola he has made a rock 'n' roll movie, the Tom Petty documentary *Runnin' Down a Dream* (extra points for using Petty's worst greatest hit as the title). The most Advanced part of that project is the running time: it's four hours, which seems like a pretty long time for a movie about a guy who has written pretty much the same (awesome) song for thirty years. Finally, I can't think of a better movie than *The Last Picture Show* or *Paper Moon*, but he never had the sustained period of excellence that is required of an Advanced Artist.

Robert Altman certainly met the sustained-excellence standard, but he never really changed during the course of his career. Of course, he made many different types of movies, but none of them would have been particularly surprising to his original fans.

All the way until his last movie, he made *Nashville*-style movies, with big casts all talking at once. There were some exceptions, most notably *Popeye*, which starred Robin Williams with Shelley Duvall as an uncanny Olive Oyl. *Popeye* was a musical with a cast of actors who were not singers, which is fairly Advanced. Harry Nilsson, a first-rate lunatic, wrote the music with the help of Van Dyke Parks, Brian Wilson's Bernie Taupin. It says a great deal about the movie that Vincent Canby didn't think too much of Williams's performance, but he was wild about the performance of Altman's grandson, who was a baby at the time of filming.

Martin Scorsese is another obvious candidate for Advancement who nevertheless doesn't quite make the cut. He began his career making gritty movies about New York but then went Hollywood. He directed the video for Michael Jackson's "Bad," did two rock-concert movies (*The Last Waltz* and *Shine a Light*), produced a documentary about George Harrison, and, best of all, made a Bob Dylan documentary. He's also done commercials for American Express (the Advanced love American Express commercials), which shows that he's not afraid of selling out, and he made *Kundun* and *The Last Temptation of Christ*, which shows he's at least interested in religion, both mystical and conventional. But ultimately his movies are just not adventurous or irritating enough to qualify for Advancement. He is a master, sure, but not Advanced.

Steven Spielberg may be too much of a master for his own good. In this way he is a lot like Eric Clapton, who supposedly never plays a bad note (which is why he is so boring). Spielberg almost always manages to be perfect, even when he is taking what should be huge risks. I'm pretty sure he could make a hard-core porn movie and it would bring out the little kid in all but the crustiest of critics. Spielberg's only hint of Advancement was *1941*, an "elephantine" period comedy according to *The New York Times* review. In that same article, the writer compared *1941* unfavorably to *It's a Mad, Mad, Mad, Mad World*, because both movies were "made by a director who has no special knack for being funny." However, though *1941* got the worst reviews of any movie of his before or since, it was still nominated for three Oscars. That is quite boring. It's a shame that the film brats couldn't have learned more from Stanley Kubrick, who managed to avoid being boring even while avoiding the bad note.

Stanley Kubrick: Taster's Choice

I don't have to convince anyone that Stanley Kubrick was a genius, so we can skip the tour through his achievements and move right into the last years of his life, when he secured his place as one of the few Fully Advanced directors.

In a documentary about Kubrick's life in pictures (*Stanley Kubrick: A Life in Pictures*), Sydney Pollack reveals that the man who brought us *Spartacus, Lolita,* and *A Clockwork Orange* was fascinated with a series of Nescafé commercials that appeared on British TV right around the time of his death. Overt directors of his era are reluctant to admit that they even watch TV, much less that they are inspired by commercials. The idea of Kubrick eagerly awaiting the appearance of a Nescafé ad is amusing and could be used to show that he had "lost it." But Pollack's point was that despite his stature as a Great Artist, Kubrick was still open-minded enough to see something meaningful in a coffee commercial. It may be that ability to see something that others can't that led him to work with Tom Cruise, the Nescafé of actors.

By the time Kubrick had announced his intention to begin filming *Eyes Wide Shut,* about ten years had passed since he had made his last movie, the widely acclaimed *Full Metal Jacket.* His reputation as an artist had grown despite (or because of) the layoff, as had his reputation as a perfectionist. Like self-indulgence, perfectionism is one of the common "weaknesses" of the Advanced. And Kubrick absolutely was a perfectionist, but with a difference: For others, the pursuit of perfection was just vanity. Kubrick, however, was capable of achieving perfection, and he knew it. That is why he demanded endless takes in pursuit of just the right performance and why he could be cruel to his actors to get the emotion he was looking for. You may not condone or, more probably, understand, his methods, but you can't argue with the results. Shelley Duvall seems to have been completely traumatized by her experience on the set of *The Shining*, but she has never been better (except maybe in *Popeye*).

So it was somewhat surprising that a perfectionist would cast Tom Cruise and Nicole Kidman as the lead actors in what would end up being his final film. It was surprising because, as noted earlier, Cruise had always been more of a "movie star" than an actor. And though critics had some respect for the "hardworking" Kidman, her previous collaborations with Cruise (*Far and Away* and *Days of Thunder*) were not classics, unless you use American Movie Classics' definition. It was surprising, too, for a supposed recluse to cast the most famous Hollywood couple, especially since there was endless speculation in the tabloids that their marriage was a sham. What isn't surprising is that not only did he coax out the best performances of Cruise's and Kidman's careers but the movie looks more and more brilliant with each passing year. One wonders how great the movie would have been had he made the movie with one of his original choices for the lead role: Woody Allen.

Woody Allen: Crimes and Misunderstandings

Woody Allen is the best American director and screenwriter of his generation.

It's likely that you were expecting a "but" after that sentence, such as "but he hasn't made a good film since *Deconstructing Harry*," "but he casts himself as the romantic interest for women much too young and pretty for him," "but he doesn't spend enough time on his movies," and so on. However (I had to avoid "but"), there is no qualification necessary. He is the best, and that's all there is to it. Whether he is Advanced, however, is another question and deserves some consideration.

One of Woody Allen's great artistic crimes is that he makes a movie basically every year. By working so quickly, he has opened himself up to a complaint that has been repeated basically every year since 1986: his movies don't go deep enough because he doesn't spend enough time writing the script, cajoling performances out of his actors, reshooting, and editing. We've been led to believe that an established artist must spend a certain amount of time on each movie. Presumably there is a perfect amount of time to work on a movie, but unfortunately the only people who know the amount only criticize movies rather than make them. Also, the requirement seems to apply only to Woody Allen. If a twenty-six-year-old Afghan woman had made *Sweet and Lowdown* on a small budget in less than a year, it would be seen as proof that the only reason Hollywood filmmakers like Steven Spielberg need huge budgets and years of developing a project is to satisfy their egos. But Allen was born in Brooklyn, so critics focus on the poorly developed character played by Uma Thurman.

The fact is, some artists work slow, some fast. Hank Williams believed if a song wasn't written in twenty minutes, it probably wasn't going to be any good. If Allen's time-based critics are right, if Hank Williams had spent enough time, "Your Cheatin' Heart" would have been ten times better if only he had spent an extra three hours working on it. It could be that had Williams spent a little longer on songs he abandoned, they would have turned out to be good or maybe some of his songs that were just okay could have been classics. But it's just as likely that if he had obsessed over every note, he would never have written a great song. He just wasn't wired that way, and neither is Woody Allen.

The reality is that critics always seem to want him to make a different movie from the one he's made. If it's a comedy, they want a drama. If it's a drama, they want a comedy. If he's in it, he shouldn't have been. If he's not, the actor in the main role is an inferior version of him. If the movie is breezy, it should be dark. If it's dark, it's pretentious. And if his next movie took five years to make, you could bet that there would be critics who would use it as the latest evidence that he has lost it. I say the latest evidence because people have been explaining why he's lost it since 1978's *Interiors*. For someone who makes movies so fast, his decline has been amazingly slow.

Just as interesting to me is why people seem so angry at a filmmaker who has made so many funny movies. When I first moved to New York, I saw *Manhattan Murder Mystery* on its opening day, and it was one of the most enjoyable moviegoing experiences I've ever had, likely because there are so many inside jokes that only New Yorkers get. After that I made sure to watch each new Woody Allen movie the day it came out, and each time it was a magical experience. I remember walking out of *Everyone Says I Love You* next to Penn Jillette (of Penn and Teller) and overhearing his comment: "What can you say? He's a genius." And I've never heard a bigger laugh than when Allen's character in *Deconstructing Harry* says that every hooker he commissions says that the job beats waitressing, adding, "That must be the worst fucking job in the world." However, after *Deconstructing Harry*, something changed. But it wasn't Woody Allen.

When I saw *The Curse of the Jade Scorpion*, there was just about the same amount of laughter coming from the audience as during the previous movies, but when it ended, the people around me angrily denounced what they had seen instead of talking about the best jokes, as I had come to expect. I'm not saying that *The Curse of the Jade Scorpion* was a particularly great movie, I just got the feeling that people had only been waiting for a sign of weakness so they could start hating him. It reminds me of a story my Aunt Peggy used to tell about an airplane that crashed shortly after liftoff. It crashed onto a highway, and before the rescue crew could make it to the scene, many of the passengers' wallets had been stolen. It was as if some people had been planning for that very moment, biding their time until a plane went down so they could put their wallet-snatching plan into action. Woody Allen's plane had barely hit the ground before his wallet was gone.

Allen's crimes outside his art probably contributed more to his perceived decline than his offenses on film. It makes sense that people are mad at him as a person because of the whole Soon-Yi situation and that it would make them predisposed to disliking his movies. Even though I've always tried not to let artists' personal lives affect my judgment of their work, I could see how someone would find Allen's behavior so detestable that they couldn't bear to watch his movies. But it seems to me that people weren't really *that* offended, at least not enough to stop buying tickets to see his movies, until he made a movie that most people—and, perhaps more important, most critics—didn't like. Maybe it took seeing Charles Winchester III in a Woody Allen movie instead of Hawkeye Pierce for there to be a universal sense of moral clarity.

It's also not too surprising that Allen's fans would eventually abandon him, because he has never openly courted them. The most famous example of his (supposed) ambivalence toward fans was his brutalization of film festivals, *Stardust Memories,* which has been misconstrued as an Advanced Irritant. The first time I saw that movie I didn't feel insulted at all, though I admit I was in Paris and had been drinking wine and cough syrup. It was only months after seeing the movie that I learned that it was not satirizing the film business, the egotism of the artist working within the film business, and fans' misplaced worship of artists with whom they have no actual connection. It was not a movie about an artist who reviles the business of movie making yet is complicit in its sins. It is not

about a selfish man who can't be faithful to anyone and roman-
ticizes his own self-destruction regardless of the people who are
dragged down with him. No, it was none of those things. It was
actually a monument to Woody Allen's contempt for his fans, especially the oily, funny ones. It never occurred to me that he wasn't
using Fellini-esque characters as homage to *8½*, he was actually
telling us that we, *his* fans, are ugly and borderline retarded. It's
striking to me that those who actually believe those things about
Stardust Memories don't allow for the possibility that Woody Allen
thinks his fans are retarded *because they are fans of his*. If there is one
thing about which Allen has been absolutely consistent, it has been
his contempt for his own art, except for whatever is his most recent
film, which, in true Advanced style, he always says is his best.

Even though *Stardust Memories* wasn't a true Advanced Irritant, he is certainly capable of irritating people. The best example
may be following *Annie Hall,* his most successful movie in terms of
reaching a wide audience, with the grim, Bergman-inspired *Interiors.* As far as Advanced Irritants go, this movie is in a league with
Bob Dylan's going electric at Newport, Lou Reed's *Metal Machine
Music,* and James Joyce's *Finnegans Wake.* As Vincent Canby wrote
in the original *New York Times* review, *Interiors* was not so much
Allen's first "serious drama" as his first movie that wasn't meant
to be funny as well—there was plenty of drama in *Annie Hall*—
but it was still a culture shock, and "not to be prepared for it is
to embark on a Miami Beach vacation having just taken a total
immersion course in seventeenth-century English literature." I
would say it's more like being plucked from your Miami Beach
vacation and landing in the middle of the biggest crisis yet faced
by the most depressing family in the history of film. But you get
the idea. This bit of "culture shock" created the first real rift in
the relationship between Woody Allen and his fans. It would be
repaired with *Manhattan*—which he tried to prevent from being
released because he was so unhappy with the final product—but

there was a rift nonetheless, one that would widen over the years the more he has grown as an artist.

As we have seen earlier, the only thing people hate more than their favorite artist growing is that artist staying the same. Weirdly, Allen is regularly accused of both crimes. When most people hear the phrase "Woody Allen movie," they think of a comedy (at times dark) starring Allen and a beautiful woman whose relationship will not work out in the end, plus some talk about death, morality, therapy, and perhaps the limits of the intellectual life. Reviewers enjoy comparing his most recent movies with past efforts (unfavorably, of course), implicitly suggesting that he just keeps making the same movie over and over. Of course, you could make a thousand movies about doomed yet funny relationships that wrestle with the great questions of our existence and there would still be room for thousands more. But unlike, say, the universally acclaimed Alfred Hitchcock, Allen doesn't just make one kind of movie. He has made farces (*Sleeper, Bananas*), straight dramas (*Another Woman, Husbands and Wives*), murder stories (*Shadows and Fog, Manhattan Murder Mystery*), period pieces (*Sweet and Lowdown, Radio Days, The Purple Rose of Cairo*), serious crime stories (*Match Point, Crimes and Misdemeanors*), ridiculous crime stories (*Take the Money and Run, Small Time Crooks*), a musical (*Everyone Says I Love You*), a fake documentary (*Zelig*), and on and on. So while he certainly has a unique and characteristic style, there is not another director who has such a diverse body of work.

What I admire most about Woody Allen is that he continues to reach out in new directions and discover new inspirations. Because he releases his movies each year, we see more of his process than that of other filmmakers, so occasionally he'll put out a subpar movie or two, but typically they are followed by something brilliant and completely different from what you had come to expect from him. *Match Point* is a great example of this. Kicked out of New York for budgetary reasons and forced into using Scarlett Johansson instead of Kate Winslet, who wanted to spend time with her family, he took his movie to London and got a great performance out of Johansson, winding up with another of his countless "returns to form."

There aren't many directors of Allen's age who can connect with young actors, yet he routinely finds new faces to populate his universe and finds a way to make them belong there. It's surprising he even knows these younger actors exist, much less invites them to be in his movies. This connection with younger actors shows that he is not out of touch. He certainly prefers certain elements of an earlier era (especially music), but not liking something new is completely different from not knowing it exists. It reminds me a bit of my grandfather, who lived in Aiken, South Carolina, and seemed completely shut off from my world. Yet he somehow knew everything that was going on with my boss at the time (Martha Stewart) and seemingly everything else going on in the world. But though he knew what was going on, he didn't really care about it as much as he did about the fish he'd caught earlier in the week or the pound cake he'd made that he bragged tasted just like Sara Lee. If you were ninety, it would be foolish to be any other way. So if Woody Allen chooses to have his twenty-something characters listen to Billie Holiday instead of Gwen Stefani, it's not necessarily because he hasn't heard of Stefani, it's just that he doesn't like her music and it would feel false to include her music in one of his movies. Besides, some young people actually have heard of music pre–Paul McCartney.

Woody Allen is not a perfect person, and he doesn't make perfect movies. But he has made more great films than anyone else in the last forty years. A true artist, he has traveled fearlessly in whatever direction seemed to him the most fertile, ignoring his fans and critics alike. As the world around him has changed, he has been able to discern what was valuable in each new era and fold it into his art without ever losing sight of who he is and what he wants to accomplish. He is so genuinely self-effacing that he cannot understand why people would care so passionately about his work. Yet at the same time he trusts his own vision completely, to the point where he will leave New York for London or Spain because he doesn't want to have to justify himself to a banker who fancies himself a moviemaker. He essentially invented a form of comedy that was borrowed by the Zucker brothers in movies like *Airplane,* and that still packs theaters today in works like *Scary Movie* (though, like a cassette copied too many times, it has lost its integrity with each iteration). He is responsible for more one-liners than anyone else since Mark Twain. He is the best director working today. He is the best screenwriter in the last fifty years. For any one of those three accomplishments he could qualify for Advancement. Since he has all three, he belongs in the upper echelon of Advanced Artists. Unfortunately, he would turn down the invitation to join the club, since it would have him as a member.

Chapter Twelve

Marlon Brando:
The Third Fat Man

From his introduction to the world in *A Streetcar Named Desire* to his mesmerizing and perplexing performance in *Apocalypse Now* to his final role in the *Godfather* video game, Marlon Brando was better—and weirder—than just about anyone else. And like most Advanced Artists, his weirdness often obscured his genius, especially for those who were born after he had achieved Plus-sized Advancement.

Like his weirdness, Brando's looks also obscured his greatness. When he was a young man, Brando was so incredible-looking that he didn't really need to be a great actor to be successful. If he had been merely a Tom Cruise or even a Tom Green, people still would have bought posters of him in *The Wild One* just because he looked so great. As long as he was beautiful, then, one could always say that he benefited as much from his appearance as from his acting skills. His solution was to release his inner fat man, knowing that if people were to see past his physical decline, he would have to act his fat ass off. I'm not saying that he got fat on purpose, but I am saying that he knew all the ramifications of his obesity, yet he kept eating ice cream.

What's My Line?

When preparing for his role as Kurtz in *Apocalypse Now*, Brando decided not to read *Heart of Darkness*. If a lesser actor were to make the decision not to prepare (at least in the traditional sense) for a role like that, it would be easy to dismiss it as laziness. But if Brando had been merely lazy, he would have read the book, shot his scenes, picked up the check, and gone back to Tetiaroa. Instead he waged war with Coppola and in the process found the essence of a character of numinous complexity. It may seem counterintuitive, but Brando's unfamiliarity with the Kurtz of the book allowed him to fully realize the Kurtz of the movie. After all, he was appearing in *Apocalypse Now*, not *Heart of Darkness* (there were hardly any helicopters or surfing in Conrad). Reading the book would have slanted his take on the character in the same way it would have had he watched another actor playing Kurtz in an earlier version of *Apocalypse Now*. He didn't want to play Conrad's version of the character; he wanted to invent, with his director, a completely new interpretation. It was a new horror he was after, and he found it.

Not memorizing his lines was nothing new for Brando. Since becoming powerful enough to get away with it, he had preferred reading off cue cards placed strategically around the set, on cameras and costars' clothes. Later he switched to a more technologically Advanced system: during filming he wore a tiny earphone that looked almost like a hearing aid, through which his assistant fed him his lines. (Orson Welles preferred a teleprompter.) On *Apocalypse Now*, he improvised and read poems by T. S. Eliot. It sounds ridiculous for an actor to use cue cards, but what is ridiculous for anyone else is actually quite logical for the Advanced. So it was for Brando.

The reason Brando didn't want to learn his lines was that he was committed to authenticity. From the beginning of his acting career, Brando strove for realism in his performances, so it bothered him that actors always say their lines as if they didn't have to think about what they were saying. A playwright reworks the lines of a play until they are exactly right, and Brando thought it was ridiculous for a character to be able to express those fully formed ideas without even an "uh" or "um." Early in his career, when he was still a stage actor, Brando toyed with different techniques to approximate reality, the most famous being mumbling, but never felt satisfied. It took a jump to the movies to provide him with the solution to his problem.

Let's discuss briefly the difference between acting in a play and appearing in a movie. For a major play, the actors rehearse together endlessly, the show is rewritten, the show tours around smaller cities, it is rewritten some more, and only then, after the actors fully understand their characters, the flaws in the staging are smoothed over, and the lines are exactly as they should be, is the play ready for Broadway. The play is performed for a different audience every night, and the actors are all in different moods every performance. In this environment, it is possible for an actor to approximate reality. When filming a movie, an actor rarely has rehearsal time with fellow actors, the only audience is the crew, and the filming is out of sequence.

Ironically, all the preparation required for putting on a play—the rehearsals especially—allows the actors to be more spontaneous. They read their lines as written, of course, but they develop a sense of space between the words, resulting in something much more organic. If you are completely in character, you can listen to the other characters and react in ways that are natural to your character. And since the same person might say the same thing differently in different situations ("these pretzels . . . are making me thirsty!"), actors can choose to say the lines the way they feel their characters would say them based on how they feel in the moment. It's not reality, but it's closer.

It might have been too close to reality for Brando, who left the stage because it was too much of a grind to appear in several shows a week, always as the same character. There was *some* laziness involved in his decision—he liked having to work only three months a year and for lots of money besides—but it was also a way for him to keep his sanity. His Stanley Kowalski was mesmerizing to audiences because he allowed himself to feel everything the character felt. Brando was basically a gentle and peaceful man, so one can only imagine how much it took out of him to play such a brute, even if he did play him with some sympathy. I certainly wouldn't want to do it, especially if I could make a lot more money and have nine months a year to live on my own island paradise.

The movie business, though, presented a different kind of challenge, which was as soul-sucking as raping Blanche DuBois six nights a week and twice on Saturday. How can you achieve authenticity when you barely know the people you're working with, your director may not know what he's doing, you're performing in front of the crew or curious onlookers, and you spend most of the day sitting in your trailer waiting to be called to the set? Different actors handle this differently. Val Kilmer and Daniel Day-Lewis won't let people call them by their real names on set, so they can stay in character all the time. Brando might have done this, but then he would have been in a similar situation as when he worked on Broadway, only instead of having to be someone else a few hours each day for several months, he would have had to be someone else twenty-four hours a day for three months. The solution was Advanced Genius: if you don't want to appear to know what you're going to say before you say it, don't.

You might be saying, "He's an actor, shouldn't he just act like he doesn't know what he's going to say?" There is some merit to that if you are some kind of Overt purist. In any kind of acting, the power of a performance depends on so much more than just an actor reading his lines effectively. Onstage, bad lighting, bad costumes, and bad audiences can all destroy a performance that would have been thought brilliant in different circumstances. The acting is the same, but it is diminished by other elements that have nothing to do with the actor. Movies are even less about the actor's performance. In addition to lighting and costumes, there are the editing, the score, the cinematography, and other mechanical aspects of the movie. Not only can a good performance seem bad, but a bad performance can seem good with the correct lighting and a good editor.

Brando certainly understood this, and, like any Advanced Genius, he took the limitations of his medium and turned them into advantages. For instance, he learned to befriend the lighting guy and the rest of the crew so that he would be shot under the most favorable circumstances. And if he felt a scene should be done one way and the director thought it should be done another way, he would do it the director's way poorly on purpose, several times if necessary, until the director relented and allowed him to shoot it his way. While these tactics may sound crass or petty, the purpose was to ensure that his performance was effective. The same goes with the cue cards. Instead of learning his lines, he learned the truth of his character, so he didn't have to fake spontaneity. What is the point in trying to *appear* spontaneous when you can actually *be* spontaneous?

Again, if a less talented actor tried to be like Brando, it wouldn't have worked because most actors need to know their character's lines to understand who that character is. Brando, though, came at characters as an improviser would, getting to know the character by his relationships and the circumstances of his life. The actual words he says are not as important as how he says them. Christopher Guest used this method in *Waiting for Guffman* and *Best in Show* to nearly universal praise, but because Brando performed in traditional scripted movies, people think he was just a big fat lazy actor who couldn't be bothered to learn his lines.

Brando did not go to much trouble to refute the perception that he was lazy or any of the other misconceptions people had about him, especially in the press. He felt that journalists had "written their articles [about him] in their heads" before they even met. So they would ask him questions about something off the wall like the sex life of fruit flies. In that situation, he could either answer the question seriously or refuse to answer. Either way he came off like an asshole. But if he played the role of "the eccentric Marlon Brando" and gave bizarre answers, then at least he kept his dignity. The problem was that people started to believe that he really was eccentric to the point of losing respect for him as an artist. The persona made it nearly impossible for him to be taken seriously in his work. He was up to that challenge, in my opinion, and even if you don't agree, he at least got the satisfaction of making an ass out of a reporter who likely wasn't fit to be shining Brando's shoes. Which, as we'll see later, he made himself.

Stupid Movies, Smart Moves

Brando was passionate about his art, but he was not above taking on "stupid movies" for the money. Even in the best of circumstances, he felt that an actor was basically a prostitute. He was accused of selling out for going to Hollywood, which he says was "in a way" true, but he knew what he was doing. In his mind, Hollywood stood for "avarice, phoniness, greed, crassness, and bad taste," but there was an advantage to working there: "You only have to work three months a year."

As I noted earlier, the Advanced can at times make bad art, but

it is usually for a good reason. Unlike Orson Welles, who took acting roles to fund his movies, Brando used his bad-movie money for
causes that actually affected people, such as the civil rights movement. As a believer in Advancement, I wouldn't think any less of
him if he did dumb movies to pay for the construction of a replica
of the New York City skyline on his island in Tahiti. But even if
you don't subscribe to the Theory, surely you can agree that working
a few weeks on a bad movie is a small price to pay for a cause as
unassailable as civil rights for all Americans.

Brando also fought for the rights of other actors, if somewhat
indirectly. In his early years, he refused to sign a long-term contract
with a studio, making him one of the first free agents in Hollywood. Enough actors followed his lead that the studio system fell
apart, leaving the actors in charge. In his Middle period (his self-
described "Fuck You Years") he used his hard-won freedom to set
his price for appearing in a movie: 11.3 percent of the gross. Don't
bother trying to figure out the significance of 11.3 percent; he just
pulled it out of a hat. Of course, that didn't stop him from insisting
on that amount and threatening to blow up the production in the
middle of filming if it was necessary to get his 11.3 percent. An
Overt person might have a problem with this behavior, but he was
fighting for artistic freedom for his fellow actors, which ultimately
results in better movies. Plus, you don't get to buy an island unless
you make sure you get paid.

Most of Marlon Brando's life from the time he bought that
island until his death was classically Advanced. He mixed in widely
accepted, traditionally good work with behavior that was seemingly
designed to destroy his career. For example, after having a forget-
table decade in the 1960s (at least in the commercial sense), he was
nominated for an Oscar for his performance in *The Godfather*. He
didn't believe in awards for acting (you would think that is an Overt
stance, but Brando said repeatedly that he just personally didn't like
awards and that people he respected enjoyed awards shows, which

was okay with him), but he also realized that if he were to win he could shine a spotlight on an issue that most people never wanted to acknowledge: the ongoing mistreatment of Native Americans by the U.S. government. So he compromised by sending an Apache named Sacheen Littlefeather to receive the award for him and read a speech he had prepared about this issue. He did win, of course, but she was not allowed to give the speech. So she spoke briefly and was whisked away.

Now, I have to admit that until I read Brando's autobiography, I thought that this was a classic Advanced Irritant move, with a bit of multiculturalism thrown in. But Brando had devoted a great deal of time and even risked his life for this cause (while helping to mediate a standoff between the National Guard and a group of Menominee Indians who had taken over an old Alexian Brothers novitiate), so sending Littlefeather to give a speech was not so much an indictment of award shows (his intention was to point out the damage the film industry had done to the image of Native Americans) as a heartfelt plea for America to finally make right what had been so wrong for so many years. Of course he knew that many people would ridicule him, just as they did for mumbling onstage, but his reputation was less important to him than advancing a cause, even if the cause was a lost one. Like Tolstoy's spreading his version of Christianity instead of writing another great novel, this is another example of Quixotic Advancement. Brando was like Tolstoy in another way: he reveled in inventing and repairing things that would make life better for the inhabitants of his island. He was like a mixture of Levin and Paul Gauguin, which is a pretty rare and amazing combination.

He was a strong believer in science, especially the potential for mapping the human genome. It is in this context that I would suggest to you that *The Island of Dr. Moreau* is not evidence of Brando's decline but an extension of his belief in the future of humanity. This was another cause he felt strongly enough about to lend his name to, regardless of the public's reaction. He was aware of the pitfalls of genetic tinkering, which is obvious if you watch the movie, but I think he also knew well that science fiction tends to inspire future scientists. The movie wasn't well received by critics, but Brando's target audience wasn't critics, who after all aren't going to contribute to the world in any meaningful way. He was after Sci Fi Channel addicts who are weird enough not only to like a movie as ludicrous as *The Island of Dr. Moreau* but also to aspire to realize its vision. Maybe it wasn't a great movie—I'm not convinced it's not because I love it—but considering the kinds of roles that men of Brando's age are normally offered, it was likely the only one that came across his desk that at least had the potential to change someone's world and, in turn, change the whole world.

One more item in the Tolstoy vein: according to Robert Lindsey, the coauthor of Brando's autobiography, meeting Brando for the first time was an interesting experience. They talked about a variety of things, including "physics, Shakespeare, philosophy, chess, religion, music, chemistry, genetics, scatology, and psychology." They also touched upon the topic nearest and dearest to Tolstoy's heart, shoe making.

Brando is the third of the Three Fat Men of Advancement, along with Elvis and Orson Welles. He is actually quite a bit like Welles in many respects: Both were brilliant artists from the beginning of their careers. Both supposedly peaked too young. Welles's first movie was supposed to be a faithful adaptation of *Heart of Darkness*. Brando was in *Apocalypse Now*, where he fought to make the movie more like the book, even though he hadn't read it. They both had very little regard for movies yet were very passionate about filmmaking. They both enjoyed making up stories about themselves when they were young. Brando's last role was in a video game version of *The Godfather*, and Welles hosted a TV special that featured Angie Dickinson, Burt Reynolds, and the Muppets. (Not exactly similar, I admit, but still awesome.) The only mention of Brando by Welles that I've found is his comment that Brando was truly ashamed to be an actor. They didn't work together, which is too bad, because they might have made something that we all could have been ashamed of.

Chapter Thirteen

Steve Martin: Advancement Is Not Pretty

Steve Martin's story is an old story, a story you've probably heard before. It was never easy for him: he was born a middle-class white child . . .

When Steve Martin was five years old, his father moved the family to California because he dreamed of a career in show business. His dream didn't work out, so he ended up in the real estate business to provide for his family. Martin writes in his memoir, *Born Standing Up* (an essential for students of Advancement and the source of much of the information in this chapter), of the impossibility of getting his father's approval and his solution to that problem: he stopped talking to him. But he also escaped to Disneyland, which was new at the time, where he sold guidebooks. His father's aloofness and the Disneyland experience combined to lay the foundation for what he would become. The former because Overtness is often a tactic used by young people to get back at their parents in a backward way of seeking if not love then attention. The latter because he learned that Disneyland was not some bourgeois salute to animated commercialism manufactured by an anti-Semite. For Steve Martin, there was actual magic in the Magic Kingdom.

No, really. He worked at a magic shop when he outgrew the brochure business.

Another important lesson he learned early in life was that magic was hard work. At first he tirelessly practiced magic tricks, then juggling, banjo, and later his comedy act. The Advanced are not only the most gifted artists, they are also often the hardest workers, and Steve Martin understood that. As he went from performing in melodramas at Knott's Berry Farm (a roadside attraction with a theater) to doing five minutes at coffeehouses in San Francisco all the way up to when he was touring the country playing for thousands of fans who knew his act as well as he did, he was constantly refining his act.

That act, at first, was a study in Overtness. For example, as he became less interested in sawing a lady in half and more intrigued by philosophy, he added a closing bit to his act: "I'm not going home tonight; I'm going to Bananaland, a place where only two things are true, only two things: One, all chairs are green; and two, no chairs are green." As he puts it, he "loved implying that the one thing I believed in was a contradiction" (page 75). That is a perfect description of the Overt mission, and it also shows you that at its core, that mission is both defined by its relationship to something else, and fruitless besides. His time at Knott's Berry Farm would ultimately prove much more fruitful.

When the hippie era began, he kept his square haircut until he found out there were more girls for guys with long hair and beards. A surprising number of people, even the Advanced, turn their backs on their true selves to meet girls. (Or maybe it's not so surprising.) Martin finally caved, grew out his not-yet-gray hair, and bought a bunch of turquoise jewelry. His comedy act was getting more absurdist all the time, but since he also looked absurd, the act didn't have the kind of power it would during his white-suit days. There's nothing surprising about an Overt comedian being Overt, and if you're going to do unsurprising comedy, you might as well be doing "take my wife . . . please" jokes in the Catskills. But a guy in a suit doing absurdist comedy was something new altogether. Martin puts it best: "Instead of looking like another freak with a crazy act, I now looked like a visitor from the straight world who had gone seriously awry" (page 144).

As a novice entertainer, Martin felt fine about using other people's material as long as it got laughs. Even the line that may have saved him from getting fired from *The Smothers Brothers Comedy Hour* was made up by his roommate. But eventually he made the decision that he would have to do original material at all costs. It wasn't enough for him to do original material in a style that existed, he wanted to invent a completely new form of comedy, one without jokes. He was still Overt and dealing in opposites (traditional comedy has jokes, so new comedy should not have jokes), but he was moving toward Advancement. In fact, his onstage persona actually was Advanced. His attitude was that he didn't care if he was bombing or didn't even allow for the possibility that he *could* bomb. His credo was "This is funny, you just haven't gotten it yet" (page 112). Reviews of this new comedy-free comedy act were unsurprisingly chilly, but looking back, it was funny and they just didn't get it.

His act truly came together when he started to wear a suit, which, like everything else he had done, was chosen carefully. When Martin decided that it was time to lose the hippie look, he remembered the advice he had received earlier in his career, which had been percolating underneath his consciousness. The advice, given to him by a veteran performer, was that the guy onstage should look better than the audience. To Martin, this meant that he needed to wear a suit, but what kind? He wanted to wear a white suit for visibility's sake, but he was concerned that John Lennon already owned the white suit. Nevertheless, he went with it, which was a pretty good idea.

Another important step in his development was his avoidance of political humor. There's nothing wrong with that type of humor, of course, but it's not too hard to get people to laugh at politicians, especially if you are reinforcing the audience's opinions. Steve Martin decided he didn't need Richard Nixon to kick around precisely because he was such an easy target. In those days, though, a comedian who didn't talk about politics, especially one who had been a hippie, was superficial, old-fashioned, or even complicit in the sins of the U.S. government. If you look back at the comedians of that era, however, you'll see that it was typically the ones talking about politics who seem old-fashioned, while Steve Martin's comedy still seems fresh. Like so many of the Advanced, his art was both ahead of its time and timeless.

After years of honing his act, Steve Martin became the biggest star in the history of stand-up comedy, playing to huge audiences who were so enthusiastic that he no longer had to work to make them laugh. He then made *The Jerk*, which was wildly successful (it was also the first R-rated movie I ever saw, one of my fondest memories of childhood). It was time, in other words, to walk away from stand-up forever and make a brutal Depression-era musical featuring the tap-dancing Christopher Walken. *Pennies from Heaven* is a classic Advanced Irritant project. It's one thing for a comedian to do a drama (the opposite of a comedy), but this movie was nearly unclassifiable. There was absolutely no chance that people were going to like it, and one wonders what chain of events allowed it to be made. Which is not to say that it is bad, but it was such obvious career suicide, it's surprising that there were so many people willing to assist him. I guess that's Hollywood.

The strange thing is, Steve Martin *likes* Hollywood. Even as his act became a parody of comedy, he still respected the art form, which is something the Overt often miss. He worked very hard to learn the rules of performing before he even considered breaking them, and that was why he was more than just another freak with a crazy act, even before he put on the suit. In a way, he broke the letter of the law but not the spirit. He loved show business, and comedy specifically, so much that the best way he could honor it was to blow it up. As original as he was, though, he was part of an unbroken line of comedians from Bob Hope to Lenny Bruce to George Carlin to himself, and since his retirement every comedian has been influenced by his comedy, even if he doesn't know it.

Speaking of comedians not knowing how much they owe the performers who came before them, I was working at *Best Week Ever* when Martin hosted *SNL*. While there were some good skits and bad ones, there was one particularly unfunny scene where he played an old wannabe surfer; the premise was that he really wanted to hang out with a group of cool young surfers. The surfers had funny names, which he kept rattling off in the hope that the repetition of the absurd names would build comedic momentum, but it never really got funny. The following Monday the guys around the office at *Best Week Ever* were talking about how embarrassing that skit had been and how Martin should just go away. As you know, he did plenty of groaners in the hallowed early days of *SNL* too, so really nothing had changed. But since he is old, a bad sketch means that Steve Martin has forgotten how to be funny. And of course that's a load of bullshit.

The even bigger load is that he just phones in performances in mediocre family comedies to fund his art collection. As I wrote in the introduction, this idea takes it for granted that it's easy to make a movie that appeals to millions of people. It's my belief that he relishes the challenge of making family comedies that are actually funny. Plus, he understands that he can't be a wild and crazy guy anymore because he isn't wild and crazy anymore and faking it wouldn't work. For example, the reason his surfer sketch didn't work is that it was a lot like the comedy he used to do, and he had already perfected the art of silly names (paging Dr. Hfuhruhurr).

There is something more than just the challenge of making funny family movies that keeps him in the *Cheaper by the Dozen* business: he likes reaching a wide audience. This may seem to be antithetical to Advancement, but the greatest artists of all time are not considered as such because only a few people like them. The true greats are the ones who reach a mass audience even though they are totally unique and even weird. Steve Martin became the comedy Elvis by making jokes about Socrates while playing a banjo and wearing bunny ears. Then he turned his back on that and somehow became everyone's favorite dad. It's tempting to say that he is drawn to family comedies because he'd like to make up for the fact that he didn't have children and had a troubled relationship with his own father. But since I don't know him, I can't say that for sure. Even if it were true, it wouldn't make him any less Advanced.

That brings us to the end of our time with Steve Martin. If there's one thing I'd like for you to take away from all this, it is that whatever else you want to say about him, you can't say that he doesn't know exactly what he is doing. Since the time he was a teenager, he has made careful decisions about where he wanted to take his genius: magic, banjo, comedy, acting, writing. He has spent a life collecting but was never reluctant to throw out what wasn't worth carrying. Considering he has been one of the most successful entertainers in the last thirty years with only a few flops sprinkled in, you have to conclude that he pretty much always makes the right decision. And if any of you is offended by anything you've read here, well, excuse me.

Chapter Fourteen

Fine Artists, but Are They Advanced?

Unlike Steve Martin's, my knowledge of painting is limited to one survey class in college, taught by a professor with hairy arms and an eye for lady undergrads. That and my time working for the Greek and Roman and finance departments at the Metropolitan Museum of Art are the extent of my qualifications for judging painters and other fine artists. So I'll stick to just a few that I feel strongly about, knowing well that there will be somebody who knows more than I do who can demolish everything I write. Since we're talking about art, though, there is someone else who knows even more than *that* guy and can demolish everything he wrote. I have an added advantage because the latter was my girlfriend in tenth grade. So on that sturdy foundation, I begin.

Modern art is not necessarily more Overt than other periods, but it does seem that way. Michelangelo may have been completely Overt, though I doubt it, given the religious nature of his greatest works. But I understand he was quite an irritant to the pope, so who knows? Leonardo da Vinci seems Advanced, what with inventing helicopters and painting half-smiling socialites as Andy Warhol would do much later, but he could have been an Overt Renaissance Man for all we know, and the truly Advanced from that era have disappeared because the Advanced Genius Theory wasn't around to rescue them from critical disapproval. Rembrandt Harmenszoon van Rijn (not that other Rembrandt), I'm guessing, was sort of on a par with Paul Newman: always good, always appreciated. He had some financial problems, though, because salad dressing hadn't yet taken off in Leiden. Raphael (going by your first name alone is a form of Advancement; see Prince Rogers Nelson) died too young to make an Advanced name for himself, at least more Advanced than the one he already had.

Jumping ahead a few hundred years, Vincent van Gogh also died too young and was about as Overt as you can get. His art, though, may have been Advanced, since not many people cared too much about it while he was living. Georges Seurat helped move painting forward, but I might be partial to him because *Ferris Bueller's Day Off* (and the Smiths) meant so much to me when I discovered him. Paul Gauguin strikes me as a good candidate for Advancement in the late nineteenth, early twentieth centuries. Not only was he a true original whom few understood, he was also a first-class jerk. But his embrace of internationalism smacks of the Overts' idealizing of other cultures, different from the Advanced love of island nations, plus he drank too much. Perhaps had the syphilis not gotten to him, he would have kicked the booze, made nice with the authorities, and painted propaganda posters for the East India Trading Company. Oh, the scourge of sexually transmitted diseases!

As we get firmly into the twentieth century, the picture gets clearer. Dada is Overt. The surrealists are totally Overt, especially Salvador Dalí. (The only difference between Dalí and the Overt is that he was Overt.) Piet Mondrian was interesting but Overt, Marcel Duchamp was Advanced. Edvard Munch was Overt, but whoever owns the licensing rights to his work is clearly Advanced. Pablo Picasso probably deserves more than a couple of sentences, but it almost goes without saying that he was Advanced. Of course he was incredibly influential and consistently ahead of his time, but it took me a trip to Wikipedia to learn that his last works were dismissed by an art world gone crazy for abstract expressionism. Once people realized that abstract expressionism was just a bunch of paint slung around on a canvas by drunk guys who couldn't be trusted alone with a woman, they realized that Picasso had anticipated neoexpressionism. Another temporary victim of the paint slingers was Andy Warhol. He will get much more than a few sentences because he is integral to Advancement, and not only because he discovered the Velvet Underground.

Andy Warhol: Canned Advancement

In the beginning of PBS's *American Experience* documentary about Warhol, there is an interview with him in which he is asked whether his Brillo box sculptures were original, to which he replies, "No." The follow-up question is whether, if indeed the art wasn't original, the sculptures were just a joke on the public. Warhol says no to that as well, remarking that they were easy to make and gave him something to do. The exchange is revealing for what it doesn't reveal: If they weren't original, why are we talking about them? If he was joking, what was the joke? If they were so easy to make, why didn't someone else do them first? And finally, if he wanted to do something that was easy, why did he give up his life as one of the most successful and sought after commercial artists in New York? You can watch the interview over and over trying to find some satisfactory answer to these questions, but Warhol never gives you a clue as to what he's really feeling, or so it seems. We know that the Advanced enjoy lying to clueless interviewers, but Warhol was up to something even better: he is being so honest that you *think* he's lying.

Andy Warhol was a combination of Picasso, Elvis, Brando, Liberace, James Joyce, Ed Sullivan, Thomas Wolfe, Sam Phillips, and Sam Walton. He changed the way the world looked at art and the way artists looked at the world. He turned mass-produced goods into art and art into mass-produced goods. He discovered the Velvet Underground. He was gay, religious, ruthless, sensitive, a pure artist, and a pure businessman, and, according to David Hickey, changed supermarkets forever. He was a poor boy from Pittsburgh who made the big time through old-fashioned hard work. He wore black leather, sunglasses, and a silver wig that was short on the sides and long in the back. When you put it all together, he was the most Advanced Artist (Fine Arts Division) of the twentieth century.

A Genuine Appreciation of Little Things

"Genuine" is not the word typically associated with Andy Warhol, but as you learn about him and hear people who knew him talk about his work, you realize that he was just that, genuine. Some admirers of Warhol like to say that Warhol's background—the sickly son of immigrants living in an Eastern European enclave in Pittsburgh—made his rise to the top of the art world "unlikely." Apparently they're under the impression that most great artists were scions of rich families from Westchester. But their unfamiliarity with the American Dream aside, it was that background that laid the foundation for everything that was Advanced about Warhol.

As a child he contracted a serious illness that kept him out of school, leaving him bedridden with little more to do than stare at the ordinary objects around him. This helped develop his ability to concentrate on an object and see in it something profound that one might miss otherwise. As George Plimpton remarks in the documentary, staring at common objects brings out something uncommon about them. I'm sure that you can see how this relates to his Campbell's soup can series, but it also relates to how an Advanced person sees the world. To achieve the Advanced state of mind, it is sometimes necessary to immerse oneself in work that is not immediately gratifying and requires multiple listens or viewings, depending on the art. This state of mind also allows you to see beauty or meaning in things that others don't see.

What is important and Advanced of him was that he really did feel a reverence for things like Campbell's soup cans, even more than Kubrick and his Nescafé commercials. Wealthy or even middle-class kids can put an ironic distance between themselves and canned food, but Warhol's parents came from a country where food was not something you took for granted, so a can of soup was genuinely beautiful. Warhol's soup cans resonate so deeply with everyone, from art critics to those who have never set foot in a museum, because the work was absolutely sincere. This doesn't stop some from reading a wink into the work (if there was a wink, it was a wink about the winkers), but for most, Warhol is like an emotional ventriloquist, able to transfer into your heart the appreciation he felt for Campbell's soup.

His upbringing was not just about temporal things; as a child, he went to Mass several times a week with his family, and the church was decorated with richly colored images of saints aligned in a gridlike pattern. This grid, which he stared at for several hours a week, is strikingly similar to the way he would display his celebrity portraits. Remember that he continued to go to church with his mother every Sunday for many years, so Warhol chose not to take the Overt route of mockery or the base profanation of religious imagery of an artist like Robert Mapplethorpe. Instead he took what was beautiful and powerful about the Catholic Church and used it to add something of the divine to his portraits, though the subjects were in most cases far from sainthood. The Overt have their *Piss Christ*, but the Advanced have the Christ within Liza Minnelli and Elizabeth Taylor.

Just Another Winning Loser

Once Warhol moved from Pittsburgh to New York in 1960, he achieved success relatively quickly as a commercial artist, which ironically made it difficult for him to find a place in the "real" art world. He couldn't convince galleries to show his work, partly because he was judged to be too figural (abstract was the only way to be). The art-buying public apparently agreed, as he couldn't sell a painting in his first show. He had such trouble finding galleries for his work that he had to rely on less traditional spaces in which to display his paintings, such as the ice-cream parlor/restaurant Serendipity. Had he been a failure in the commercial sphere, he might have been taken more seriously early on, but artists are supposed to be starving, not filling up on ice cream (except for Marlon Brando).

One of the interesting stories from the PBS documentary is about Warhol's early fascination with Truman Capote, whom he came to idolize. Warhol basically stalked him for a time, and predictably Capote dismissed him as a loser. That's one of the reasons I think Capote was not Advanced, though, in fairness to him, it's difficult to get too excited about a stalker's potential as an artist. However, Warhol himself was open to whoever happened to come by the Factory and was even able to make stars out of some of them, despite their having zero talent. When you compare Capote's lack of recognition of greatness staring him in the face (or rifling through his garbage) to Warhol's ability to transform the dregs of the New York underground into celebrities, you can understand the Advanced world's negative judgment of Truman Capote.

Nearly everyone agreed with Capote's judgment that Warhol was a loser or a creep. His early Pop Art works were not well received, and some weren't received at all. Even the soup can exhibition got little notice in the art world, though he did get some recognition by some in the mainstream press who found the soup cans intriguing in a "look at *this* weirdo" kind of way. (If the cans were happening today, the articles would appear in the "Life" section of *USA Today*.) This early failure, so typical of the Advanced, would shape what Warhol would become for the rest of his career. Because it caused him not to change who he was—which is how lesser artists react to adversity—but to be even truer to his own vision.

This reaction to criticism is also typical of the Advanced, who are blessed with supreme self-confidence, though they are sometimes cursed with a compulsion to seek out ways to make life more difficult for themselves. For instance, Warhol wanted to be seen as a beautiful person, yet he wore rumpled clothes and terrible wigs on purpose, even before he was famous. While this may have been merely a self-destructive impulse, it seems more likely that he was just dabbling with being an Advanced Irritant. There are countless examples of his Irritant behavior: when asked to paint something for the New York World's Fair, he produced a series of mug shots. When the work was rejected, he suggested a painting of Robert Moses instead. Finally he decided to paint over the mug shots with silver paint, and that was the final product

Another way he irritated people was by saying that he wasn't original and had no ideas of his own. For an artist to say this is really unthinkable, and for one as talented as Andy Warhol to make this claim is truly maddening. I think this is one case where he embraced an opposite, because the quickest way to be original in a world full of people claiming to be original is to call yourself a copycat. Still, this is not exactly the path of least resistance for someone who wants to succeed in his chosen field. And he made no secret of the fact that he wanted to succeed, both artistically *and* financially.

Warhol's naked ambition is seen as fundamental to his decline as an artist, as if most artists paint for the love of it and give their paintings away for free. It's true that he turned himself into a sort of industry, but he did it creatively and successfully. So it's hard to see why he should be criticized for it. One of his grave sins was putting just as much energy and thought into making money as into his art. He even said that "good business is the best art." Surely, like James Brown, his modest upbringing had something to do with his nearly obsessive need to make money, but I suspect that after seeing up close the art world where he was arbitrarily hated and then just as arbitrarily worshiped, he saw that the world of business at the very least rewarded hard work, and no one worked harder than Warhol. In fact, while he was surrounded by people "expanding their minds" by using drugs, he took diet pills to lengthen his workday.

The reason Warhol was surrounded by the mind expanders is that he liked to mingle with the Overt. This is not unusual for the Advanced, though I've never been able to figure out why, unless it is because there are just so few Advanced people and no one likes to be lonely. (I have thought at times that the Advanced embrace some form of God because they are looking for a peer.) Whatever the reason, Warhol's Factory was a sort of Promised Land for dime-store weirdos, and he welcomed them all without question, like some kind of silver-wigged Statue of Liberty. His open-door policy left him vulnerable to attack, most notably in the form of an assassination attempt by a man-hating playwright who confused his willingness to tolerate her with a desire to produce her work. But it left him vulnerable to criticism as well, because if you let losers hang around with you, people will blame you when they inevitably fall, especially if you are a winner. For example, Warhol was often compared with Dracula, sucking the blood of innocents. But to that I would say that at least victims of vampires are immortal.

Take the case of Edie Sedgwick, whom he is accused of treating terribly, using her to further his career, and then throwing her out when he was done with her. But who benefited more from that relationship, the unknown, untalented socialite or the greatest artist of the second half of the twentieth century? The fact is that she was going to fall with or without Andy Warhol, but with him her descent had witnesses. He may have been an enabler, but to say that he was to blame for her fate would be like blaming the cliff instead of the lemmings.

Sedgwick became famous because of her appearance in Warhol's movies, which he had taken up because he supposedly had given up painting. I think this was an overly simplistic (and Overt) explanation on his part. It seems to me that the truth is that, like Elvis and John Lennon, he turned to films out of love and a need for a challenge. His movies, such as *Sleep,* were living soup cans, a close examination of moments that go by without notice. You may think that anyone could film someone sleeping, but if you've ever watched a movie by someone with no talent, you know that he would somehow ruin it. Warhol understood that though a sleeping person is physically still, that person's mind is active. It's a still life, but the fruit is in a blender.

Another great "still life" is *Empire,* a roughly eight-hour static shot of the Empire State Building. On its face, this idea is ridiculous. Who wants to look at a building for eight hours? But there's not much difference between *Empire* and Claude Monet's Rouen Cathedral series. As interesting as *Sleep* and *Empire* were, they are merely examples of an Advanced Artist failing in another medium. The reason he made movies where "nothing happened" was that he wasn't able to make movies with traditional narratives. When his films became more conventional or at least featured actors speaking, he worked as Chuck Berry does with his pickup bands, giving his subjects just enough to go on so they could improvise. Though this technique did produce a number of magical moments, Warhol used it as a crutch because he had so little talent (unlike Brando, who used improvisation because he had so much). He made the most of his limited ability, but that is not Advancement.

What is Advanced was the period after Warhol had recovered from the assassination attempt. Gone were the leeches, replaced by whatever the opposite of leeches are (I just know they wear suits and have college degrees). This, too, opened him up to criticism from those who thought he had become too business-oriented. Here again is a perfect illustration of why the Advanced just have to do whatever is in their best interests. If you are as successful as Andy Warhol was, people are going to do all they can to tear you down. If you run an open studio where the freaks run wild, you are a vampire sucking the life out of helpless victims. If you close yourself off, you've gone corporate and are no longer an artist. Somehow the Advanced tune all this out and continue on a path of their choosing. For Warhol this meant painting pictures of socialites, running a magazine, and appearing on his own show on MTV, *Andy Warhol's Fifteen Minutes,* which was one of the last gifts he left before his tragic death.

His death was tragic, not only because it came as the result of a careless mistake following a routine operation but because he would have enjoyed what the world has become since then. With Photoshop, Pro Tools, After Effects, and other software, it has never been easier to create art. And sites like YouTube make it even easier to share that art with the world. I'm not the first to say it, but everyone really can be famous these days, even if it's just for filming your son after a dentist appointment. I can't help but wonder, though, if the world that he helped to shape makes it less likely for another Warhol to emerge. Does a kid today ever take the time to study something like soup cans when he can watch a mash-up of the Snuggies commercial and the trailer for *The Name of the Rose* instead? I think probably not, but Warhol wouldn't have been too worried about it. He did, after all, leave much of his estate to the "advancement of the visual arts," so he would have embraced the new technology regardless of the changes it might bring.

Andy Warhol's body rests at St. John the Baptist Byzantine Catholic Cemetery outside his hometown of Pittsburgh. Advanced to the last, he was buried in a silver wig and sunglasses.

Chapter Fifteen

Writers

Judging writers is hard for me because I've read very little fiction that has been written in the last fifty years. This is completely Overt of me, of course, but every time I try to read something by someone still living, I can't shake the feeling that there's a Balzac novel I should be tackling instead. So I've been reluctant to apply the Theory to authors, which isn't to say that there aren't Advanced writers; it's just that due to my narrow focus on the classics, the writers I know most about weren't living in the Modern Advanced era and are therefore hard to categorize. For instance, Flann O'Brien was a great writer, but a drunk who didn't believe in himself enough to be Advanced. But is embracing a cliché actually a sign of Irish Writer Advancement? Thomas Wolfe had the Advanced temperament, but was he or his editor, Maxwell Perkins, the Advanced one? And what of John Kennedy Toole? He couldn't find a publisher for *A Confederacy of Dunces* during his lifetime but thanks to his mom and Walker Percy, it turned out to be one of the most celebrated books of all time. Would he have Advanced if he had lived long enough? I just can't say. The only thing I'm certain of is that Allen Ginsberg was Overt.

J. D. Salinger

You can't get much more Overt than J. D. Salinger, either, but he would definitely qualify for Advancement if he were to choose to accept the challenge. He achieved enough as an artist, he has irritated plenty of people, and there was a great deal of Eastern philosophy in his books. I don't think being a recluse necessarily qualifies you for Advancement, though many Advanced Geniuses do go through periods where they seem to disappear. But usually the Advanced recluse is really just not willing to talk to journalists and the other things that one does for publicity. They still have friends and go on vacation to the south of France, they just make sure they keep their bikini tops on so photographers won't take pictures of them for *Us* magazine. Salinger, though, appears to have really checked out, other than the occasional lurid affair and trip to the grocery store. So what would it look like if Salinger were to Advance? Given the nature of his work and the life he has led since he stopped working, you might think it would be Advanced if he were to write a sequel to *The Catcher in the Rye* or make it into a movie starring Hayden Christensen. Or he might be better served by writing a science fiction novel, setting up a Facebook profile, or maybe creating a *Catcher in the Rye*–themed online poker game called "Texas Holden." But if you and I can imagine it, it's probably not Advanced.

Truman Capote

As you know, Truman Capote is Overt, even though he apparently threw a great party and Andy Warhol worshiped him. It strikes me as rather dramatic of him not to have finished another book after *In Cold Blood,* but not in a good way. Apparently he toured with the Rolling Stones to write an article about them, which gives him rock-'n'-roll points, and he certainly had plenty of Advanced friends. Ultimately, though, he was a less talented, more drunk Marcel Proust, whom he sought to emulate with a tell-all book that ended up being more Kitty Kelley than *In Search of Lost Time.* (The latter, by the way, can be summarized thus: Marcel embraces Advancement.) Sadly, the real Marcel didn't live long enough to enjoy the fruits of his Advanced breakthrough. He probably would have enjoyed Kitty Kelley very much.

Hunter S. Thompson

I didn't think much of Thompson, so I never developed an opinion about his Advancement. I knew that a lot of smart people liked him, and he invented a style of journalism with an Overt name, "gonzo." (Words with a *z* in them are almost always Overt: see Thomas Pynchon.) I knew he was an incredible irritant to just about everyone, though people liked that about him, so I'm not sure if that really qualifies as being an irritant. He did drugs and drank, but I don't think he ever renounced that practice as an Advanced Genius would. He always wore sunglasses. I liked the Bill Murray version of him, but that was just a movie and probably had as much to do with liking Murray as it did with the actual Thompson. Still, the real Thompson did write a lot about sports, which is obviously in his favor, but his writing style was always Overt. Overall he lived what I would say was a Refined Overt life. It was his death or, more accurately, his funeral that made me change my mind about his Advancement.

Having a weird funeral ceremony is not impressive on its own. According to AARP, there is even a unique-funeral industry. But

Thompson's manner of being laid to rest was so ridiculous, that it launched him into Advancement. Literally. The sound track was "Spirit in the Sky," a rock song about Jesus by a guy with a Jewish name (Norman Greenbaum). Thompson had commissioned a monument to himself, a large statue of a fist, which was his trademark. Spotlights lit up the monument and the surrounding clouds. There were fireworks and an eleven-piece Japanese band of drummers dressed in kimonos. Then his ashes were shot out of a cannon while the mourners drank champagne and sang along with Lou Reed's "Walk on the Wild Side." However he may have fallen short of Advancement while he was still alive, surely he made up for it with the most Advanced funeral in history.

William Faulkner

I count Faulkner among the Advanced for many reasons, but mainly because I don't like his books until I'm finished with them. I find myself missing being in his world, no matter how unpleasant my time in it was, a lot like how New Yorkers miss street noise when they're in the country. Honestly, I used to think that it was possible I liked him because someone who has an English degree and is a southerner besides is pretty much required to. Now that I'm older, though, I see that as bewildered as I was when reading him seriously the first time (by serious I mean having to write a paper about it afterward, requiring me to remember the characters' names), I was "getting it." Not all of it, of course, but part of his genius was that his writing is so confident that you end up taking his side. He's like the Bill Brasky of literature: part real, part myth, and if he made love to your wife in front of you, you'd probably weep at the beauty of the spectacle.

I'd like to believe that I've caught up with him somewhat, with the help of the Snopes trilogy, which was recommended to me by some kind Amazon user who described it as a good place to start out if you want to understand Faulkner. I think this is true because, like Lou Reed rerecording VU-era tunes, much of it was written later in his career and dealt with characters and events from other novels that were more Overt. Of course, he changes those characters and events to fit in with his new story, but even those fictionalized versions of stories that were fiction in the first place help you grasp what he was trying to achieve. I say "help you" because most of us never really grasp Faulkner, any more than you could reassemble the actual faces of the models who posed for *Les Demoiselles d'Avignon*. This is so because he is dealing with myths, which collapse when approached with flat-footed literalism.

I'll step away now from literary criticism and focus on Faulkner's Advancement, more familiar ground for me. He sold out to magazines, went to Hollywood to write screenplays based on Ernest Hemingway and Raymond Chandler books, and abused alcohol. His books were not widely accepted in America, even after he was given the Nobel Prize. He was ahead of his time in the South, counseling reform in race relations, which caused him to be vilified. Late in life, he felt that his best work was behind him and he became more of a public figure than a writer, much as Einstein became a voice for humanity rather than physics. This is one area where I feel that he wasn't Advanced (assuming he was telling the truth); most Advanced Artists do not see the decline in their creative powers because there is none, though I believe that had he gone sober and practiced kung fu, he would have died in the middle of his greatest novel yet.

Thomas Pynchon

He seems incredibly Overt to me, but that's probably because the book of his I'm most familiar with is *Vineland*. I understand that it was a critical disappointment, so perhaps I discovered him after he had already Advanced, which made me think that he just stank. To be honest, I probably could have loved the book if it hadn't featured a character named Zoyd. You just can't get any more Overt than a name starting with Z. It's sort of like how any movie set on another planet makes a point of showing a sunset with multiple moons or suns. We get it, we're in a weird place. And so it is with Z names, and that does include all forms of Zooey. He wrote the liner notes to a Spike Jones album, which could be deemed Overt because Jones is so wacky, but he also wrote the liner notes for Lotion's second album, 1996's *Nobody's Cool*, stating, "rock and roll remains one of the last honorable callings, and a working band is a miracle of everyday life." This attitude certainly merits further investigation into Pynchon, but I've got *A Harlot High and Low* staring at me from my bookshelf, so it will have to wait.

James Joyce

As I've written, Advancement is a personal thing, having as much to do with you as it does with the genius being considered. The Grateful Dead means absolutely nothing to me, so I would never say it could be Advanced, although the Dead made zillions of dollars off hippies who thought they were a part of some kind of traveling commune. And then there was the merchandise (skis, ties, and so on) and sponsoring an Olympic basketball team, complete with tie-dyed uniforms. None of that matters because its music is so bland to me. But if you are one of those hippies who bought Mickey Hart his mansion, the Dead could be Advanced because you think its art qualifies.

Advancement can also be personal in another way, as illustrated by my relationship with James Joyce. First things first: he's my favorite writer. I think "The Dead" is the best thing ever written, especially the last few sentences, which make me cry nearly every time I read them. What is amazing about him is that, much like Faulkner, Joyce moves me even when I don't understand fully what he's talking about. Even better, he has helped me understand things that I wouldn't have been capable of understanding without having read him. When I read *Dubliners* the first time, I knew I liked it but I wasn't really getting it. A few years later, I finally caught up with him and was knocked out by just about every word. The same thing happened when I read *A Portrait of the Artist as a Young Man* as a junior in college: I read it and loved what I understood. After I graduated from college, I reread it during my obligatory trip to Europe, and it changed the way I saw the world and myself. I tried *Ulysses* as a senior in college and didn't get it at all. A few years later, I read it again with a guide, which helped a lot, but I still felt as if I were reading a book in a different language with the help of a Joyce/English dictionary. I got the meaning of the words, but I missed how they worked together. Finally, a few years later, I was able to truly enjoy the book. One day, I know, I'll finish and love *Finnegans Wake*.

I guess you could say that Joyce is always ahead of my time, and that is what I mean by another kind of personal Advancement. We all develop in our own time, and the period of your life when you discover artists can have an impact on whether they seem Advanced to you. Of course it matters whether artists are ahead of their time in the sense that they anticipate cultural movements, but it is also important when an artist can give you a glimpse into your future self.

Chapter Sixteen

Advancement and the 2000 Presidential Election

Today's political environment would seem an unlikely arena in which to find examples of Advancement, especially if you subscribe to the Overt opinion that today's politicians are somehow less honorable than those in the past. But there have been Advanced politicians as long as there has been politics. For example, Nero was the classic Classical Advanced Irritant; Benjamin Franklin and Thomas Jefferson were Advanced Founding Fathers; and Abraham Lincoln was the Advanced emancipator. But it would be silly to think that political Advancement would suddenly disappear even if you believe, as I don't, that twenty-four-hour news and bloggers have dumbed down our national discourse.

William F. Buckley was a conservative voice in the wilderness when it looked as if the Democrats would control Congress forever. He stood by his beliefs and was eventually vindicated by the ascension of Ronald Reagan to the presidency. Whatever you think about him, you have to admit that he was right when a lot of people thought he was wrong. Plus he wanted to legalize marijuana, if that softens you up a bit. You could also say that Barry Goldwater, he of the unshakable conservative principles, was Advanced in the same way as Buckley, though I don't know what Goldwater's policy was on weed. More recently, Newt Gingrich was borderline Advanced as he led the "Republican Revolution" in 1994. Of course, that revolution was a failure, so I can't say he was too much of a genius or ahead of his time. But he did shut down the government twice, which basically destroyed the public's opinion of the Republican Party, so he may qualify as an Advanced Irritant. On the other side of the aisle, not only was Bill Clinton the most gifted politician of the last half of the twentieth century, he was also the greatest Advanced Irritant in the history of the presidency. His affair with Monica Lewinsky was just another example of a genius needing a challenge to overcome. Plus he likes rock 'n' roll, wears dark sunglasses, and had Lou Reed play a show at the White House. Now, that's Advancement. What's more, his behavior laid the foundation for what would be the most Advanced presidential election ever.

First let's talk about Al Gore, who is the most Advanced American politician of our generation. Gore, more than any other politician—or public figure, for that matter—has been the victim of the older-brother resentment I spoke about in chapter one. He has been right about everything for the last forty years, and it annoys everyone, especially the press. Even more annoying is that he is one of the rare know-it-alls who actually does know it all. That's why the "invented the Internet" meme spread so easily. He never said that, and he really did sponsor two important pieces of legislation that made the Internet more accessible, but he is ridiculed anyway because few in the press want to stick up for him and set the record straight. He was mocked, too, for his environmentalism, not to mention his lockbox concept, which doesn't sound all that funny these days. (A trillion dollars might have come in handy in late 2008.) The truth is that he has been consistently ahead of the curve in technology and science, but those are not qualities usually appreciated in a candidate for a major political office. In fact, while he was Bill Clinton's vice president, Gore seemed to abandon some of his principles to position himself as a future presidential candidate. Enter Ralph Nader, the second most Advanced American politician of our generation.

For years Ralph Nader dedicated his life to consumer activism, writing the book *Unsafe at Any Speed*, which did for cars what *The Jungle* had done for meat, advocating for clean energy and peace and generally being a pain for anyone trying to slip one past the public. He also popped up on *SNL* from time to time, most memorably for me in the Carl Sagan "Global Warming Christmas Special." Eventually he set his targets on the political system, which had become so beholden to big-money donors that there was no difference (that he could see) between the two major parties. His decision to run for president was welcome news to many who felt the same way, and he got a fair amount of support considering he didn't have a chance to win. That support, the story goes, came at the expense of Al Gore and "cost him the election." If you read Bob Somerby's "Daily Howler," you know that Nader was the least of Gore's problems getting elected, as he was given the most ridiculously unfair treatment a candidate had received since Dan Quayle.

Given the immediate outcome, it's certainly tempting to label Nader's run in 2000 (and especially in 2004) as nothing more than the highest-stakes Advanced Irritant move in history, but I think it was a genuinely Advanced act, which ultimately benefitted the progressive cause. (I'm not advocating for that cause, exactly, but he certainly was hoping that his candidacy would result in a more progressive government.) Let's take a close-ish look at the circumstances of that election and you can decide for yourself what to label Nader: during his presidency, Bill Clinton abandoned the progressive agenda—gays in the military, universal health care, not bombing people—in favor of centrist-friendly initiatives, especially welfare reform. Al Gore had not done much more to advance the progressive agenda, even regarding climate control. Finally, George Bush was a likable buffoon running on a compassionate-conservative platform. At the time Nader was probably correct about the lack of difference between the parties before the election, but he didn't see that there were hidden distinctions that would appear only as a result of an extraordinary event, such as a terrorist attack—though, as he has pointed out, after September 11, 2001, Democrats were just as supportive as Republicans as President Bush rolled back civil liberties and led us into a war against Iraq.

Nader ran less to win than to make the point that the Democrats could not take the progressive wing of their party for granted. He succeeded. What's more, it can be argued that:

1. His call for a more progressive party paved the way for Howard Dean's strong early showing in the Democratic primaries in 2004.
2. Dean used the Internet and netroot organizations to raise money in ways no one had ever seen.
3. After failing to gain the nomination, Dean then became the chairman of the Democratic Party and instituted a fifty-state strategy that made many old-guard Democrats angry because it seemed like a waste of resources.
4. The Obama campaign used Dean's strategy to raise huge sums of money from small donors.
5. This strategy allowed Obama to further Dean's fifty-state strategy while diminishing the need for big-money donors.
6. Reduced dependency on big-money donors limited their potential influence on the Obama administration.
7. This came about only because the Democrats ran a progressive candidate who was against the war in Iraq, is for universal health care, and promotes wind, solar, and other clean-fuel technology.

8. Finally, had Gore been elected president, a role he was not suited for, he wouldn't have made *An Inconvenient Truth* (which could potentially wind up saving the planet), won the Nobel Prize, and ascended to the position of most Advanced American politician ever.

While Nader's run in 2008 borders on Quixotic Advancement, it took eight years for me to see the wisdom of his campaign in 2000. So maybe I'll get back to you in 2016, when I might understand what he was thinking at the time.

Chapter Seventeen

The Advanced World of Sports

Most of us will never be elite athletes, so we watch college and professional teams to live vicariously through them, spending a few hours a week in a world with no real repercussions in our real lives. The Overt, however, respond to their own physical ineptitude by dismissing sports as a waste of time played by idiots and followed by morons (or the other way around). It is a badge of honor in the Overt world not to know anything that is happening in the three major U.S. sports, just as it is not to know which bands are currently in the Top 40 or not to have seen any of the top-grossing movies of the year. To the Overt, physical gifts are inferior to intellectual gifts and the two are not compatible, as though every push-up eats away a little bit of the brain. Watching a game on TV is a waste of time at best and morally repugnant at worst, and actually going to a game is beyond all comprehension. There are exceptions: It is okay to watch a less popular sport, especially soccer, which the Hyper-Overt might even insist on calling football to show their disdain for all things American. It is also okay to go to a minor-league baseball game, as long as you are going for the beer and irony (wearing ironic T-shirts or jerseys for teams with funny names is also acceptable). In any case, to have an emotional attachment to a team in any sport is a sign of warped priorities.

The Advanced view is that there is no good reason to reject sports unless you honestly don't enjoy them. Playing the guitar or painting or acting is a physical act that is really no different from making a layup or putting a football where only your receiver can get to it. It involves the mind and body working together in concert, and some people are better at this coordination than others. Yes, a lot of idiots play and watch sports, but a lot of idiots play guitar and listen to music. But there are a lot of athletes who combine incredible skill with a unique intellectual insight into how to play games at a different level. Think of Bob Cousy, who was obviously blessed with physical gifts but used his mind to develop those gifts into something no one had ever seen before. Whether this intelligence applies to life off the court is irrelevant. He was brilliant at his chosen field of expertise and shouldn't be dismissed for, say, not reading Kant any more than Kant should be dismissed because he couldn't make a no-look pass.

There is also much more to sports than the game on the field. As sports have evolved, the games have become incredibly complex, requiring sophisticated strategies. If you do not take the time to truly understand this complexity, your opinion of it is worth no more than the rock musician who thinks free jazz is just a bunch of guys masturbating in fedoras. How can you possibly say that football is a dumb game if you don't understand how a defense adjusts when the running back goes into motion, leaving an empty backfield? Obviously coaches need to be strategic, but it takes an agile mind for a player to react to the nearly endless set of possible outcomes on the football field. It may look like a bunch of guys smashing into one another, but what's actually going on is more complex than a chess match. Not only must a player be prepared to counteract the strategy of the opposing players, by trying to decipher their moves, he must also be prepared for the opposing players to punch him in the testicles while fighting for a fumble in the bottom of a pile. Chess pieces hardly ever do that.

Not only is it Advanced to like sports, but there are people who play, write about, and broadcast sports who are Advanced as well. For an athlete, though, Overt and Advanced are sort of turned upside down. Dennis Rodman was Overt when he looked and played like a regular basketball player, and he was probably Advanced when he looked as if he were in the Spiders from Mars. Broadcasters are pretty much locked into whatever jacket they are forced to wear by the network they work for, so we can judge them only by what they do and at best what they wear in their spare time. Sportswriters are supposed to be slobs, which makes it kind of difficult to decide what an Advanced writer should look like, so we can only judge them by their work as well. But judge them all I most certainly will, starting with the guys who play the game.

Doing It All: Michael Jordan

Michael Jordan is famously competitive, and I suppose it is his drive to be the best at everything that helped him become not only the greatest athlete in my lifetime but the most Advanced athlete as well. Not only did he carry UNC to a championship as a freshman, hitting the game-winning shot in the closing seconds, he won six NBA championships and countless scoring titles, and should have won the MVP every year he played. But it was the years he didn't play—and the years he "shouldn't have" played—that make him Advanced. It was during those periods that Jordan managed to outdo both Jim Brown and Rickey Henderson by leaving on top (twice), playing minor-league baseball, acting, and "tarnishing his legacy" by playing into his forties.

In his early, innovative period, Jordan was cut from his high school basketball team by an obviously Overt coach. Somehow, though, in just a few years he willed himself to become the player who would help win that national championship, showing early on the desire for challenges that characterize the Advanced. After leaving UNC he went to the Chicago Bulls and became the best player in the league, though Overt critics said he was too selfish to win an NBA championship. He proved them wrong three times over, and then, when there were no more challenges, he quit basketball to play in the Chicago White Sox minor-league system. Though we've all had time to absorb it, this was an incredibly weird move for which there was simply no precedent. It would be like Muhammad Ali leaving boxing after beating Sonny Liston to play in the Chicago White Sox minor-league system.

As soon as he began playing baseball, the ridicule began, with *Sports Illustrated* taking the lead. To be fair, he did have trouble hitting a curveball, but the guy hadn't played baseball since he was a teenager! To give an idea of how hard it was for him to get used to playing baseball again, try going to a batting cage after not hitting for a few years and see how hard it is to connect even on dimpled balls from a pitching machine hurled any faster than 50 miles per hour. His numbers were actually pretty respectable given his rustiness plus the intense scrutiny of members of the media just waiting for him to fail.

I think if he had stuck with it he might have at least made it to the big leagues, though he would have never been as great as he was a basketball player. But every Advanced Genius needs a reunion, so Jordan went back to the Bulls. This was almost as bold as playing baseball because no one expected him to do well at baseball, but he had been the greatest basketball player on the planet, so if he failed in this comeback, the writers would be even more brutal. But it turned out to be yet another challenge he would be up to: he won three more championships, then retired on top, again, after hitting the game-winning shot against the Utah Jazz. It would have been the perfect bookend for a legendary career that effectively started with that shot against the Hoyas. It *would have been* if Michael Jordan hadn't been so Advanced.

Let's take a quick detour to look at his Advanced exploits off the court. He was a champion sellout who responded to criticism for not speaking out about politics by saying "Republicans buy shoes, too." Of course, he would have been criticized for speaking out as well, so I say that was the right play. He was a great host on *SNL*, appearing in three all-time great sketches ("If you want real hardcore porn, look for the box with my picture on it"; playing Sweet River Baines, the first black player on the Harlem Globetrotters; and his interview with Stuart Smalley: "I don't have to dribble the ball fast, I just have to be the best Michael I can be"). He starred in a movie with Bugs Bunny and was in a video with Michael Jackson. And then there was his time with the Washington Wizards, which takes us back to the court.

As weird as it was to see Jordan in that number 45 jersey during his first comeback with the Bulls, at least it was a Chicago uniform. Seeing him in that Wizards uniform, though, was completely unsettling. More unsettling was finding myself caring about the Wizards, the very definition of an afterthought in the NBA. The logical place for him to play would have been either Charlotte, since he was from North Carolina, or New York, because he always said how much he appreciated the fans there. He could have even chosen to play for a team like the Clippers, which has been comically inept for decades, so if he won anything there people would have been amazed. But he chose the Wizards (who were too chicken to keep their old name, the Bullets), a team that was always bad-to-okay but without any identity. Like his time in the minor leagues, his stint in D.C. was ultimately a failure, but a noble one. I think it was because he had become so Advanced that he couldn't be a teammate anymore. He just couldn't understand how to communicate with the Overt players on the team. (Picking Kwame Brown in the NBA draft was a rare non-Advanced moment for Jordan, I admit. Or at least I think it was.)

There was a time when I entertained the notion that maybe Jordan really had done the wrong thing coming back that third time. It was painful to see him missing dunks and watching young guys blow past him. But I was forgetting one of the principles of Advancement: what makes us love the Advanced when they were young is the same as what makes us stop loving them when they are old. Yes, it would have been poetic if he had stopped playing after that shot against the Jazz. But if he had been the kind of guy who would do what others wanted, that shot would never have happened. He would have given up basketball after being cut from his high school team and probably become a pretty good baseball player.

Quitters Never Win, but They Are Sometimes Advanced

Michael Jordan is not the only athlete to commit the sin of playing past his prime. Athletes are like rock stars in that they are required to be young, and the people they please the most—their fans—are the first to turn against them as they age. Jerry Rice was run out of San Francisco to make room for Terrell Owens because he had "lost a step." Never mind that he was still far superior to 90 percent of the rest of the league, as he proved when he went to the Oakland Raiders (the most Advanced NFL team, due mostly to Al Davis) the next year. Even so, sportswriters wrote that it was strange to see him in the black and silver; they felt it was their duty to register their disappointment that Rice didn't play his career for one team. Of course, there aren't many sportswriters who work for the same company their whole careers or would turn down more money from another company out of loyalty, but never mind all that. They want Rice to do what *they* want him to do, not what makes him happy or even what is best for the game. When Rice did finally retire after being cut by the Broncos in preseason, sportswriters gleefully wrote what a sorry thing it was that he should go out that way. That's stupid, of course. Rice went out competing, not quitting, and isn't that what being an athlete is all about?

Other examples of players "playing too long" and "tarnishing their legacy" are Willie Mays's stint with the Mets, Joe Namath's brief tour with the Rams, and Emmitt Smith's time with the Arizona Cardinals. But Rickey Henderson hung on longer than just about any other past-his-prime professional athlete, going so far as to play minor-league ball in Newark, New Jersey, in his midforties. Tom Verducci wrote a story some years back about Henderson's time there, when he was trying to show that he could still play well enough to be in the major leagues. In the piece, Verducci relayed an anecdote about a call Henderson made to Kevin Towers (the general manager of the Padres) one off-season. Towers wasn't available, and this is the message Henderson left on his answering machine: "Kevin, this is Rickey. Calling on behalf of Rickey. Rickey wants to play baseball." In an age where athletes are thought of as greedy and selfish, Rickey just wanted to play baseball, so much that he exposed himself to scorn and mockery by playing in the minor leagues in his midforties.

Of course, people had been mocking Henderson most of his career because, among many other things, he liked to refer to himself in the third person and apparently enjoyed standing naked in front of a mirror, swinging a bat, and repeating "Rickey is the greatest." I'll admit that this behavior was somewhat erratic, but if he had said anything else, he would have been lying, because he really was the greatest. And if I were built like him, I might enjoy seeing myself nude in the mirror too. Whether I would do it in a locker room in front of other people, I can't say. At any rate, his final attempt at making it back to the major leagues was simply Rickey being Rickey. And Rickey was being Advanced.

Henderson's Advancement began on the field, where he wore mirrored sunglasses and was freakishly great in all facets of the game. But his batting stance was particularly Advanced. He crouched down extremely low, which gave him a microscopic strike zone. He also had a good eye, so if the ball was outside that small strike zone, he wouldn't swing at it. And since he was the best base stealer of all time, a walk to him was almost as good as a double. He was the one player where the old saying "A walk is as good as a hit" was true and not just a way to encourage an uncoordinated kid not to swing in the hope that the pitcher will walk him.

Henderson was also frustrating to pitchers on the base paths, as he distracted them into worrying more about him than the batter. His crouch, his eye, and his base-stealing prowess all combined to make him the most Advanced Irritant in baseball since Ty Cobb. Remember, though, Henderson hit more lead-off home runs of any hitter in history, so he wasn't just a walking machine or slap hitter like Ichiro Suzuki. He just did whatever it took to get on base. It was that spirit of doing whatever it took that took him to the Newark Bears. The Overt might not understand it, but few people ever understood Rickey except for Rickey, and Rickey, as Rickey would tell you, was going to be Rickey no matter what anyone said.

Sportswriters write quite a bit about protecting the legacies of aging athletes like Henderson, but there aren't many—if any—examples of stars who have walked away because they were interested in protecting their own legacies. The few athletes who have gone out on top didn't do it because they were worried about their place in history: Barry Sanders retired early, but he was more interested in protecting his body than his legacy. He could have broken the all-time rushing yardage record, but he decided that it wasn't worth it to endanger his future health for a team as lousy as the Detroit Lions. Sandy Koufax, an Advanced Jewish athlete who wouldn't pitch in a World Series game because it fell on Yom Kippur, also left on top, but that was due to arthritis, so he really had no choice. Jim Brown, after starring in both football and lacrosse at Syracuse (Lou Reed's alma mater), ran for more yards than anyone in the history of the NFL but then retired when Cleveland Browns owner Art Modell insisted he leave the set of the movie he was working on (*The Dirty Dozen*) to come to preseason practice. He clearly made the right choice; not only did he save himself from physical wear and tear that could have left him crippled as an old man, but *The Dirty Dozen* turned out to be a classic, and Modell himself would prove to be completely disloyal to the Browns. Jim Brown's most Advanced move, though, was when he publicly contemplated (in black leather and dark sunglasses) coming back to football in his forties when it looked as though Franco Harris might break his record. Brown apparently didn't respect the way Harris ran out of bounds to avoid getting hit, which is fascinating coming from a man who effectively ran out of bounds on his career.

Sportscasters

Of the 10,000 or so sportscasters working on TV these days, about 750 have interesting insights into the game on the field, 200 can consistently speak English with fluency, and maybe 25 are interested only in enhancing the game for the viewer. So, as with most art, excellence is rare in the world of sports broadcasting, and only occasionally does a sportscaster come around who would even understand Advancement, much less be Advanced. If there's a sportscaster out there who *would* understand Advancement, it's Bob Costas. But as you'll see, understanding and being are two different things.

I think Costas is one of the greatest broadcasters of our generation, but he's just a bit too eager to please to be Advanced. He's the kind of guy who tends to agree with just about anyone he's talking to, almost to the point of being a sort of less funny Zelig. Whomever he's talking to, whether it's an athlete or a musician or a fellow journalist, he seems to take on the role of the exact person the interview subject would want to be talking to. If he's talking to an old-school basketball player like Bill Russell, he'll pull out an anecdote about James Naismith. If he's talking to LeBron James, he'll talk about having dinner at Lupa with Jay-Z and Beyoncé. If the interview is with someone serious and important, he dresses like a square, but if it's with someone cool, he dresses down. This was especially true on his late-night talk show, *Later with Bob Costas*.

I guess what bothers me most about him is that he acts as if he's familiar with everything having to do with whoever happens to be sitting in front of him because he's a big fan. You just know that what actually happened was that he read a couple of books a few days before and had his staff put together a list of interesting facts. For example, when he interviewed Max Weinberg on *Later,* you would have thought that he had been assiduously studying every move of Weinberg's career with the E Street Band. But even if he really did follow Weinberg, you still get the feeling that he was doing so as a robot would. A social robot, who was storing away data about all the members of the E Street Band to bring up at parties in New Jersey and, if everything went according to plan, his own late-night talk show.

In direct contrast to Bob Costas, you never got the feeling that Howard Cosell was being anything other than completely honest about who he was. If he didn't like someone, he had no problem saying so, even if the object of his dislike was the sport he was covering or the network executives paying his salary. I came across a quote from Robert Lipsyte in Cosell's obituary in *The Washington Post* that speaks to this: "He is the only broadcaster in America who can be the promoter, the reporter, and the critic of an event packaged and merchandised by his own network." Cosell was not only honest, he was also right most of the time. He defended Muhammad Ali for refusing to go to Vietnam because it was against his religious beliefs, saying that "what the government did to this man was inhuman and illegal under the Fifth and Fourteenth amendments. Nobody says a damned word about the professional football players who dodged the draft. But Muhammad was different; he was black and he was boastful." And though he was at his best calling boxing matches, he turned his back after the ridiculous Larry Holmes/Randall "Tex" Cobb fight because he was fed up with the brutality, hypocrisy, and "sleaziness." If you've followed boxing at all the last twenty years, he was pretty spot on. He also spoke out against baseball's reserve clause, which restricted players from switching teams, and he criticized the hypocritical Olympic movement. The biggest argument for Cosell's Advancement other than his "hair" may be that in 1975 he premiered his own live variety show on Saturday nights called *Saturday Night Live*. Unfortunately for Cosell, Lorne Michaels was even more Advanced.

Marv Albert is like a combination of Costas and Cosell, being able to travel very easily from topic to topic with a wit that is acerbic yet ingratiating. He's great enough and weird enough to be considered Advanced, but I'm not sure his sports-folly reels qualify him for being innovative, and the only way he made his fan base upset was with his sex life. It may be that he is innovative in ways that I don't see as a nonbroadcaster, but I feel pretty confident with the label of Merely Great.

John Madden was great *and* innovative: he took a coach's mentality to the booth, preparing for games by looking over films and talking to coaches and players, which helped him enlighten viewers' understanding not only of what was happening but why. He also has appeared in countless commercials, was criticized for thinking that he is more important than the game, wore black when he coached the Raiders, and hosted *SNL*. His bus strikes me as somewhat Overt, but it was plastered with ads for Outback Steakhouse and other sponsors, which makes it more acceptable from the Advanced point of view. To take a page from political reporting, I'm going to say Madden is in a Lean-Advanced state.

SportsCenter has produced a lot of interesting sportscasters, including Dan Patrick, Keith Olbermann, Chris Eisen, and Kenny Mayne. Interesting, but not Advanced. But Chris Berman is one ESPN personality who may have become Advanced but pissed it away. I loved the nicknames he gave to players, thought it was clever the way he called the NFC North division the Norris Division, and admired his Ivy League heritage, even though it was just Brown. But he never grew as an artist, either by renouncing his old style or taking that style to a place that could continue to be interesting (maybe nicknames as obscure and long as an Alanis Morissette album title). He just does the same thing over and over, only louder. I sort of like that he calls himself "the Swami" but the way he shortens the name to "the Schvahm" is nothing more than Overt self-aggrandizement. Plus I have a hunch he thinks that the act is funny for reasons other than his lack of special ability to pick games. The verdict is: Overt Irritant.

Another man known for predicting the outcome of NFL games was Jimmy "The Greek" Snyder, who was credited by *The New York Times* as having brought gambling to the "forefront of televised sports." Not only could he pick NFL games, but it is said that he bet ten grand (you have to say "grand" when talking about betting) on Harry Truman to beat Thomas Dewey at 17-to-1 odds, so he was aware of what was going on in the world outside of sports. Add into the mix that he was in *Cannonball Run,* and you see that he merits a close look. Like Bob Dylan and David Bowie, he changed his name: he was born Demetrios Georgios Synodinos (and raised in Steubenville, Ohio, just like Dean Martin). But what is great is that he changed his name to sound more American but then called himself "The Greek." It would be like Robert Zimmerman calling himself Bob "The Jew" Dylan. Entertaining as he was, ultimately he doesn't quite merit Advancement, and not just because of the ill-advised comments that got him fired from CBS. The reason he doesn't cut it is that he was often as vague in his predictions as the New Year predictions by *The Star* (a celebrity living in Hollywood will have trouble with the law but will get away with it!). If he had been truly Advanced, he would have gone out on a limb, gotten it wrong, and then been just as bold the next week. Perhaps with more research, possibly into his previous life as a businessman, I could turn up evidence that he really was Advanced, but I wouldn't bet on it.

The 1985 Chicago Bears: The Most Advanced Football Team Ever

There will never be agreement among football historians over which was the greatest pro football team of all time. Some say it was the Otto Graham Browns, others the Vince Lombardi Packers. The Steelers in the '70s, the Montana/Young/Rice 49ers, and the Aikman/Smith/Irvin Cowboys also come up in the conversation, and legitimate arguments can be made for them all. Which team you choose usually depends on your age or on what part of the country you grew up in. But no one can deny that the 1985 Chicago Bears were the most Advanced football team of all time.

You may be asking how a *team* from a *single year* qualifies despite the going-solo requirement and fifteen-year rule. It's possible that the Bears are so tempting to call Advanced that I've sacrificed my principles. But the individuals who formed the team had all played football for more than fifteen years, and the team broke up very quickly after winning the Super Bowl. In fact, you could say that it happened immediately after, because not only did part of the team carry Mike Ditka off the field, the defense carried Buddy Ryan. It was a great gesture, but one that suggests a fractured locker room.

The Bears certainly fill the superficial requirements: First of all, they wore black uniforms. This is a small point, but it does have a hand-of-fate quality. Second, their quarterback, Jim McMahon, wore black sunglasses on the field and had short hair in the front and long hair in the back. Third, that quarterback got in trouble for selling out: he wore a Nike headband during a game, which was against the rules of the NFL. McMahon responded to this hypocritical rule (the NFL is lousy with commercialism, after all) in true Advanced Irritant style: during the next game he wore a plain white headband with the name of the commissioner written on it. In black, of course. There was also William "The Refrigerator" Perry, who was not only incredibly talented but also incredibly fat. Of course, nowadays, most linemen are even bigger than the Fridge, so in that respect he was quite ahead of his time.

There have been plenty of teams with a bunch of characters, but what set the '85 Bears apart was that in addition to being a collection of entertaining personalities, they were the best team I've ever seen. The manner in which they won was pure Advancement: the defense was run by Buddy Ryan, who created the 46 defense, which used the blitz in ways no one had ever seen before. Ryan was also an Advanced Irritant who once got into a fistfight with another coach during a game when he was with the Houston Oilers. Another coach on *his* team, that is.

The head coach of the Bears was Mike Ditka, who later coached the New Orleans Saints and traded all his draft picks for Ricky Williams, then wore a black dreadlocks wig in a press conference about Williams. Ditka was a tough tight end who learned the game from some of the best minds in the game, including George Halas and Tom Landry. Ditka and Ryan were like the Lou Reed and John Cale of the NFL in that one was something of a purist while the other was innovative, sometimes just for innovation's sake. That's not to say that Ditka couldn't be an innovator, too. He did let the Fridge play fullback, which was both hilarious and effective. I've always found it Advanced that the Fridge scored a touchdown in the Super Bowl while Walter Payton didn't.

The Bears had the characters and the coaches to qualify for Advancement, but they also had the players. Walter Payton was among the best running backs ever to play the game. The 46 defense required players who were not only physically dominant but also cerebral. And that's just what Ryan had. The team was loaded with Pro Bowlers who weren't just vicious hitters but also understood the intricacies of the game. Their strong safety, Gary Fencik, went to Yale and wasn't even the smartest guy on the team (Mike Singletary takes that honor).

Speaking of Fencik, he was a literature major at Yale with a minor in poetry, which makes his participation in "The Super Bowl Shuffle" all the more laudable. Yes, the most Advanced pro football team of all time even embraced rap, long before it became fashionable for athletes to release hip-hop records. The 49ers had made a song the year before the Bears Shufflin' Crew, but it was disco, which was decidedly behind the times by then. The Bears' song and accompanying video represent probably the most Advanced moment in the history of sports, right up there with the Carl Lewis version of the national anthem and *Kazaam*. Not only did it reference McMahon's Overt punk roots, it spoke to Singletary's affinity for Eastern culture. The Shufflin' Crew were trailblazers in another way as well: their song was nominated for a Grammy, one of the first rap songs to be so honored, which opened the door for future hip-hop acts such as Kanye West and Outkast.

The only argument against the Bears' place as the most Advanced pro football team of all time is that they won only one Super Bowl. But they had many good years, and I would argue that the longevity requirement doesn't really apply to team sports, especially in the era of free agency. Plus, Ryan was bound to go solo like all Advanced

Geniuses, and that he did, coaching the Eagles and the Oilers with some success, but neither he nor Ditka would win another Super Bowl. But that's not surprising, as they would never have another group of athletes Advanced enough to understand their methods. But for that one glorious season, they had a team that was so Advanced, you know they were good, blowing our minds like they knew they would.

Chapter Eighteen

What Might Have Been and What Might Yet Be

Since Advancement didn't exist—or at least wasn't recognized—until the early 1990s, it's difficult to say if it would have been possible to tell in 1964 that Bob Dylan would one day be doing women's underwear commercials and Marlon Brando would be appearing in video games. But now that we do have a sizable list of Advanced Geniuses from which to learn, we can look backward at their early careers to find clues to their future Advancement. These clues may make it possible to pick out current artists and others who may one day Advance. I can't predict how the next generation will Advance, but I can at least identify those who have either achieved enough to qualify or at least show enough promise to indicate that one day they will qualify.

Unfortunately, many promising artists haven't lived long enough to achieve full Advancement. For instance, Kurt Cobain was conflicted in the way an Advanced Artist never is, wishing he could enjoy rock stardom like Freddy Mercury but still keep his status as a disaffected punk rocker. But I do think that if he had had the courage as an artist to go forward with what he truly believed in, he might still be with us today. He probably would have remained Overt, but I would take a living Kurt Cobain over a dead one any day, no matter how Overt.

Cobain is a member of the 27 Club (rockers who died at the age of twenty-seven), which also includes Brian Jones, Jim Morrison, Janis Joplin, and Jimi Hendrix. I don't think Jones would ever have Advanced, but only because he was an under-the-radar kind of a guy. Morrison was one of the few artists of the late-1960s era to put Woodstock and the hippie movement in general into its proper perspective (it's just kids having a good time, and that's always good). He certainly had the leather covered, and he sang the blues pretty well for a poet/Lizard King. But one question will always remain for me: If he was such a rebel, why did he show such a slavish devotion to rhymed couplets? Was he just a lazy writer, or was this some early sign of Advancement?

I'd really like to think that Janis Joplin would have embraced Advancement. While her music was mostly blues-based rock 'n' roll, there were other elements to it that she could have developed. She could have gone cabaret (like Bette Midler, who played a version of her in *The Rose*) or country (like k.d. lang?). Perhaps it would have been Joplin who did her interpretation of the American songbook rather than Rod Stewart. Maybe she would have sung with Sting and Bryan Adams. Now, that's a world I would like to live in.

But of all the members of the 27 Club, Jimi Hendrix seems like the one most likely to Advance. All of his contemporaries report that seeing him for the first time was like looking into the future. Brian Eno refers to him as the first proper electronic musician. And though I don't think Hendrix would have become as preppy as Eric Clapton, it would have been interesting to see what would have happened to him after he ditched the headbands and boas. Might he have given up on the guitar completely for the synthesizer?

Would he have played on Paul McCartney solo records instead of Steve Miller? Might he have been in Cream or the Traveling Wilburys? Or would he have written a song for Rob Thomas instead of Carlos Santana? Whatever his path would have been, I feel confident that it would have been Advanced.

Buddy Holly didn't live long enough to make it into the 27 Club, which is incredible (and unbearably sad), considering what he accomplished. Though he died at the age of twenty-two, he is among the most influential rock musicians of all time. What is so tragic is that he had such Advanced plans for the future: he was going to learn flamenco guitar and collaborate with soul and gospel singers, and he had registered for classes at the Actors Studio, where James Dean and Marlon Brando studied. The kicker is that he wore dark sunglasses during his wedding. One day I'd like to make a movie about an alternative universe where Buddy Holly decided not to do that last tour and became the most Advanced Artist of all time, more Advanced than Lou Reed, Marlon Brando, and Orson Welles put together. And of course the perfect person to play the role of the older, Super-Advanced Holly would be Gary Busey.

There are plenty of other artists who might have Advanced but died too young: John Belushi, River Phoenix, James Dean, and, more recently, Heath Ledger. Any of them could have ended up the next Marlon Brando or the next Marlon Wayans. But there is nothing sadder than contemplating what might have been, so let's move on to what might yet be.

Musicians

The members of Radiohead are a fair bet because they are certainly one of the great bands of the last fifteen years or so. The most obvious choice would be Thom Yorke, but I think Johnny Greenwood may be the dark horse. I do have my doubts about them because they seem pretty committed to Overtness. For example, most people thought it was pretty brave of them to put out a record like *Kid A* after having such monumental success with *OK Computer,* but if they really had guts, *Kid A* would have come first. Doing it the way Radiohead did is like Pearl Jam's giving up making videos *after* selling a zillion records: is it really that much of a sacrifice? And it's not as if *Kid A* was truly alienating, like *Metal Machine Music.* Ultimately, *Kid A* is all atmosphere and no meaning, even if you read between the lines. Just about every weirdo band who has heard Brian Eno's solo records and can afford the toys could make a record like that, but either they can't force their record company into letting them release it or they are more ambitious. Radiohead has made some great music over the years, but if it really wants to Advance, it needs to embrace its inner "Creep." And then break up, of course.

I would love it were R.E.M. to Advance, but even though it easily qualifies, the only one in the band who has come close is Mike Mills, with his shiny suits and long bleached-blond hair. Bill Berry became a farmer, which is great but not Advanced, and Pete Buck is exactly the same as he has always been, at least from what I can tell. That leaves Michael Stipe, who, for all his promise, can never break free from Overtness. He's come a long way from the *Murmur* days, when he hid behind his hair and mumbled lyrics, but though I think he'd like to Advance, he's still Overt at his core. Unfortunately, this lack of Advancement has made R.E.M. seem somewhat stale, with only a few songs on each album coming close to pre–*Automatic for the People* material.

Among younger musicians, the Killers seem like poseurs to me, but Lou Reed loves them, so they have to be taken somewhat seriously. However, I have a suspicion that they are going to disappear in the next year or so, at least in America. Coldplay wishes it could Advance, but Chris Martin will just have to settle for being married to Gwyneth Paltrow. Trent Reznor is not young, but he does dress in black leather and is now clean and more pumped up than Joe Piscopo. Amy Winehouse is talented enough to Advance, so maybe one day she'll clean up *her* act and be the next Eartha Kitt or Nancy Sinatra. Or perhaps Britney Spears could take over that role if Winehouse isn't up to it. The duo who make up Gnarls Barkley are above average, but they seem just a bit too self-conscious and ironic to ever fully embrace Advancement. It's almost as if they are a loving parody of Advanced music, but, loving or not, there are no parodies in Advancement.

I'll leave it to you to try to figure out what R. Kelly is.

You know already that I'm not much of a hip-hop aficionado, but I have to believe that Kanye West is an ideal candidate for future Advancement. Not only does he already have the look, but his first big hit was a song about Jesus. And he has recently taken to singing instead of rapping, even though his voice is not conventionally pleasing. His singing reminds me of how two-year-olds sing: he doesn't quite carry the tune, but he is so happy to be doing it, you can't help but love the sound. Little kids also have supreme confidence in their singing because no one has told them what good singing really is, and Kanye's got that too. I'm not saying that he has the intelligence of a child, of course, I'm just saying he is as free as a child, which makes for compelling art.

Outkast has done just about everything right, from making movies to producing a double album that is essentially two solo records, appearing in cartoons, and making the some of the most interesting music of their era. Still, I can't help but think that they are too aware of Advancement, and, like Gnarls Barkley, it seems as though they're just pretending (very well). Ludacris seems like a better horse to back, as he is just as interesting as Outkast but he seems to sincerely not give a fuck. Not to mention that he did the unthinkable, making Sum 41 seem authentically hard core (and nicking the title of a Beatles song at the same time).

It may by somewhat predictable of me to say so, but Beck strikes me as the musician most likely to Advance. He's always been linked with Radiohead in my mind because they both had breakout hits about ironic self-loathing—"Creep" and "Loser"—at around the same time. And while either of them could have been the next Timbuk3, both were able to escape the one-hit-wonder curse to become highly respected, even revered, musicians. This was more of a challenge for Beck, whose song would have nested comfortably between "Fish Heads" and "Someone Ate the Baby" on *The Dr. Demento Show*. Not only did he overcome longer odds than Radiohead, he did it in a more interesting way.

Neil Young once said that he hoped Beck would be the future of music. This was around the time of *Odelay*, which was similar to *Mellow Gold* but tighter and better produced. It blended rock, hip-hop, and Beat poetry with contemporary imagery and '70s-kid irony. He was compared to Bob Dylan, which I guess should have been my first clue that there was something more to him than "Beercan." Still, even though there was a hint of something dark in his music ("Pay No Mind" in particular), there was so much jokiness going on that it was hard to feel anything real. I didn't really need another Ween in my life.

It was *Midnight Vultures* that really opened my eyes, even though that was perhaps even more ironic (see "Debra") than his previous work. What was different to me was his focus on the songs rather than the sounds. Plus he got accomplished musicians to play with him, which showed that he wasn't going to make any excuses about his music, which was becoming much more conventional. After he broke up with his girlfriend, he rocketed past conventional to "boring." Only, if you listen enough, his music since *Midnight Vultures* has been much more interesting than his earlier stuff. The first few records were just a collection of bells and whistles intended to set him apart from the competition (he discussed this strategy with Terry Gross on *Fresh Air*), while what we've heard the last several years is the music of the real Beck, or at least the Beck of today.

I'm reluctant to mention his religious background, but he was raised by Scientologists and apparently has not renounced his faith, so I should discuss it at least briefly since religious belief is often a part of an artist's Advancement. People get pretty excited about Scientology, with the general consensus being that anyone who would belong to the movement must be an idiotic dupe. This may in fact be true, but some incredibly successful people seem to really be into it, and it isn't any crazier than Buddhism or other belief systems that are more hipster-friendly. In any case, he was pretty quiet about the topic for a long time but came clean about it just as his music was getting more fascinating. I don't think it's a coincidence that just as he was feeling comfortable enough to tell the truth about himself, his music improved.

Directors and Actors

The first name that came to my mind when thinking about the future was Paul Thomas Anderson (sometimes Overtly known as P. T. Anderson), because not only does he have the talent, but he also seems to be aware of his Advanced predecessors. In fact, he copies them so shamelessly that it comes off as audacity rather than mere thievery, especially in the Scorsese shots in *Boogie Nights* and the beginning and end of *There Will Be Blood*, which felt like outtakes from a Stanley Kubrick production. (Talk about drinking somebody's milk shake.) Plus he cast Kubrick fave Tom Cruise in one of his movies, which is just a great move any way you look at it. I give him some credit for casting Quasi-Advanced Burt Reynolds in *Boogie Nights*, though it wasn't as much of a leap as casting John Travolta in *Pulp Fiction*, and he could always use irony as an excuse if he hadn't worked out so well. He has been accused of overusing showy camera work, much like the Coen brothers, but that's just Overtness. The real question is whether those shots come off, and I think they do.

There Will Be Blood seems to me the most promising of his movies, though I can't quite say why. There is something in that movie that wasn't in his earlier ones, though it might have just been Daniel Day-Lewis. For instance, the spectacularly great ending might have been unsatisfying if he hadn't cast Day-Lewis in the role, so he is to be commended for that. But with an actor that talented (there aren't many), you just turn on the camera and let him do his thing. If he is to Advance, Anderson will have to get that kind of performance out of an actor who isn't already so compelling. Perhaps a sequel to *There Will Be Blood* starring Scott Wolf? If he doesn't Advance, Philip Seymour Hoffman may, as long as he stays away from Anderson. They are both much too comfortable working together, and comfort does not breed Advancement.

Tim Burton and the good-looking version of himself, Johnny Depp, seem as though they are on the road toward Advancement. Burton's most Advanced achievement was *Mars Attacks!*, but he has also married a movie star, made a Batman movie starring Michael Keaton in the title role, and remade *Willy Wonka*, while Depp was in a movie based on an amusement park ride and its two sequels and the *Wonka* remake. Points off for living in France.

Christian Bale has what it takes if he can just make up his mind. Not only did he play Batman (there's that man again), but he also defined Overtness for us. And Ewan McGregor has already been in a musical and starred in the *Star Wars* prequels, plus he played the most Advanced character in *Trainspotting*.

Peter Jackson is someone to watch. He pulled off the impossible, making a movie version of *The Lord of the Rings* that met with the approval of geeks everywhere. He could have made any movie he wanted to after the *LOTR* trilogy, but he followed it up with a remake of *King Kong* for some reason and cast Jack Black as the lead for some other reason. He also lost a ton of weight; wild weight swings seem to be a sign of Advancement (see Robert De Niro, Orson Welles, Marlon Brando, Elvis), though usually the Advanced get bigger, not smaller. Maybe his weight loss is Overt, but I don't think so. He also wears black all the time and has absolutely horrible hair.

Wes Anderson is brimming with potential, having made three of the best movies of the last twenty years, *Bottle Rocket*, *Rushmore*, and *The Royal Tenenbaums*. He is still clearly Overt, but I was pretty excited when he made an American Express commercial (just like Robert De Niro, Jim Henson, and Martin Scorsese), which shows that he rejects the notion that only sellouts do commercials. That the commercial is generally regarded as his best work since *Tenenbaums* makes it all the more exciting. His sometime partner Owen Wilson is amazing, but despite *You, Me and Dupree*, I don't think he'll ever actually Advance. Anderson could make it, though.

Mike Judge is a definite possibility. It takes a pretty strong sense of self to produce something like *Beavis and Butt-Head* without feeling the need to remind everyone that he is not as dumb as his characters. I have to add that while they were "dumb," they were incredibly perceptive and especially sensitive to Overtness. For instance, upon seeing a Pavement video, they remarked, "They're not trying very hard. They need to practice." Adding, in a subtly mocking tone, "They went to *college*." If that is not the most precise takedown of Pavement, I've never heard it. Another great comment was noting wryly, "That guy's *old*" in a Metallica video where a wizened old man was used to make the video seem weird. Judge is obviously not against selling out, as there was tons of Beavis and Butt-Head paraphernalia for sale. I still have their *Ensucklopedia* in my bathroom, as a matter of fact. Finally, his movies never get the credit they deserve. *Office Space* did very little business in the theaters, and *Idiocracy* (*1984* with Jet-Skis) was completely misunderstood by audiences in test screenings, which encouraged studio executives to give the movie the *Citizen Kane* treatment, releasing it in just a few cities and letting it disappear. Luckily, like *Eddie and the Cruisers*, both movies got second lives on cable and are now recognized as the classics they are.

I'd like to see Pedro Almodóvar Advance, but I'm not sure what that would look like. *Mission: Impossible IV* is my standing guess for any great foreign director, but I don't know how he could squeeze transsexuals into an *M:I* movie. Ang Lee did *The Incredible Hulk*, which is sort of like Batman, so perhaps he has some plans for Advancement. Baz Luhrmann hasn't done quite enough to be considered seriously, but *Moulin Rouge* showed a healthy respect for Advancement. Werner Herzog has the temperament for Advancement, but he's much too committed to being weird to ever make a full commitment. But I am impressed that he made a fictionalized movie version of his own documentary.

Finally, I would have never thought that Quentin Tarantino could Advance, but I've recently opened my mind to the possibility. I am particularly impressed with his decision to direct episodes of *CSI, ER,* and *SNL;* he also appeared as a judge and "mentor" on *American Idol.* More controversially, he seems to be the only person concerned that Joseph Goebbels's comedies and musicals are not better known. *Kill Bill* was the equivalent of a double album, and he once played an Elvis impersonator on an episode of *The Golden Girls.* As I look back on these accomplishments, I'm almost convinced that he won't be Advanced in the future but that he is already Advanced.

A New Category

The world of cooking might be one of the last, great, unexplored territories. Mario Batali, Tom Colicchio, and particularly Anthony Bourdain could be Advanced chefs. Bourdain has given up drugs and cigarettes, sold out by doing a show on the Travel Channel (though doing TV is pretty acceptable in the culinary world), and actually made nice with Emeril Lagasse. But without eating a chef's food, I can't really judge whether his artistry is up to the Advanced standard. Plus, I don't like fish, so I'm sort of disqualified. I do know that if a chef has a great reputation and sells frozen food or opened a restaurant in Las Vegas before it became acceptable, that chef deserves some recognition.

There are other artists, chefs, athletes, businessmen, politicians, and scientists out there who may one day Advance, but the final candidate I want to talk about is the most exciting of them all: you.

Chapter Nineteen

The Advanced State of Mind, or How to Like Everything

By virtue of being average, you and I are really not capable of true Advancement. But if you follow the principles of Advancement you can achieve the Advanced state of mind, which enables you to see the greatness hidden in the works of Advanced Artists. By doing so, you can help prove the correctness of the Advanced Genius Theory. Here's how: The one hole in the theory is that many of the works by Advanced Geniuses continue to be seen as inferior. As long as this is the case, we can't say that they were ahead of their time. However if you and I, plus enough other people, begin to love the later work of the artists covered in this book, then we prove that the Theory is correct. In other words, your believing the Theory makes it true.

So that's what you can do for Advancement, but what can it do for you?

The Advanced State of Mind

As I wrote in the introduction, Overtness has evolved from defining a stage of artistic development to describing anyone who rejects certain kinds of clothes, music, books, entertainment, and other symbols that are not consistent with the image he wants for himself. In other words, just about everyone. But while Overtness is the human condition, it's possible to overcome it, even if one isn't a genius. This is known as the Advanced state of mind, which makes it possible to enjoy what others detest.

What I find so liberating about the Advanced state of mind is that it helps you approach the world with an attitude of "How can I like this?" rather than the Overt position "Why shouldn't I hate this?" The Overt make it nearly impossible to enjoy anything outside what they have predefined as worthy of their free time or entertainment dollar. What Advancement does is puts you in touch with that part of yourself that wants to sing along with "I'm Still Standing" because you loved it when you were a kid, before you were aware that Elton John wasn't cool. The Advanced Genius Theory says that a good song is simply a song that you love, regardless of what everyone else thinks. You can Advance, then, only when you believe in yourself.

But what do the Overt believe?

To answer that, I've assembled a list of topics, giving first the Overt point of view and then the Advanced take on each one. I've limited myself to subjects I've heard actual Overt people talk about, but I don't want to name any names, as it is not my intention to embarrass anyone but merely to illustrate the differences between the Overt and Advanced states of mind.

Books

I'm going to break my promise right away about not naming names: If you want to see Overtness in the world of literature, go to the Strand in New York City. The employees there hate you because you haven't dedicated your life to reading books, as they want you to believe they have. They would be glad to tell you this if they were capable of gladness or would ever talk to you without having to be forced. Of course, most major cities have a bookstore where customers are Philistines, tolerated only because you have to sell books to someone. And you don't have to work in a bookstore to be Overt about them. The Overt view books as the supreme means of learning, entertainment, and apartment furnishing—but only certain books, of course. Stephen King, John Grisham, and Tom Clancy do not write literature, according to the Overt, they write "popular fiction." You might think that you'd be safe with a writer like Vladimir Nabokov, but try to say you think *Lolita* is his best book and watch how quickly you'll be dismissed by the Overt book expert. An author's most popular work cannot also be his best work. A truly good book must be somewhat obscure but embraced by certain influential critics. It must feature the word "tumescent." It should have an antihero. It should end in the middle of the story. It should be very long. Anything less is probably not worth your time, unless you are at the beach, which the Overt never condescend to visit because they don't like the sun.

First of all, a good TV show like *The Wire* or *The Sopranos* is equal to a good book (more on TV below). And even if a show isn't as well written and acted as those two shows, you are still allowed to like them if they give you pleasure. You are not required to spend your leisure time in a productive way if you don't want to. There is nothing that makes books inherently superior to other forms of entertainment, and the distinction between "literature" and "popular fiction" is a false one. Charles Dickens was the popular fiction of his day (and even now his reputation suffers for it), but he influenced countless authors of "literature," including Leo Tolstoy.

The Dickens of our time is probably Stephen King, whose crimes as an artist include writing lots of books of the wrong genre and selling lots of those books. But the guy can tell a great story, which is a rare skill, and he can get people to sit down and read them, which is even rarer. Yet he is dismissed by serious readers, I think, because his stories are *so* good that it's as if he didn't even write them, they were just plucked out of the sky fully formed. King's situation is similar to Paul McCartney's: he has the ability to write such great melodies that critics take it for granted and look for something else in his music to criticize. King certainly has a natural talent for telling stories, but all the writers of serious literature were also born with gifts, only those gifts are not appreciated as widely and are therefore seen, erroneously, as more precious. Stephen King was born to write books you can't put down, just as James Joyce was born to write books that challenge people's understanding of what a book can be. Both writers succeeded in what they set out to do, so why not be Advanced and like both of them?

Idols

Overt

I once overheard a conversation between a Starbucks barista and his customer that is a perfect example of Overt joy sabotage. The customer asked about the cover of "The Rainbow Connection" playing at the time (he had never heard the song before, not even the Kermit version!), and the barista started talking about *The Muppet Movie* and how great it was. Then he allowed his Overtness to get the best of him when he declared that anything Muppet-related since Jim Henson's death was "not the real Muppets." I'm guessing that his rejecting the post-Henson era was a twisted form of tribute, but I can't imagine that Henson would have wanted people to stop liking the Muppets, especially a new generation of kids, who will love his creation just as much as my generation does.

Which leads us to the greatest sin of Overtness: ruining things for everybody else. It's one thing to deny yourself the pleasure of something you consider beneath you, since you're hurting only yourself. It's quite another to make other people feel bad about something they like. The worst example of this is *Kill Your Idols*, a beyond-pointless book that invents new ways for you to dislike music that everybody knows is great, such as *Exile on Main Street* and *Sgt. Pepper's Lonely Hearts Club Band*. The book's thesis is the opposite of my favorite quote by Mark Twain, who said that Wagner's music is "better than it sounds." To the *KYI* crew, everyone's favorite music is worse than it sounds, only we're all too dumb to realize it.

Advanced

Some have voiced concern that Advancement's seemingly unquestioning embrace of idols is a little too close to the dangerous parts of Friedrich Nietzsche's philosophy. But that's hooey on a couple of levels. First, I'm as unfamiliar with Nietzsche as the people who compare his philosophy with mine. In fact, I have to use spell check even to type his name correctly. Second, I don't think you should cede Sudetenland to Bob Dylan, I just want you to give *Infidels* another try. Plus, those of us who believe in Advancement don't unquestioningly embrace our idols, they have to earn our respect first. And once that is earned, we don't just abandon the relationship when they do something we don't understand, we try to understand it. If anyone is not asking enough questions, it's the Overt, who reflexively reject anything that doesn't fit within their arbitrary rules for what constitutes quality. Advancement says that it may be an error to give your idols too much credit, but this is much less corrosive than not giving them enough, as the editors of *Kill Your Idols* would have us do. Let's put it this way: there's so much out there to hate, why would you go out of your way to hate something you love?

Love Songs and Happiness

Overt

The Overt automatically dismiss movies and books that celebrate love and feature "happy endings," preferring something bleak or ambiguous (leaning toward bleak). I believe this is more a symptom of youthful ignorance rather than being out of touch with one's feelings. When you're young and Overt, you don't want to be finished with *anything* because that would bring the end of possibilities.

Take *The Graduate*, for instance (I'm limited to the movie because I've never read the book). If Benjamin had married Elaine at the end of the movie, their future would have been set. Instead we last see them, smiles fading, riding on a city bus staring off into the distance, with some vaguely depressing but not explicitly pessimistic Simon and Garfunkel to hammer home the uncertainty of their future. There are many more adventures to come for these two, including their likely dramatic breakup. He did have sex with her mom, after all. As you get older and your views on life Advance, you realize that uncertainty becomes as stale as any other routine and that a stable relationship with someone you love is not the end of the story but the beginning of a better one. But young people don't want a stable relationship, they want to go scuba diving in swimming pools, take their dates to strip clubs, and have affairs with their engaged friend's parents.

Songs like Paul McCartney's "Silly Love Songs" or Stevie Wonder's "I Just Called to Say I Love You" are criticized for being cloying or trite, but is it any less trite to declare that those songs are trite? What, after all, is the problem with a song that extols the virtues of love, the most profound emotion a human being can have? Is it because the topic of love between a man and a woman has been exhausted as a subject for art? Is it because it is so profound that a songwriter shouldn't even attempt to write about it? Or is it because people are uncomfortable with the subject and make fun of it, like a little boy hitting a little girl because he likes her but is incapable or afraid of expressing it? That seems more likely to me, because most of us are much more embarrassed about what we love than what we hate because saying you love something makes you vulnerable in a way that hate or sarcasm never will. But, as always, the easy way out is the least productive because those who can't express their feelings are usually consumed by them and end up forming terrible bands. Now, that is an unhappy ending.

Hollywood

Overt

The quality of a movie, so the Overt might say, is inversely proportional to how much money and publicity are behind it. Points are also taken off if too many people like the movie. So "Hollywood" movies like *Independence Day* or *Runaway Bride* are obviously pure dreck. Or impure dreck, as nothing pure could come from Hollywood. If a movie stars the wrong actor or has a tie-in with Taco Bell, it is impossible for it to have any merit at all. The Overt are made fun of a lot for distinguishing between "films" and "movies," so I don't need to do it, but that compulsion to categorize art so narrowly is the essence of Overtness.

The Overt are the first to disparage the sound track for being too weepy, the writing for being too clichéd, the plot for being too far-fetched, and so on. As is their habit, they are so enamored with what they don't like that they never give themselves the chance to find things they do like about the work or the work as a whole. However, if a movie was poorly financed, an Overt filmgoer will forgive any number of sins, such as a poorly constructed narrative and sloppy camera work, with the idea that the shortcomings improve the movie because otherwise it might be too slick. It's sort of like how Overt critics are bothered that the Eagles had the audacity to write country-tinged rock songs that were recorded well and played with precision. If Hank Williams had come along in the 1970s, you can be assured that he would have recorded his music as well as possible. Sure, the recordings he made were charmingly lo-fi, but first of all I can almost guarantee that he wished they had sounded more like a live room, and second, the Eagles would have been dishonest if they had tried to make albums that sounded like old country records that were made with inferior technology, and third, the best country musicians are extremely slick themselves (just listen to the hi-hat playing on George Jones's "He Stopped Loving Her Today"). But back to the movies, it's as if the Overt can tolerate only a certain amount of craftsmanship, and anything that exceeds that limit is discounted as phony.

Advanced

Any movie can be good, no matter who stars in it, how much money it took to make it, how many car chases are in it, or how many people like it. And making a high-quality Hollywood movie is much more difficult than making a great independent movie. Let's look at Steven Spielberg and Steven Soderbergh, a pair of directors whose names are so similar, I can hardly believe the luck that they illustrate my point so well. Making a movie like *sex, lies, and videotape* is a piece of cake compared with making *Schindler's List* because no one had any expectations of Soderbergh at the time (plus, James Spader is always amazing), so he could just make a weird little movie for little money and if it bombed, no big deal. But think of the risk that Spielberg took making *Schindler's List*. Here's an enormously successful Jewish director taking on the dominant event of the twentieth century, in black and white, no less. If he'd failed, he would have incurred the wrath of just about everyone. Of course he didn't fail, but he is still held in lower esteem than directors who make their movies when no one is looking. Incidentally, Soderbergh eventually recognized the limitations of the independent spirit and went Hollywood.

MTV

Overt

People of a certain age (people younger than me) would probably be somewhat surprised to find out that MTV used to air only music videos. No *Real World*, no *Parental Control*, no *Date My Mom*. Instead you got a steady rotation of Tom Petty, Pat Benatar, and Tom Petty again. Despite the limited material, we kids couldn't get enough of it, and we watched it for hours on end. Or so it seemed. What we actually did was watch for a little bit, change the channel when a commercial or song we didn't like came on, flip around, and eventually come back. Once advertisers figured this out, the executives at MTV realized they had a problem that required action. So they started airing shows like the game show *Remote Control* so the kids would stick around for more than five minutes at a time. But it was *The Real World* that permanently changed the way we watched MTV. Or, if you are Overt, the way you don't watch MTV, because the Overt felt that by abandoning the all-videos, all-the-time format, MTV had sold out. Never mind the fact that it existed in the first place because the founder of the network realized that there was an opening in the marketplace for an all-music channel. The problem was that MTV did such a good job of presenting itself as cool that people were shocked to find out that the people at MTV actually cared about making money. Thus the ridiculous notion that a business can sell out.

Advanced

The really amusing part about the whole story is that people of another generation (people older than me), thought that MTV was going to kill music because it created stars out of musicians who couldn't play but looked great in a video. Overreacting to generational shifts is a big thing for the Overt. Each new wave of Overt people is convinced that whatever is new is worse than what they have grown accustomed to, ignoring the fact that what they have grown accustomed to was new before they became accustomed to it. The funny thing is that the people who worried about MTV's tendency to make stars of bands like Duran Duran that were flashy and good-looking fell in love with Elvis when they saw him on *Ed Sullivan* because he was flashy and good-looking. And of course the generation before that saw Elvis as the end of music, and the generation before that thought the bobby-soxers had lost their minds, and so on.

MTV was great when it started out, and the music-videos-only format was probably ideal, but it wouldn't be around today if it hadn't switched to more traditional programming. To its credit, MTV's traditional programming wasn't exactly traditional. It actually invented reality TV as we know it, and though Overt people would say that was a bad thing, it is not MTV's responsibility to ensure the quality of its imitators, and *The Real World* was a great idea; this is similar to blaming *Jaws* and *Star Wars* for the blockbuster mentality that people pretend is so bad for movies.

Television

Overt

If there is a common enemy for the Overt, it is the television. The nicer the television, the more the channels, it is thought, the emptier the soul of the person who owns the set and subscribes to the deluxe package. The optimum situation for an Overt person would be not to have a television in his or her apartment (or, if they are really Overt, "flat"), but if for some reason it is unavoidable, an old, crappy black-and-white TV is the only way to go. Also, it should be hidden away, as not to upset the aesthetic of the room, and propped up on important books, their titles showing. While the Overt do not want TV to be a part of their lives, their repudiation of the medium is a central part of their worldview. It is not necessary to discern between good TV and bad TV, because the thing itself is evil and will "suck you in." People who sit on the couch and watch TVs are "zombies," while people who smoke cigarettes and drink coffee for three hours are "interesting." While there is no such thing as good TV, somehow reality TV is seen as particularly vapid; scripted shows are the lesser of the evils. Needless to say, the Overt watch neither but feel that if a script exists, there at least has to be a writer involved. MTV was the only acceptable form of television when it came out for a generation of Overt viewers, but every generation before and since has seen TV for what it is: evil masquerading as cool. The only acceptable channel is of course PBS, but only the news and a few documentaries. Ken Burns is not to be trusted because he appeals to too many people, which has somewhat diminished the importance of their Channel 13 or WGBH tote bags as a sign of superiority. The classic Overt bumper sticker says it all: KILL YOUR TELEVISION.

Advanced

Just as painting, poetry, opera, folk art, movies, and every other art form can be bad (and often is), so can TV. The Advanced person sees no reason why we should hold television to another standard than all other forms of art. And certainly if one is to invest in a television, it is a waste not to get the best set with the most options in your budget range. Yes, it is tempting to watch too much TV if you have a lot of channels, but if someone feels as though he is "wasting" too much time watching, all that is required is to turn it off. Meanwhile, having as many choices as possible ensures that viewers will be able to watch something that they deem worthwhile—whether that means a sitcom, a documentary about ant colonies and what we can learn from them, a Werner Herzog movie, whatever—when the set is on. And if it is a movie the viewer chooses, shouldn't that movie look as good as possible? With the technology we have today, you can almost replicate the cinema experience in your living room. If you live in a big city and have the opportunity to watch art movies and foreign films in the theater, of course you would prefer that. You'll also probably pick the theater with the biggest screen and the best sound (unless you are seriously Overt). But if you don't have that option, it's nice to have a big TV with surround sound. Sure, you might end up watching a few episodes of *The Nanny* that you regret, but that's a small price to pay to be able to watch *Grizzly Man* the right way. Plus, you probably like Fran Drescher more than you admit to yourself anyway.

Once you have achieved the Advanced state of mind, something amazing happens: you start to like *everything*. Not only will you appreciate Advanced Artists' most challenging work, but you'll also experience with an open mind the parts of popular culture that otherwise might have tormented you, such as "We Built This City," movies based on TV shows, TV shows based on movies, radio commercials featuring two people pretending to have a casual conversation about a product, and Fox News.

What's more, though you will like everything, you won't necessarily lose the ability to discern between levels of quality. You can still have "good taste." It's just that the question becomes *how much* you like a work of art rather than *whether* you like it. This is far superior to traditional good taste, which is predicated on what one rejects. The Advanced accept everything, including everything the Overt enjoy—acid jazz, abstract expressionism, French New Wave, NPR—but they won't ruin your party by insisting on playing music no one's ever heard of. So not only will Advancement give you back your favorite artists, help you enjoy things you've always hated, and put you in touch with your true self, it will get you invited to more parties.

One final tip: when you are at one of those parties, you might not want to mention how much you like Sting's latest record.

Acknowledgments

Endless thanks to my mother, father, and brother, Skipper. Thanks to Jeffrey Rotter, Andrew Beaujon, and Scott DeSimon. This book would not exist were it not for their inspiration and encouragement. And thanks to Brant Rumble, Pam Sanderson Lyon, and Daniel Greenberg, who made things easy.

Finally, thanks to Oran, Caroline, and, especially, Jenny.

Index

Beck, 46, 234, 235

Beckham, David, 143

Belushi, John, 231

Bennett, Tony, 116

Bergman, Britt, 2, 9, 34, 55, 56, 70, 75, 91, 94, 113, 129, 145

Berle, Milton, 72

Berlin (album), 74–75, 78

Berman, Chris, 224

Berry, Bill, 232

Berry, Chuck, 58, 60, 91, 106–7, 119, 198

Best, George, 4

Best Week Ever (blog), 37, 188

Black, Jack, 236–37

Blanchett, Cate, 83

Blige, Mary J., 126

Blondie, 61, 64

Bloom, Harold, 2–3, 50

Bogdanovich, Peter, 163

Bono, 56–57, 84, 121–22, 128–30

Booker T and the MGs, 60

books, Advanced State of Mind about, 242–43

Bourdain, Anthony, 238–39

Bowie, David, 4, 31, 56, 72, 73, 91, 95–97, 106, 119, 128, 136, 224

Bowie, Iman, 96

Brando, Marlon: Actors Studio studies of, 231; and Coppola, 163; and Dean, 151; and directors, 178; in *The*

Godfather, 51, 163, 174, 182, 229; Holly compared with, 231; improvisation of, 175–79, 199; and journalists, 179; and Oscars, 180–81; and science, 181–82; and stupid movies, 179–83; and Warhol, 193, 195; weight of, 93, 174, 182, 237; in *The Wild One*, 23, 174

Brasky, Bill, 204

broadcasters, sports, 215, 221–25

Brodsky Quartet, 134

Brown, Bobby, 40

Brown, James, 60, 97–101, 102, 131, 197

Brown, Jim, 215, 221

Brown, Kwame, 218

Bruce, Lenny, 10, 86, 188

Buck, Pete, 232

Buckley, William F., 208–9

Burns, Ken, 250

Burton, Tim, 236

Buscemi, Steve, 40, 42

Busey, Gary, 231

Bush, George W., 130, 211

Byrne, David, 40, 94

Cage, John, 28

Cage, Nicolas, 41–42, 43

Caine, Michael, 151–52

Cale, John, 226

Canby, Vincent, 164, 170

Madden, John, 223–24
Maddox, Lester, 99
Madonna, 46, 95, 136–38
Malkovich, John, 42
Manowar, 159
Mapplethorpe, Robert, 194
Marangoni, Carlo, 131
Marcos, Imelda, 40
Marcus, Greil, 68
Marr, Johnny, 142–43
Marshall Tucker Band, 71–72
Martin, Chris, 232–33
Martin, Dean, 145–46, 224
Martin, George, 116
Martin, Steve, 5–6, 8, 18, 184–89
Massey, Raymond, 150–51
Matlock, Glen, 141–42
Mayne, Kenny, 224
Mays, Willie, 111, 219
McCartney, Paul, 7, 23, 64, 111–20,
    134, 172, 231, 243, 246
McGregor, Ewan, 236
McGwire, Mark, 89
McLaren, Malcolm, 133, 140
McMahon, Jim, 226
Mellencamp, John, 45, 116
Melvoin, Wendy, 104
Men at Work, 141
Menudo, 114
Mercury, Freddie, 64, 229
Merely Great, 7, 223
Metal Machine Music (album), 68,
    76, 78, 83, 96, 170, 232

Metal Machine Trio project, 90
Metallica, 237
Michaels, Lorne, 17, 135, 223
Michelangelo, 190
Midler, Bette, 108, 230
Mike and the Mechanics, 104
Miller, Steve, 120, 231
Mills, Mike, 232
Ministry, 137
Minnelli, Liza, 195
Mistral (album), 11, 75, 77, 79, 125
Modell, Art, 221
Modest Mouse, 66, 73, 143
Mondrian, Piet, 69, 191
Monet, Claude, 198
Monkees, the, 140
Moore, Scotty, 59
Morrison, Jim, 116, 139, 151, 230
Morrissey, 84, 86, 142–43
Moses, Robert, 196
MTV, 87, 199, 248–49, 250
multiculturalism, 44, 92, 146, 181.
    See also world beat
Munch, Edvard, 191–92
Muppet Movie, The (movie), 155–56,
    243–44
Muppets, the, 182
Murphy, Eddie, 42, 43
Murray, Bill, 203
Myers, Mike, 150

Nabokov, Vladimir, 242
Nader, Ralph, 210–11, 212

Presley, Elvis (*cont.*)

    guitars of, 92; impersonators of, 38, 238; as innovator, 92; in Las Vegas, 92, 93; Lennon comment about, 115; look of, 92, 93, 95; Martin as comedic, 189; in Middle Advanced stage, 46; in movies, 93, 198; Overt stage of, 92; and *Rattle and Ham* movie, 128; as rebel, 92; and religion, 46, 92; and rock and roll, 92; and rock-'n'-roll lifestyle, 59; as second tier of Advanced Musicians, 91–95; as selling out, 92; and U2, 129; and Warhol, 193; weight of, 93–94, 95, 182, 237; and why we love geniuses, 17; and world beat, 64

Prince, 101–4

professionalism, 59–62

Proust, Marcel, 57, 203

Public Enemy, 129

Public Image Limited, 141

Pullman, Bill, 45

punk, 60–62, 64, 116, 133, 134, 227

Purple Rain (movie), 102, 104

Pynchon, Thomas, 203, 205–6

Quarrymen, the, 115

Quayle, Dan, 210

Radiohead, 231, 232, 234

Ramone, Dee Dee, 65

Ramones, the, 60–62, 65

rap, 65–67, 99, 227

Raphael, 191

Rat Pack, the, 145–46

Reagan, Ronald, 208

Real World, The (TV show), 248–49

Reed, Lou: as Advanced Musician, 2; and Bono, 128, 129; Bowie's recognition of greatness of, 96; and characteristics of Advanced Genius, 4, 136; commercials of, 2, 45; covers of, 78–79; and critics of Advanced Genius Theory, 11; decline of, 2; and drugs, 70, 72; Dylan compared with, 69–70, 81, 82, 83, 89–90; experimentation by, 79; failures of, 79; in Final Advanced stage, 50; guitars of, 77–78, 79; Halas compared with, 226; Holly compared with, 231; as innovator, 70–71; as inspiration for Advanced Genius Theory, 2, 70, 75, 89–90; and journalists, 76–77; and Killers, 232; look

of, 2, 55–56, 69, 77–78, 79;
Metal Machine Music of, 68,
76, 78, 83, 96, 170, 232; as
most Advanced Musician
ever, 68–69, 70–79, 89–90,
91; Orbison compared
with, 143; Overt period for,
68, 71–72, 74, 76, 77–78;
Pandora station named,
95; rebelliousness of, 74;
and rock-'n'-roll, 58, 72;
Sinatra as, 146; and Sting,
125; Syracuse as alma
mater of, 221; and Velvet
Underground, 2, 58, 70, 71,
72, 75, 77, 78, 205; "Walk
on the Wild Side" of, 2, 11,
72, 73, 74, 100, 143, 204;
White House performance
of, 209

Reeves, Keanu, 132–33

reggae, 64–65, 86

R.E.M., 25–26, 28, 65, 122, 232

Rembrandt, 191

Renoir, Jean, 27

Replacements, 131

Reynolds, Burt, 182, 235

Reznor, Trent, 96, 144, 233

Rice, Jerry, 218, 219

Richards, Keith, 107

Rivers, Nick, 151

Roberts, Julia, 152

Rock, Chris, 22

rock-'n'-roll: and Advanced
Musicians, 57–62, 68;
Bowie's use of term, 96; and
characteristics of Advanced
Genius, 113; and Clinton,
209; as cornerstone of
Advanced Genius theory,
146; lifestyle of, 59; 1996's
comment about, 206; and
professionalism, 59–62; and
rap, 66; and relationship
of past and present,
30–31; saving power of, 72;
stereotype of, 58–59; what
is, 58–59; and world beat,
64. *See also specific musician
or band*

Rock 'n' Roll Animal (album), 72, 75,
77

Rodgers, Nile, 96

Rodman, Dennis, 10, 215

Rolling Stone magazine, 68, 71, 74,
84–85, 130

Rolling Stones, the, 58, 63, 107–10,
112, 203

Rollins, Henry, 64

Ronstadt, Linda, 84

Rooney, Frank, 23

Rose, Axl, 103, 148

Roth, David Lee, 102, 141, 148

Rotten, Johnny, 86, 133, 140–42

Run-DMC, 65, 66

Russell, Bertrand, 15

About the Author

Jason Hartley is a writer, musician, and online marketer. He holds a BA in English from the University of South Carolina. He has worked professionally as a dancer and choreographer and has studied at the American Dance Festival, Dance Space, Inc., and Movement Research. He has written for *Esquire,* Spin.com, and VH-1's *Best Week Ever* blog. Since 2004, Jason has maintained his own Web site, Advanced Theory Blog. Originally from South Carolina, he now lives in Georgia.